The Quest for
CITIZENSHIP

The Quest for
CITIZENSHIP

African American and Native American
Education in Kansas, 1880–1935

KIM CARY WARREN

The University of North Carolina Press *Chapel Hill*

© 2010 The University of North Carolina Press

All rights reserved. Designed by Courtney Leigh Baker and
set in Merlo with Barrel display by Tseng Information Systems, Inc.
Manufactured in the United States of America. The paper in this book meets
the guidelines for permanence and durability of the Committee
on Production Guidelines for Book Longevity
of the Council on Library Resources.

The University of North Carolina Press has been
a member of the Green Press Initiative since 2003.

Library of Congress Cataloging-in-Publication Data
Warren, Kim Cary.
The quest for citizenship : African American and native American
education in Kansas, 1880–1935 / Kim Cary Warren.
p. cm.
Includes bibliographical references and index.
ISBN 978-0-8078-3396-4 (cloth : alk. paper) — ISBN 978-0-8078-7137-9 (pbk : alk. paper)
1. African Americans—Education—Kansas—History. 2. Indians of North America—
Education—Kansas—History. 3. Racism in education—Kansas—History.
4. Segregation in education—Kansas—History. 5. Educational change—
Kansas—History. 6. Education and state—Kansas—History. I. Title.
LC2741.W37 2010
371.829′960730781—dc22
2010010141

Portions of Chapter 6 first appeared in "'All Indian Trails Lead
to Lawrence, October 27 to 30, 1926': American Identity and the Dedication of Haskell Institute's Football Stadium," *Kansas History: A Journal
of the Central Plains 30 (Spring 2007): 2–19. Used with permission.*

cloth 14 13 12 11 10 5 4 3 2 1
paper 14 13 12 11 10 5 4 3 2 1

For Luke and in memory of Mom

Contents

Part III

NEW LEADERS IN THE TWENTIETH CENTURY

Illustrations

Acknowledgments

There are four groups of people who made this project possible from the start to the finish: those who recorded their thoughts and educational experiences, probably having no idea that a future historian would find their words so fascinating; those who taught me how to use such sources to craft a tale worth reading; those who provided resources to move the research and writing forward with steadiness; and those who stood by with support and never-ending encouragement. Without all of those groups, this book would not have come into being, so I am grateful for each of them.

My academic interest in the humanities sparked when I was an undergraduate at Yale University trying to find my way through a major in American studies. The fact that Ann Fabian and Nancy Cott are such superb teachers and scholars played no small part in my decision to become a historian. Margaret T. McFadden and Lee Winthrop also helped to move me forward in college. In graduate school at Stanford University, it was Estelle Freedman who supported me throughout this entire writing process by allowing me to explore my own ideas and helping me marshal my arguments and forms of expression. She is a mentor in the truest sense of the word and has brought me to levels of thought and dedication that I never imagined possible. I am also grateful to Stanford faculty who shared their expertise and trained me in the art of historical inquiry, especially Richard White, Joy Williamson, Michael Thompson, and David Tyack. The staff in the Department of History at Stanford, especially the late Gertrud Pacheco, also deserve praise.

My friends wisely taught me that producing scholarship is not an individual struggle, but rather a series of community efforts in researching, teaching, and learning. Thanks to Shana Bernstein, Marisela Chávez, Dawn Mabalon, Rachel Jean-Baptiste, and especially Cecilia Tsu for reading the pages that I decided to keep, as well as the ones that I did not. Roberta Durham, Valerie McGuire, Sile O'Modhrain, Nimmi Paulraj, and friends from the Peace Corps and CCSAS deliberately made my life in Palo Alto easier and more enriching so that I could concentrate on my studies. A special word of appreciation goes to Patricia Charles Brown and Candace Brown Janowitz for prodding my forward momentum from my California days into the present. Rockhurst University provided ample support so that I could simultaneously write and facilitate service-learning projects. My colleagues at the University of Kansas tracked down sources and helped me to navigate the complicated world of academe. I extend a special word of thanks to the Department of History staff, Pam LeRow in the College of Liberal Arts and Sciences, and those who offered gracious and substantial feedback on various parts of this project, including Luis Corteguera, Jonathan Earle, Steven Epstein, Megan Greene, Eve Levin, Elizabeth MacGonagle, Rita Napier, Leslie Tuttle, and Marta Vicente. I am especially grateful for all of the support from members of the Junior League, the KC-KU writing group, the Gender Seminar, the American Studies program, Women, Gender and Sexuality Studies program, and the School of Education, especially Giselle Anatol, Tamara Falicov, Marni Kessler, Ann Rowland, John Rury, Ann Schofield, and Sherrie Tucker.

Generous funding allowed for research trips and time to concentrate, so I thank the Department of History and the Institute for Research on Women and Gender at Stanford University, the Mellon Mays University Fellows Program at the Woodrow Wilson Foundation, and the Andrew W. Mellon Foundation. After seeing a remarkable exhibit on desegregation at the Smithsonian National Museum of American History, Jack and Kathleen Kelly generously funded a trip to Washington so that I could see it, too. While at the University of Kansas, I have been fortunate to receive funding from the New Faculty and General Research Fund through the KU Center for Research and a Vice Provost Book Subvention award from the Hall Center for the Humanities. Kathy Porsch is a remarkable grants coordinator and deserves much praise for helping me to transform my ideas into fundable proposals. A very special word of thanks goes to the National Academy for Education/Spencer Foundation staff, faculty fellows, and scholars, especially William Reese, Patricia Graham, and Benjamin Justice for providing several opportunities to substantially revise this book.

The organizers of Shifting Borders of Race and Identity, a project funded by a Ford Foundation grant held by the University of Kansas and Haskell Indian Nations University, welcomed me into their fold and ultimately helped me to further engage in an ever-expanding field of African American–Native American scholarship. I especially thank James Brooks for his comments on a conference paper, James Leiker and Barbara Watkins for co-editing *The First and the Forced* with me, and Victor Bailey and Zanice Bond de Pérez for skillfully guiding the project for three years.

Archivists and librarians liberally made materials available and pointed me to sources that I never would have found on my own. I am indebted to the staff members at the Kansas City, Kansas Public Library, the Wyandotte County Historical Museum, Special Collections at Wichita State University Libraries, the Haskell Indian Nations University Cultural Center and Museum, the Kansas City, Kansas and Fort Scott school districts, the Manuscripts and Archives Collection of the Sterling Memorial Library at Yale University, the National Ministries Division of the Presbyterian Church, and the Presbyterian Historical Society. Deborah Dandridge created an incredible number of paths for my research at the Kenneth Spencer Research Library, and Bobbi Rahder got me started with my study of Haskell Indian Nations University. Tami Albin and Ada Emmett at the University of Kansas Libraries, Tim Rives at the National Archives and Records Administration–Central Plains Region, Mary Conrad at Sumner Academy, and Arnold Schofield at the Fort Scott National Historical Site proved to be essential, enthusiastic, and amusing guides. Virgil Dean and his colleagues led me to vital sources at the Kansas State Historical Society and gave me permission to incorporate material in Chapter 6 from my article "'All Indian Trails Lead to Lawrence, October 27 to 30, 1926': American Identity and the Dedication of Haskell Institute's Football Stadium," which appeared in the Spring 2007 issue of *Kansas History: A Journal of the Central Plains*. Outside of the archives, a number of generous collaborators shared their own comments, works in progress, and photographs and letters with me, including Philip Deloria, William Hart, Mildred Buster Hart, Susan Gardner, Elizabeth "Jing" Lyman, Peggy Pascoe, and Kirk Sharp.

I have always relied upon and admired the books published by the University of North Carolina Press and am humbled to be included among its group of authors. Chuck Grench and Katy O'Brien ushered this project through important developmental and production stages with astute attention to both the historian and the history being written. Tiya Miles and Wilbert Ahern invested their valuable time and wisdom in this project. They were terrifically thorough with their reviews of the manuscript and kindly provided precise insight to make my arguments stronger and more cohesive.

During the many years that this book transformed into its final incarnation, I was fortunate to have a community to support and sustain me and my work. Numerous friends and cousins put me up, let me borrow their cars during research trips, listened to my ideas, asked smart questions, clipped newspaper articles, and made repairs on my house—none of which I took for granted. Over the years, an amazing transformation happened as several friends became family and many family members became friends—I am fortunate for those experiences. I especially appreciate that during the last phase of this project their roles became increasingly important as special aunts, uncles, cousins, and grandparents to my son and to me. An enthusiastic appreciation goes to all of the cousins, aunts, and uncles who claim the Crnic family as their own, as well as to the Mahers, the Petersons, the Salems, the Thuts, the Youngs, Alex Williams, Phil Johnson, Myra Jenkins, and Julia Schulte. On a number of occasions, Dan and Shane McEnany provided comic relief, and Cara McEnany danced into the world just in time to get her name in print. Extra special words of gratitude go to my sister, Angie McEnany, my cousin, Jennifer Sease, and my friend, Babs Mullins, who have always gone beyond the call of duty. My appreciation would not be complete without acknowledging the ancestors who encouraged my early scholarly attempts, especially Mary I. Crnic, Armerike Warren, and Gertrude Shumway. As for Luke Warren, he has been nothing short of an extraordinary light in my life and a gift beyond description. Now that the project is finished I dedicate this book to his future, as well as to the memory of the one who made everything possible, Carol Warren—my mother, my inspiration, and my first teacher.

The Quest for

CITIZENSHIP

Introduction

In 1944, G. B. Buster, a longtime African American teacher, gave a college commencement speech imploring churches, community organizations, and government leaders to sound a "clarion call" that would finally solve the largest social problem in the United States—racial tension between whites and people of color. If members of the larger society were to continue fostering "race prejudice, discrimination, arrogance, insult, and exploitation of minority groups," the entire country would feel the harm. Therefore, he charged his audience, comprised mostly of African Americans, to work together with whites in pressing for the enforcement of equal civil rights for all Americans.[1] A few years earlier in 1941, Henry Roe Cloud (Winnebago), a well-known Native American activist and educator, addressed a group of superintendents of Indian agencies and reservations. He criticized the federal government for its past record of destroying Indian cultures and praised the more recent efforts toward preserving cultural practices, studying traditions before they completely disappeared, and encouraging self-government among Native American tribes. He hoped for a day when Indians could embrace the kind of political organizations, industries, and economics modeled by the dominant society without having to give up their own arts, religions, and aesthetics—two sets of values that many whites had often thought of as incompatible.[2]

In each address, Buster and Roe Cloud, respectively, represented long-held desires of twentieth-century African Americans and Native Americans with regard to American citizenship. Black parents, leaders, and teachers like Buster had been working for decades for social integration and equal rights in their schools and in other public places. When they spoke of citizenship, they expressed their longing for complete inclusion with all of the accompanying rights and privileges. At the same time, Native American students, teachers, and activists like Roe Cloud had pushed back against decades of assault on their own cultures, beliefs, and traditions and instead said that they could claim identities as American citizens by embracing the behaviors, habits, and practices that whites demanded while simultaneously holding onto their traditional customs. Inclusion and integration for African Americans and autonomy and bicultural identities for Native Americans provided the focal point for each group's understanding of what it meant to be an American in the twentieth century, even though those notions stood in exact opposition to the ideas that white reformers had originally outlined for them a few decades earlier in the 1880s and 1890s.

The Quest for Citizenship tells the story of how, during the last decades of the nineteenth century, in the midst of confusion about the status of Indians and blacks in the United States, white reformers opened separate schools for children from each group in order to fit them into the dominant culture's definitions of American citizenship. At the time, most whites considered Native Americans and African Americans outsiders, vulnerable to forced migration, violence, and warfare or to colonization and removal. Missionaries, educators, and government officials—whom I call reformers—referred to the longtime exclusion of Native Americans and blacks from American identity as the "Indian Problem" and the "Negro Problem," and those who tried to solve each problem considered themselves to be friendly advocates whose educational campaigns were intended to elevate students' status in American society. They operated under similar ideologies and used similar curricula in black and Indian schools, yet there were distinct differences between the ways in which education prepared students for citizenship roles depending on their race. For Native Americans, segregated education required children to move away from Indian reservations and aspire to full assimilation. Segregated schools purported to prepare them for transition into public schools with white students and ultimately into work environments with white adults. The possibility of intermarriage between whites and Indians could perform the final step toward integration of Native Americans into white society; or as one reformer argued, intermarriage "gradually narrow[ed] down the racial cleavage."[3] Reformers hoped that by learning to speak English, attending mandatory Christian services, and engaging in so-called American activities—joining the YWCA or the Boys Scouts, for example—Native American children would eventually become indistinguishable from white Americans. Altering students' cultural attributes, (e.g., hair, dress, and language), would eradicate their "Indianness," thereby transforming their various tribal identities into a single American one. Conversely, white reformers almost always designed segregated education for African Americans with the intention of preparing students for a lifetime of marginalization. Black students were to be transformed into citizens who would make contributions to the larger society through their labor in tandem with, but distinctly separate from, whites. Reformers believed that blacks would neither blend with nor disappear into white society in public schools or through marriage because their racial category was considered to be less mutable than the tribal identities of Native Americans. Instead, they wanted African American students to conform to a set of values and behaviors to help them become well-trained laborers, domestic workers, and farmers—positions that would subjugate them to distinct and permanently lower-class positions in society. A sense of duty to God and the nation guided reformers' efforts, but as benevolent as they thought they were being, reformers never truly viewed members of minority groups as their equals. Inevitably the schools they created pushed African Americans and Native Americans outside of mainstream American society.

Despite the determination of reformers to create their own versions of minority citizens, both Indians and blacks ultimately created new versions of American identities for themselves. Native American students often ran away from school, shared their forbidden traditions, and found other means of protest while they were in school. On behalf of African American students, parents and other advocates not only contested the inferior condition of their schools, but also took advantage of segregated environments out of view of white school boards to develop curricular and extracurricular programs infused with race pride. In the twentieth century, when Native Americans became teachers themselves, they also encouraged their students to take pride in their heritage and adopt pan-Indian identities while simultaneously developing a sense of biculturalism that allowed them to integrate into white American culture whenever they desired. Both African American and Native American teachers showed their students that it was possible to move away from the predetermined definitions of American citizenship established by white reformers, and thus Indians and blacks reversed the intentions of white missionaries, teachers, and government leaders by redefining what it meant for them to be American.

Although blacks and Native Americans responded to similar educational campaigns in the 1880s and 1890s, they reacted differently to the expectations that their segregated schools established. Dissimilar perceptions about the role of the law in their lives guided each group's actions; that is, African Americans, believing that they had always been integral to the nation's history, sought legal means to foster social change and equality, but Native Americans, not necessarily wanting to be completely absorbed into white society, grew increasingly distrustful of a government that had systematically broken up their lands and their families.[4] Therefore, African Americans fought segregation and sought legal inclusion and formal integration as ways to bolster their roles as citizens. At the same time, Native Americans recovered cultural traits that whites had attempted to destroy and protected them in order to provide a foundation for modern American identities that did not preclude Indian traditions and languages and sometimes allowed for separateness from white society. By the early twentieth century, both groups had thrown off the prescriptions for citizenship that white educators had created for them and crafted new definitions of what it meant to be an American, including taking pride in their own cultures.

It is important to note that for Indians and blacks, claiming American identities proved particularly challenging because, at different times in American history, members of these groups had been considered property, wards of the government, or even enemies of the United States Army. While these two groups were not the only minorities to suffer discrimination in the nineteenth and twentieth centuries (various populations of Asian and Latino descent being other examples), the focus in this book is on them and on their uncomfortable fit in an American society dominated in numbers and power by whites. African American and Native American citizenship status was confusing at best, sometimes filled with contradictions, and often unclear. The very survival of African Americans and Native Americans threatened the stability of white domination and existing conceptions of racial hierarchy. Martha Hodes argues that African Americans' freedom, in particular, challenged traditional notions of racial order and threatened a social system that had for so long equated blackness with slavery and whiteness with freedom.[5] Although their status was indeterminate under the Constitution, American-born blacks were formally granted citizenship in 1868 by the Fourteenth Amendment, while some nineteenth-century treaties allowed for citizenship among certain Indian tribes. But the Fourteenth Amendment certainly could not enforce African Americans' civil rights, and the 1884 Supreme Court case *Elk v. Wilkins* ruled that Indians born on United States soil were not necessarily citizens in the absence of formal naturalization. The 1887 Dawes Act also largely failed in its attempt to grant legal citizenship to land-owning Native Americans, so universal citizenship for Indians would not be granted until 1924. Such legal ambiguity combined with shifts in late-nineteenth-century Indian policy that turned Native Americans from targets for removal and extinction to targets for education and uplift added to the puzzle that was Indian citizenship.

For members of both groups, de facto (as well as de jure) segregation prevented them from enjoying privileges of citizenship even if they possessed a nominally legal status.[6]

Although the changing political and legal status of Indians and African Americans provides an important backdrop for this book, my focus is *cultural* citizenship, or a sense of belonging. Cultural citizenship, as I am defining it, is dynamic in nature, an "ongoing ideological process" that provides a useful perspective on "the ways that people have been historical agents of change," to apply pertinent concepts from Gail Bederman's categories of social organization. To be clear, I am defining cultural citizenship as a set of feelings and modes of behaving within the larger American society rather than a way of exercising a specific set of political or legal rights.[7] Therefore, I use the terms "citizenship," "identity," and "being American" interchangeably to signal a relationship to the nation in which whites, blacks, and Indians lived.

To white reformers, citizenship for African Americans and Native Americans meant specifically defined roles and purposes in the social and labor structure of the larger society; but to people of color, a claim on American identity could also be measured by the ability of individuals to enjoy the respect and protection that came with that identity: to move freely throughout their own city and other regions of the country, to live where they chose, to find jobs to support themselves and their families, to achieve some degree of economic mobility, and to influence the type of identities their children would develop. Blacks believed that real citizens could acquire liberty, improve their economic circumstances, exercise their vote, buy land, serve on juries, gain better employment, and combat institutionalized prejudice and hostility.[8] Native Americans often spoke of being able to experience tranquility with neighbors, determine their own economic futures, live in safe communities, serve in the military, own land, practice religious freedom, hold onto their cultural identities, and as Philip Deloria argues, practice elements of performance when needed.[9] Both groups stressed ideological beliefs in their own independence, intelligence, self-reliance, and right to educational opportunities, and both groups resisted and negotiated the prescriptions for citizenship that white reformers originally laid out for them. For those reasons, citizenship in this book does not simply refer to legal definitions of nationality but rather addresses an ongoing consciousness or feeling of belonging within the larger population, keeping these central questions in mind: How did blacks and Indians think of themselves as Americans? How did their notions of citizenship get influenced or crafted by white reformers in schools? How did these two groups define American citizenship for themselves despite whites' efforts to dictate those definitions?

Citizenship Training

In the nineteenth century, when the responsibility for citizenship training shifted from families to schools, educational thresholds allowed reformers to inculcate patriotism, skills for future jobs, and a sense of national identity into children. Schools became the vehicles through which reformers defined American behavior, language, work ethics, and religious beliefs for students throughout the country. Although nineteenth-century reformers spoke of the possibility of meaningful citizenship for people of color, they created curricula focusing on laborious industrial training and strict religious indoctrination while demanding conformity to their own ideas. Classrooms turned into contested terrains where funders, teachers, families, and students battled over the social, political, and economic roles that students would later play as adults in the United States. In the western region of the country, citizenship training took on special meaning because white reformers believed that students' minds were open, ideological landscapes, presumably like the geography surrounding them.

Using education as a portal to understand race and American identity between 1880 and 1935, this book shows that if we are to understand citizenship at the turn of the twentieth century, we need to examine American identities from multiple vantage points. By comparing the thoughts and intentions of three groups concerned with education—whites, blacks, and Indians—we can see how each group came to different conclusions about American identity. White teachers, missionaries, and government officials generally thought of education as the opportunity to shape their students' malleable minds and habits. This was different from the point of view of many African Americans, who viewed schools as important magnets for the modern generation of college-educated teachers that created platforms from which black middle-class communities could develop in growing urban centers. For Native Americans, schools often became a physical and figurative crossroad where Indians of various tribes could meet, develop pan-Indian identities, and then radiate their influence over fellow Indians throughout the country. Taken together, it is possible to see the importance of education and schools in what Alan Trachtenberg calls the "ongoing drama of the making of Americans." Indeed, for all involved, the idea of being American was at stake.[10]

The starting point of this book is the 1880s, or the beginning of the Jim Crow period when many whites often denied blacks their freedoms, political rights, and sometimes their lives. The 1880s was also the Indian Assimilation period when most whites turned away from policies of extinction toward efforts meant to absorb Native Americans completely into white society. With Progressive-era educational innovations in mind, this book chronicles the concerns of white reformers and the experiences of students and their parents and teachers in Native American and African American missionary, government, private, and public schools through the mid-1930s, an era when attention to the preservation of Indian cultures increased and a growing federal intervention in response to the Great Depression ushered in the New Deal.

Ultimately, *The Quest for Citizenship* tells stories that reveal three essential points. First, I argue that at the same time that white reformers launched assaults on African American and Native American cultures, they still expected the children in both groups to learn how to become Americans. They wanted students to incorporate their American identities at various degrees of inclusion, depending on their race and gender. Second, I argue that Native Americans and African Americans had distinct and creative ways of asserting themselves in response to the efforts of reformers. Most notably, Indian students negotiated their rights and identities with white reformers in relative isolation at boarding schools without the aid of adults they trusted, whereas black parents and leaders, acting on behalf of the younger generation, protested against inequality through legal channels because they wanted to effect systematic shifts toward legal integration. Third, I argue that Native American and African American teachers, many of whom had been educated in segregated schools themselves, redefined the concept of American identity to mean that their students could both maintain racial or tribal identities as well as claim a sense of belonging within the dominant culture. By both resisting and negotiating with white reformers, African Americans and Native Americans created new patterns of citizenship to define their own sense of American identity. As early as the 1910s, black teachers created an academic discipline, African American studies, to address the absence of black history and literature in their standard textbooks, and they pushed for college-preparatory curricula as well as full-scale integration into white society. Eventually, these teachers joined other leaders in the fight for integration that culminated in *Brown v. Board of Education*. In contrast, many Native American teachers resisted full assimilation into white society and therefore taught their students how to navigate their way through it while creating the pan-Indian identities and reclaiming the very traditions and tribal cultures that some white teachers had attempted to destroy in the nineteenth century. Both groups of leaders employed tools that they had obtained as students and used them for their own empowerment in ways that their teachers neither intended nor foresaw.

The Symbolic Power of Kansas

Kansas—neither particularly northern nor southern, and yet reflective of educational and social trends in *both* the North and the South—is a place that Americans have continually turned into a testing ground for ideas about the ways in which they should think about themselves. The state has long been at the geographical and ideological center of battles over freedom, citizenship, equality, and education as evidenced by the 1854 Kansas-Nebraska Act, the era of Bleeding Kansas in the 1850s, the destruction of Indian reservations by the 1887 Dawes Act, and the 1954 Supreme Court case *Brown v. Board of Education*. Although the state had been linked through communication, economics, and transportation to the rest of the nation since the mid-nineteenth century, and in many ways was forward-thinking in terms of early legislation on woman suffrage and civil rights, Kansas still seemed to be just barely keeping pace with modern developments through the first decade of the twentieth century.[11]

The philosophically progressive yet practically unresolved political nature of Kansas has allowed the state to repeatedly serve as an ideological reflecting pool of national worries about freedom and citizenship. Therefore, in this book, Kansas is not simply a fixed physical point in the geography of the United States. Rather, the symbolic power of Kansas provides an especially important anchor for understanding how whites, Native Americans, and blacks struggled with the puzzle of citizenship throughout the nation. Since American citizenship is so intrinsically tied to notions of freedom, it makes sense to turn to a state that has prided itself on free ideals to understand American identities. "Kansas was born in a struggle for liberty and freedom," suggests Richard Sheridan, and that point was not missed by those who grappled with questions about citizenship and American identity as the meaning of freedom and equality moved from battlefields into classrooms in the second half of the nineteenth century.[12]

Kansas has earned its reputation as a testing ground where arguments about slavery, state sovereignty, integration, and evolution in schools and in courtrooms have reflected national concerns about politics, the law, and morality. Recently the media have reported on school boards in Delaware and other states that have officially allowed the study of intelligent design to be added to their school curricula, but popular beliefs about this evolution-creationism debate often refer to a single state, Kansas, "Where Evolution Is Optional," as a bumper sticker touts. The idea of Kansas has become shorthand for multiple places in the United States that have endured ideological conflicts about how the nation should move forward. At the same time, Kansas boosters still claim that their state has a greater potential to provide freedom and equality for its residents than any other. During the late nineteenth and early twentieth centuries, those who migrated to Kansas did so in hopes of finding what Nell Painter has called "real freedom." For white Free-Soilers seeking an escape from the industrialization and wage labor system of the Northeast, Kansas held out hope of owning land. African Americans viewed Kansas as a place of refuge for slaves escaping through the Underground Railroad; the nineteenth-century Congregational minister Richard Cordley claimed "that not less than one hundred thousand dollars' worth of slaves passed through Lawrence on their way to liberty during the territorial period." Blacks also saw the state as a "New Canaan," or "Promised Land," during the mass exodus from the South in the late 1870s and 1880s. Even before the exodus, there were higher percentages of African Americans in the state—among the first to ratify the Thirteenth Amendment abolishing slavery—than in any other state that had not held slaves. The population of blacks rapidly increased from over 43,000 by 1880 to 100,000 at the end of the 1930s. Although African Americans comprised no more than 6 percent of the population, they were largely concentrated in the eastern part of the state and at times formed important voting blocks, from 15 to 20 percent of voters. During the era of Indian removal in the 1830s, Kansas became a destination for exiled Native Americans who were forcibly removed from Ohio and other eastern states. Kickapoos, Sac and Foxes, Iowas, and Potawatomis joined other tribes with a long history in the Great Plains region, including the Pawnees, Osages, Kiowa, Cheyenne, and Arapaho. By the 1870s, Plains Indian populations had declined so much that they could no longer resist white encroachment, but

Native Americans in Kansas totaling only 815 in 1880 did manage to increase to 2,180 by 1900 and grew slightly to 2,444 by 1910. Compared to the rest of the country, Kansas seemed both welcoming to migrating blacks and capable of accommodating Indians, whether indigenous to the area or not. And even though the state may not have provided the "real freedom" that these migrants hoped for, the reputation of Kansas as the "Free State" maintains its symbolic standing into the twenty-first century.[13]

For more than a century, Kansas has drawn people from across the nation to struggle with contentious issues that reflect problems throughout the country. John Brown anchored his antislavery campaign in Kansas and became legendary when he wielded his vigilante terrorism against proslavery proponents in 1856. Almost twenty-five years later, in the 1880s, abolitionists Elizabeth Comstock and Laura Haviland moved to Kansas to help African American Exodusters acquire promises of freedom. They had been abolitionists since they were young women, yet in their sixties and seventies, they answered a call to assist the state to fulfill its pledge of freedom for black migrants who had recently moved out of the South. In 1915, Henry Roe Cloud also chose Kansas as the site of his high school for Native American boys because he thought the heartland would be the most strategic place to train students who would then radiate their influence over Indians throughout the nation. And although the director, writer, and photographer Gordon Parks left his childhood home of Fort Scott as a teenager in 1928, the state's struggle to maintain its symbolic claim as the quintessential Free State — despite the Jim Crow segregation that permeated cities like Fort Scott — has held a prominent place in Parks's poetry and literature.

Historiographical Considerations

Construction of whiteness and nonwhiteness, along with ideas about masculine and feminine citizenship, informs this study about the making of American identities by whites, blacks, and Indians during a fifty-five-year period. Today scholars agree that race and gender are not fixed but everchanging categories that have been socially constructed in the context of certain times and locations. Matthew Frye Jacobson uses terms like "fabrication" and "invented categories" to point out that race is generated by politics and culture rather than nature; so, for example, Caucasians "are not born . . . they are somehow made."[14] However, the reformers, students, and parents discussed in this book were not likely of the same mind. Instead, to them race was most obviously signaled by skin color, and the prevailing

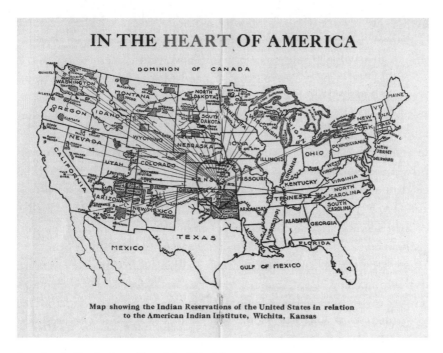

IN THE HEART OF AMERICA

Map showing the Indian Reservations of the United States in relation
to the American Indian Institute, Wichita, Kansas

American Indian Institute Map of the United States. Henry Roe Cloud opened American
Indian Institute in Kansas because he believed that a school located in the center of
the nation would attract a variety of students who would then radiate their influence
throughout the country. (Courtesy of Roe Family Papers, Manuscripts and Archives,
Yale University Library)

scientific racism supported racial hierarchies and rankings of peoples. By
1900, these notions had become what Alan Trachtenberg calls "an article of
faith among most Euro-Americans" that bound minorities to a lower status
than whites in American society.[15] Gender categories, in their minds, were
also fixed, biologically determined, and attached to traditions of hierarchy
and unequal distributions of power. Both race and gender distinctions have
been formulated to group and separate people along lines of what Jacobson
refers to as "presumed difference."[16] This book compares the ways that African Americans and Native Americans wrestled with seemingly fixed racial
and gender categories—sometimes accepting popular beliefs and often
challenging hierarchies in the hope of opening up new possibilities. In addition, with a definition of the frontier as a site for the colliding and meld-
ing of cultures in mind, I focus on the ways in which disparate ideas about
American identities clashed and then created opportunities for new ones to
emerge.[17] In order to help readers understand the ideas at play, I have often

quoted directly from the subjects who appear in these pages, allowing their individual voices to tell their own stories. I have also noted their relationship to their school, community, or uplift movement.

The scholarship on Native American and African American education is rich and contributes to the historical depth of this book. In particular, scholars have called Indian boarding schools "total institutions" that dictated every minute of Native American students' lives while they were in attendance. But they have also shown that such schools inadvertently provided common meeting grounds for students to share the very tribal customs and experiences that white reformers tried to eradicate.[18] By examining the range of ways that students negotiated the terms of their education and by analyzing the strategies of Native American teachers who took on leadership positions in their schools in the twentieth century, I argue that Indians came to define their American identities as a mixture of traditional and adopted characteristics, sometimes using those combinations as a means to educate white audiences and sometimes as a means to navigate their own careers while maintaining some sense of sovereignty in the face of continual federal interference. For their part, African Americans have a long history of using literacy as an instrument of resistance and liberation and a tool for arguing for inclusion in civil society. The scholarship on southern education is deep, and recent studies on African American education in the North have added many layers of understanding to segregation and inequality, but few scholars have tried to understand black education in a state that typically belongs to neither region.[19] This book examines African Americans in a western region of the country, paying particular attention to the ways that black parents and teachers confronted the ideologies of freedom that Kansas purported to provide for all of its inhabitants, in order to examine the simultaneous march toward legal integration and the use of segregated schools to reshape the goals of black education toward social, political, and economic uplift.

Drawing on historical sources from a set of Kansas schools, most of which were initially started by white founders, this book traces the rise of and fall of individual institutions, but not in the fashion of a traditional case study model. Instead, *The Quest for Citizenship* uses evidence about these schools to explicate turn-of-the-century reform ideology, curricula established for minority Americans, the ways in which Native American and black students and adults negotiated the opportunities and limits of segregated education, and the methods that Indian and African American graduates used to shift the contours of American identity when they became adults.

By examining the experiences of two minority groups of people, I also make a methodological shift in the study of race in the United States by moving from a traditional black/white orientation to one that is multicultural and comparative. The focus on African Americans and Native Americans, in particular, adds to the expanding field of black-Indian studies. Rather than seeking out intersections like the important work of James Brooks and Tiya Miles does, I show how similar schooling experiences ultimately led to divergent paths because of the strategies that each group employed and because of the roles that they played in shaping their American identities.[20]

Organization of Chapters

The chapters that follow thematically and chronologically lay out definitions of citizenship from multiple points of view across a half century. The book is divided into three sections: First, "Origins, Ideology, and Racial Hierarchies," which looks at how white reformers initially crafted citizenship roles for nonwhite students in the late nineteenth century; second, "Strategies of Negotiation," which explores how African American and Indian children and adults wrestled with the prescriptions that whites had laid out for them; and third, "New Leaders in the Twentieth Century," which shows how a generation of students grew into adults determined to cultivate American identities on their own terms.

The first chapter, "Reformers," concentrates on the people who raised large questions about where Indians and African Americans would live, how they would survive economically, and what roles they would occupy in the postwar society. Although they employed various methods to address what they called the "Negro Problem" and the "Indian Problem," reformers all agreed that education would be the most effective, the most universal, and sometimes the only solution to the problems of inequality that African Americans and Native Americans faced. Elizabeth Comstock, Laura Haviland, Hervey Peairs, and their contemporaries took on great responsibility for the education of blacks and Indians, but rather than alter the laws or the attitudes of the dominant society, these well-intentioned white reformers attempted to change students to fit into particular social and economic places in society. They optimistically spoke of blacks and Native Americans eventually elevating into active roles in society, and they invoked concepts of equality and freedom when they discussed citizenship training. And yet they repeatedly reinforced the very racial hierarchies that they had promised to overturn. Like many colonialists, white reformers thought more about their own status on their imagined evolutionary ladder than about those who occupied lower rungs. In the end, they followed the ideology of race hierarchy to preserve their top position above all other races.

Chapter 2, "Curriculum," shifts away from ideologies to the structures and curricula that white reformers established for Native American and black students. The uniformity and rigidity of students' daily schedules indicates reformers' belief that students could acquire citizenship by adopting a set of cultural practices and habits. Curricular and extracurricular programs at Native American and black schools resembled each other since they both required Christian indoctrination and industrial training while emphasizing conformity to ideals of Victorian, middle-class gender roles, in which boys would become farmers or laborers while girls would become housewives. Although curricula at both sets of schools were similar, this chapter shows that the intended outcomes for African Americans and Native Americans were different. While Native Americans were supposed to use their education to assimilate, and even disappear, into white society through subsequent generations of intermarriage, African Americans were to use their education to learn how to be hard workers who maintained a distinct position on the margins of white society.

Chapter 3, "Students," turns to Native American students' reactions to the teachers and curriculum at a federal Indian boarding school, Haskell Indian Institute. Students exhibited a range of responses to the confines that their school placed on them, including negotiating the terms of their enrollment with school officials and outright rebellion or arson. In a few cases, Native American parents advocated for their children's needs, but because boarding schools were deliberately located far from reservations to remove the influence of their families, the majority of students fended for themselves. In doing so, they developed their own sense of self-determination as intrinsic to their own definitions of citizenship.

Chapter 4, "Parents," examines how black adults organized themselves into groups to call for better schools and for legal integration into white schools. African Americans thought that they resided in a Promised Land, where they would have a better chance to buy land, earn fair wages, send their children to good schools, and insert themselves into the mainstream of society than they or their parents had in the South. Indeed, many found better lives in Kansas, and yet African American also pointed out the contradictions between the state's special claim to freedom and the segregationist conditions that existed there. Segregation was prevalent in schools and public spaces, but to black parents, teachers, and leaders, citizenship meant that they could use collective political action to force the legal system to make good on Reconstruction-era promises for equality. Arguing that legal segregation threatened the integrity of American society as a whole, African Americans also developed new ideas about black education that did not depend on industrial training and fought for schools that would prepare their children for more prosperous lives than their own. Unlike Native American leaders whose desire for government assistance had waned, black leaders continually demanded local, state, and federal legislatures to change the structures of oppression that they had endured.

Chapter 5, "Teachers," continues the discussion of African American advocates by examining the strategies of black teachers who resisted discrimination and fought for more inclusion in society. While they waited for their efforts to turn the tide of segregation, black reformers used creative and sometimes covert measures to insert race pride and African American studies into their educational activities. Early-twentieth-century teachers, such as William Vernon and G. B. Buster, represented a new generation of black leaders who argued that to be American meant to be fully integrated into public spaces. After they took the helm at black schools, teachers took advantage of the shield from white observers that segregated schools inadvertently provided to prepare students for college, professional jobs, and leadership. Black teachers resisted pressure from white school boards and funders to perpetually teach industrial education and instead created new pathways for their students' achievement and acceptance within the dominant society.

Chapter 6, "Identity," examines the changes that took place when former students of Indian schools became teachers themselves. By adopting bicultural identities, Native American leaders Ella Deloria (Dakota) and Henry Roe Cloud showed that to be American meant to be able to negotiate with white society as well as reclaim the very traditions, culture, and identities that their teachers had once tried to annihilate. When Native Americans flocked to a 1926 powwow at Haskell Institute to celebrate a new football stadium and World War I memorial arch, they embraced pan-Indian pride. By raising their own money for the new stadium, dressing in traditional wear, and demonstrating Indian dances, twentieth-century Indians reversed the very lessons that they had been taught in their Native American schools and reclaimed Indian heritage as part of their American identities.

By the 1930s, blacks and Native Americans contributed more readily to the formation of their own American identities. It would be their students, and, in particular, their children who participated in and led black civil rights and Indian rights activities in later decades. Specifically, descendants of Indians and African Americans raised in Kansas played key roles in watershed moments of the Indian rights and civil rights movements, the occupation of Alcatraz Island in 1969, and in the *Brown v. Board of Education* case in 1954. Comparing African American and Indian struggles to define their citizenship roles, *The Quest for Citizenship* shows that although black and Indian students did not attend school together and very few individuals in this book actually ever met, their combined experiences tell a complicated story of the hopes, disappointments, limits, and possibilities regarding Native American and black identity. By examining ideologies, structures, and behaviors, this book reveals how the large-scale efforts of white reformers ultimately failed and how small groups of African Americans and Indians resisted decades of attacks on their own cultures through campaigns involving thousands of people, millions of dollars, and decades of effort. Through persistent negotiations, Native Americans and blacks not only made changes in segregated education, but they also expanded their own of notions American identity, increased their participation as citizens of the United States, and fanned the flames of the civil rights and Indian rights movements that would explode in the 1950s through the 1970s.

Part I

ORIGINS, IDEOLOGY, AND RACIAL HIERARCHIES

Chapter One

REFORMERS

"FRIENDS OF THE INDIANS" AND
"FRIENDS OF THE NEGROES"

The Indian question is not any more difficult than
the Slavery question, and it is not very different from it.
—*National Anti-Slavery Standard*, 1 May 1869

I never could understand how he knew just where to draw the color
line, since the Indian and I were about the same complexion.
—Booker T. Washington, *Up from Slavery*

In 1879, when Elizabeth Comstock first heard about the exodus, a mass migration of African Americans from southern states to Kansas, she immediately started a collection to provide for their relief. A white abolitionist before the Civil War, Comstock had developed sympathy for blacks in earlier decades, and she also gained exceptional skill in gathering support and money for African American causes. After traveling throughout the United States and her native England for two years, Comstock had collected $60,000 in cash and goods for the Kansas Freedmen's Relief Association (KFRA), an organization which had extended the relief efforts that the federal Freedmen's Bureau had abandoned since 1868.

With her collection and her national recognition, she journeyed from the Northeast to Kansas to start her work with other white reformers to provide housing, job training, and education to adult Exodusters. For the children, Comstock helped to open the Agricultural and Industrial Institute for Refugees, a school on 400 acres of land just east of the town of Columbus, in the foothills of the Ozark Mountains; a location that white townspeople called "Nigger Hill."[1] With a curriculum that emphasized work and

"En Route for Kansas," Drawing by H. J. Lewis, *Harper's Weekly*, 16 August 1879. In hopes of better lives, thousands of African Americans migrated out of the South into Kansas during the late 1870s and 1880s and established black neighborhoods such as Tennesseetown in Topeka. (Courtesy of HarpWeek, LLC)

ignored any cultural values that the Exodusters might have brought with them during their migration, the school started with the express purpose of providing African Americans with "skills to survive and prosper."[2]

Although the sixty-four-year-old Comstock had extraordinary success in raising both money and attention for the plight of poverty-stricken African Americans, it was her religious missionary zeal that reflected the common attitude of many white reformers in the late nineteenth century. When the Institute for Refugees opened on 15 April 1881, Comstock illustrated the link between abolition and educational efforts by declaring that her work was a continuation of the project that Abraham Lincoln, "our martered [*sic*] President," had begun. "He crowned the labors of Abolitionists. It is left to the Christian Philanthropists of our age to crown his great work," she proclaimed.[3] Comstock also considered the antislavery crusader John Brown a martyred hero, who had planted a proverbial "tree of liberty" and "whose soul was still marching on." She claimed that her abolitionist and educational work naturally extended Lincoln's and Brown's legacies.[4] James McPherson would later describe the founding of schools like Comstock's as the extension of abolitionists' "missionary impulse to a new frontier."[5] Concern for the plight of African Americans pushed her own efforts, but not more than Comstock's sense of duty to her adopted country and to her Christian ideals.

In 1884, three years after the founding of the Institute for Refugees, an off-reservation, federal boarding school for Native Americans, Haskell Indian Institute, opened in Lawrence, 175 miles north of Comstock's school. While the Institute for Refugees was intended for educating "and training people of the colored race,"[6] the Haskell Institute, originally named the United States Indian Industrial Training School, was one of several Indian schools founded in the 1880s when the federal government increased its attention to the survival of Native American people. In 1882, Congress allocated $150,000 for industrial, off-reservation boarding schools. The new schools were to be located in the West, specifically in Nebraska, Kansas, and Oklahoma, where the concentration of Indians lived, and where the frontier represented new possibilities. The chair of the House Committee on Indian Affairs, Representative Dudley Chase Haskell from Kansas, had lobbied specifically for a school in Lawrence (a small town between Topeka and Kansas City) because it enjoyed the advantages of electricity, three main railroad lines, and the educational resources of the University of Kansas. Dudley Haskell succeeded with his lobby, and when the school bearing his name opened, Indian agents first drew students from the reservation day schools and mission schools in the area.[7] Twenty-two boys and girls in grades one through five entered during the first semester, and the enrollment quickly grew to over four hundred students from the entire Plains region by the end of the first school year. During the first three years of operation, Haskell Institute boasted of its mixed student population comprised of members from twenty-seven tribes; students from sixty tribes would attend the school by 1904.[8] School officials frequently recruited children from various, and often distant, reservations to keep the student body diverse and to prevent tribal allegiances from forming. Hervey Peairs, who worked for nearly four decades at Haskell Institute, described the purpose of these new boarding schools as the place where Native American children could learn the language and industries of whites in preparation for citizenship. Peairs echoed the dominant theme in late-nineteenth-century Indian reform when he defined the terms of citizenship as complete assimilation and absolute erasure of traditional cultures—a shift from earlier extermination policies that did not offer any hope for Indian survival. This optimism for Indian inclusion would eventually wane among some reformers in the early twentieth century—although not particularly for Peairs—but in the 1880s and 1890s, the plan for assimilation persisted.[9]

In the descriptions of their respective schools for African American and Native American children, Comstock and Peairs represented the ideals of white reformers who concerned themselves with the fate of these two large minority groups. Reformers came to work on behalf of Native American and black people from a variety of military, religious, and educational backgrounds; but they all held common beliefs about the nature of race in America. By the 1880s, race denoted less about nation and culture and more about biological inheritance, as it increasingly signaled meanings about social ability and intelligence.[10] Imbued with racialist thinking, white reformers understood race as a category through which biology distinguished groups from each other. As they ignored generations of racial mixing between blacks and Indians, as well as members of both groups with whites, the reformers' ethnocentrism allowed them to see themselves as both separate from and perpetually superior to nonwhite races; they imagined an evolutionary ladder on which whites permanently occupied the top rung. Considering themselves models for survival and success, they believed that they could help all other races fit themselves into the dominant narrative of European American society. When they spoke in terms of race, they heavily emphasized their belief that whites inherently possessed superior capabilities, but they also expressed compassion, contending that schools could improve the condition of Indians and African Americans.

Changing the outward behavior and habits of students would allow Indians and blacks to move up the rungs of an evolutionary ladder and ultimately improve their positions as American citizens. After several generations of education, assimilation, integration, and intermarriage, Indians might even disappear as a distinct racial group and merge with whites.[11] Although there was no national consensus on prohibiting intermarriage between Native Americans and whites, miscegenation laws preventing African Americans and whites from marrying may have led to a general distaste for intermarriage between whites and all nonwhites. White reformers were less likely to oppose intermarriage between whites and Indians than between whites and blacks, and some reformers even noted that commingling of Native Americans and whites would lead to a desirable decrease in the number of full-blood Indians.[12] While reformers did not believe that blacks would ever be absorbed into the white race, they did think that schooling would help them become better Americans, making them more productive workers and allowing them to coexist more easily with members of the dominant society. In reformers' minds, blacks and Indians would continue to suffer economic, legal, and political oppression unless whites themselves served as ambassadors to each community and established educational campaigns to transform students primarily identified by their race or tribe into adults with new American identities.

As much as they thought their intentions were strictly altruistic, whites held complicated ideas about reform. Indeed, they called for educational programs to make worthy American citizens out of Indians and African Americans—a campaign that they thought would combat the ills of racism in society. Yet at the same time, they further entrenched the notion that students' backwardness had been anchored in thousands of years of slow evolutionary development leading to a hierarchy of races where Native Americans and blacks resided at the bottom. Even though their rhetoric professed a belief in freedom and progress, their ideologies were actually fraught with inequality. As reformers perpetually embraced racial hierarchies and biological determinism, they allowed racism to emerge from their own benevolent efforts.

Intentions of Reformers

As the population in the United States grew in size and diversity, Americans had grown dependent upon schools to teach future citizens common ideals. In the 1870s through the 1890s, attendance in public elementary and secondary schools increased from nearly seven million students to fifteen and a half million. After expanding the Indian school system, Congress passed compulsory attendance laws for Native American students. Between 1880 and 1900, the number of Indian students in school quadrupled to 21,568 and would increase by more than three times by 1925. Decades of battles with the army and threats from Indian hunters and white settlers had led to a steady decrease in the Indian population to fewer than 240,000 in 1900, and yet despite this decline, the United States government steadily increased its responsibility for education and proposed to provide federally funded, common schooling for all of its Native American wards. The reservation day schools in the Sac and Fox, Potawatomi, Shawnee, and other Kansas agencies, under the jurisdiction of the Bureau of Indian Affairs (BIA), moved students into federally funded boarding schools, which became vanguards of Indian education through the 1920s. State and church priorities mixed when the federal government exercised influence over church-sponsored schools, including the Mennonite-run Halstead Industrial Institute and Baptist-run Ottawa University, which became accountable to the BIA once school officials accepted government funding to support their institutions.

On the whole, Indians neither asked for an increase in federal aid nor necessarily wanted such federal intervention, and yet spending steadily increased from $100,000 in 1870 to $487,000 in 1883 to $1.4 million in 1890, $2.9 million in 1900, and nearly $5 million in 1920.[13]

In 1870, when Congress began dramatically adding resources for Indian education, two years had passed since the government closed the doors to the Freedmen's Bureau, the federal office established after the Civil War to supervise relief and education for freedpeople. Although African Americans made up a much larger population in the United States than Native Americans and blacks welcomed federal and state aid for education, black education was no longer a national priority, and the project was left to white missionaries, public school systems, private aid organizations such as KFRA, and African American families and teachers. Although federal interest in black education waned, in Kansas, the steady increase in the African American population forced whites to address their educational needs. For example, when a great number of black army families migrated to Fort Scott in 1865, the Northwestern Freedmen's Aid Commission constructed a schoolhouse behind the officers' quarters of the military fort. Reverend W. A. Adams and his wife divided the teaching duties; Reverend Adams taught 160 children during the day and Mrs. Adams taught 75 adults in the evening. Such individual efforts could not keep up with population increases, however, so the territorial legislature allowed for taxes assessed on property owned by African Americans to be "appropriated exclusively for the education of Negro and mulatto children."[14] As the African American population increased by 40 percent between the late 1870s and 1880s, and grew to nearly 50,000 by 1890, more educational opportunities arose for black students, including the Fort Scott Freedmen's School, a public school mostly populated by children of African American soldiers who had fought in Kansas regiments for the Union. By the end of the 1880s, charity schools opened by freedmen's aid societies swelled in Lawrence, Leavenworth, Tonganoxie, and Topeka, but could no longer manage the education of all black students, and therefore, the public school system assumed more responsibility for the expansion of African American schools. Although white Kansans supported the notion that African American children should be educated, they did not necessarily call for the integration of public schools and continued to see black schooling as largely separate from white education.[15]

The approaches of Elizabeth Comstock and Hervey Peairs to African American and Indian uplift responded to specific needs in Kansas but also reflected broad, national trends. Comstock's long tradition with the abolition movement resembled the experience of many white reformers who had started campaigning for the betterment of African American people before the Civil War. Born in Maidenhead, Berkshire, England on 30 October 1815, Elizabeth Leslie Rous was raised by Quaker teachings, actively participated in abolitionist campaigns, and aided the Underground Railroad in Rollin, Michigan, the hometown of her second husband, John Comstock. During the Civil War, Elizabeth Comstock traveled extensively throughout the country ministering to hospitalized and imprisoned soldiers as well as to refugee slaves. After the Civil War, she continued her involvement in peace, temperance, home-mission welfare, prison, women's rights, African American relief, and education movements. In 1879, a stream of southern African Americans prompted Comstock to collaborate with the governor of Kansas, John P. St. John, to provide clothing, food, shelter, and education for the freedpeople. "Kansas has done nobly, but she will soon be overwhelmed," she explained to donors.[16] Recalling the outpouring of generosity from Americans who had sent a quarter of a million dollars in money and food to people starving in Ireland, Comstock hoped that white Americans would respond to black Exodusters' needs with "one-fifth as much [as given to the Irish] to aid our starving, freezing Americans!" Susan B. Anthony was just one prominent donor who responded to Comstock's far-reaching plea by enclosing a ten-dollar subscription for the KFRA in a letter to Governor St. John detailing her resolve for citizenship and equal rights for women. More than $70,000 in cash and supplies came to KFRA from other donors; $13,000 of the total was sent from England.[17]

Comstock played a critical role with KFRA's fund-raising; she also coordinated with the governor to influence legislative reform and served as spokesperson for the Institute for Refugees. For her work among the Exodusters, Comstock received no salary and, in fact, had to pay board for her visiting daughter at an aid-house. She donated over $700 of her own money when it was needed at one point. When she moved to Kansas to engineer relief efforts, she knew that the state would not become her permanent home, but she tried to uphold the ideals of freedom that the state had promised and the freedpeople had so clearly desired.[18]

Comstock claimed to understand African Americans' desire to go to Kansas to escape the racism and threat of violence that permeated the South. In public fund-raising addresses, she often stirred her listeners with anecdotes about the violence in southern states. She once spoke of a man who had migrated to Kansas with the "advance guard of the exodus. He was industrious, and in a few months earned and saved enough to buy a little home for his family." Comstock reported that he returned to the South to retrieve his family, "but he never returned." Comstock learned that, the day after the man rejoined his family, he had been seized by some white people in town who "cut off his hands, threw them into the lap of his wife, and while he was bleeding to death, said, 'Now go to Kansas, and earn a living for your family.'" Sharing such shocking stories across the country and in England, Comstock hoped to gain financial support for blacks who tried to escape the horrors of the South. Other stories about resourceful refugees who built successful lives supplemented her fund-raising lectures.[19]

Comstock used her national and international connections to expose the hardships of African Americans and to seek support for their plight. For example, when she spoke about the exodus to the *New York Tribune*, Comstock reported that there were more African Americans flocking to Kansas than ever because they had been disappointed by President Ulysses S. Grant's inability to protect their lives and property in the South. "Atrocities continue to be perpetuated upon them in the South. Hanging, shooting, whipping, mutilation have not ceased," she reported. Exodusters confirmed Comstock's claims, reporting that some southern conditions were worse for blacks after Reconstruction than during slavery, including unfair price gauging, perpetual debt, and white-on-black robbery and violence.[20]

Comstock frequently moved back and forth between Kansas and Washington, soliciting donations from charitable individuals and encouraging state and national legislators to pass bills that would aid freedpeople. Comstock even received a special invitation from President James Garfield to bring a delegation from New York to Washington to argue before Congress a proposal to allow Kansas-bound donations to enter the country duty free. Comstock argued that the overseas support for freedpeople should go directly to those in need without taxation. In 1882, while the bill was being debated, Comstock became ill, and another KFRA member, Laura Haviland, continued to push for its passage. The bill eventually passed in 1884, after several attempts. Comstock returned to New York to undergo medical treatment for a physical paralysis and a mental debility resulting from stress. Therefore, Haviland, although well into her seventies, took over Comstock's responsibilities in Kansas.[21]

Laura Haviland noted that there were many times when she and Elizabeth Comstock met opposition in their work, but both insisted that they would continue "battling for the right and for the colored race."[22] Like Comstock, Haviland was an abolitionist, a Quaker, and a longtime educator and reformer. Born Laura Smith in Kitley, Leeds County, Ontario, on 20 December 1808, she grew up in New York state and then moved to Michigan with her husband, Charles Haviland Jr. In 1845, when an outbreak of inflammatory erysipelas took the lives of Haviland's father, mother, husband, sister, and youngest child, Haviland began fifty-three years of widowhood. The loss prompted her to strengthen her resolve to help runaway slaves, distribute supplies to refugees, and aid war victims during and after the Civil War. Like Comstock, Haviland's commitment to African American uplift was rooted in abolitionism and other reform efforts. She taught school, ministered in prisons, sought pardons for imprisoned ex-slaves, engaged in temperance and mission work, and helped orphans. She also lobbied for a home for wayward girls.

Laura Haviland's experience as an educator supported her efforts with the Institute for Refugees. At the age of twenty-nine, Haviland and her husband had started a school for orphans called Raisin Institute with the mission to achieve "the perfect equality of all mankind." With that goal in mind, they schooled two or three African Americans, along with their own children and other white children, hoping "to enlighten and elevate both mentally and spiritually, and to inculcate personal freedom as the spirit of American government."[23] Like many Christian reformers, Haviland also believed that the purpose of education was to help prepare one's immortal soul for the next world.

Many of the students at Raisin Institute knew about the runaway slaves seeking refuge at Haviland's home, one of Michigan's earliest Underground Railroad stops. Although some students did not support Haviland's anti-slavery stance, she believed that none of them would betray a fugitive. The "unflinching zeal" of the school's supporters and its position as a stop on the Underground Railroad for fugitive slaves on their way to Canada gained the school notoriety as the "nigger school" or "nigger den."[24] Other than the derogatory name that Haviland's neighbors used, the integrated school existed largely without incident. Haviland even took pride in the fact that a young white girl, who had once complained of having to sit next to an African American student in class, overcame her prejudices by the time the term ended.

Like Elizabeth Comstock, Laura Haviland spoke frequently and publicly against slavery during the Civil War and continued to campaign for freed-people's rights after emancipation. To stir her listeners, Haviland often displayed items that represented enslavement from the South on her speaking engagements. She dramatically posed for photographs with the shackles,

Laura Haviland's Antislavery Portrait. Haviland moved to Kansas to open a school for African American refugees in the 1880s after spending much of her adult life as a Quaker abolitionist. (Courtesy of Burton Historical Collection, Detroit Public Library)

iron collars, and "knee-stiffeners" used by slaveholders to keep slaves from running away. At the Ladies' State Freedmen's Fair in Detroit in 1865, Haviland took along John Brown's sharpshooter, an item given to her by the antislavery radical's half-brother, J. R. Brown. This antislavery work earned her a well-respected reputation among abolitionists but also a $3,000 bounty among proslavery factions. Despite the outstanding bounty on her head, Haviland continually traveled to the South to collect information about atrocities committed against slaves and then use those stories to capture the attention of her audiences.[25]

The exodus of African Americans from the South to Kansas brought the western part of the country to Haviland's attention in the 1870s. She heartily sympathized with the thousands of African Americans who had spent over a decade in "patient hoping, waiting, and watching" for the government to make life better for them. She believed that leaving the South was the only option for many African Americans who otherwise "saw clearly that their future condition as a race must be submissive vassalage, a war of races, or emigration." After arriving in Kansas, Haviland witnessed a steady stream of migrants into the state and distributed supplies to over one thousand of them within three weeks. The total number of refugees grew beyond ten thousand in 1879 and 1880.[26] Haviland continued fund-raising efforts and made special appeals to those who had already supported black schools in the South. Touring various towns in Kansas, including Fort Scott, Leavenworth, Quindaro, Wyandotte, and Kansas City, Haviland distributed $90,000 in money and supplies to tens of thousands of refugees by 1883. A salary of $40 per month represented the first remuneration she received for her decades of work with African Americans.[27]

The Institute for Refugees stayed open until 1888, when KFRA resigned its responsibility for the school. A year before that closing, twenty-one-year-old Hervey Byers Peairs graduated from Kansas State Normal College and took a post at the three-year-old Haskell Indian Institute. Originally from Zanesville, Ohio, Peairs moved to Kansas to pursue his own education but ultimately stayed in the state for the remainder of his four-decade career in Indian reform. In his first job at Haskell Institute, Peairs taught the first and second grades, but he was quickly promoted to school disciplinarian and then to principal; he became the superintendent of Haskell Institute in 1898. Like Comstock and Haviland, Peairs's reform work moved him back and forth between Kansas and Washington. In 1910, he became supervisor of Indian schools for the BIA, but after seven years, he returned to Haskell Institute to resume his leadership position there for another ten years. In 1927, Washington called again, and he took a position as commissioner of Indian schools until 1930, when he returned to Haskell Institute for the third and final time as superintendent until his retirement in 1931.[28]

Hervey Peairs, born in 1866, was significantly younger than Elizabeth Comstock and Laura Haviland, and he entered his career in Indian education as part of a new generation of professional teachers who learned their trade through schooling rather than a series of volunteer experiences. Despite these differences, Peairs's confidence in the ability of education to transform groups of disenfranchised people into American citizens matched that of Comstock and Haviland. Peairs's career bridged the nineteenth and twentieth centuries, but his methods remained rooted in a late-nineteenth-century ideology focused on assimilation. A frequent essayist and speaker at national meetings on Indian Policy, Peairs believed in removing children from reservations because he thought that the reservation system and the issuing of rations had "marked the beginning of the deterioration of the red race." Citizenship training in schools like Haskell Institute would prepare Indians for lives outside of reservations, so that "they may be able to compete anywhere the same as other people do."[29]

At Haskell Institute, Peairs thought that his students would be better prepared for their futures if he solidified the industrial departments to ensure that the rooms were fit for such instruction. He had new buildings erected and started a library and a literary society for additional instruction. In 1910, through his position as supervisor of Indian schools for the BIA, Peairs expanded the course of study for all federal boarding schools to include three primary, three prevocational, and four vocational grades. As his role in Indian reform grew, Peairs called for greater attention to physical health, home building, and citizenship training. By the 1920s, Peairs had transformed Haskell into the leading Indian boarding school and secured his own rise to national prominence among Indian educators.[30]

Hervey Peairs believed that proper citizenship training would eventually make his students disappear into white society. Like his contemporaries, Peairs pressured Indian students to disregard their traditions and life on the reservation in order to prepare for a future distinctly different from their parents' lives. While addressing a crowd of white and Native American listeners, Peairs admitted that when he had started his work at Haskell, his impression was that "Indians were an inferior race . . . they would not take on civilization; that the best Indian was a dead one." Peairs would eventually change his perception and think of Native Americans as fit for citizenship, but only after they had gone through an assimilation pro-

Hervey Peairs, Superintendent of Haskell Institute. Peairs worked his entire career in Native American education, spending most of the time promoting assimilationist policies. (Courtesy of National Archives and Records Administration–Central Plains Region)

cess. Captain Richard Henry Pratt, the founder of the first Indian boarding school, Carlisle Institute, had most vocally espoused the "kill the Indian and save the man" philosophy, but Peairs and his contemporaries quickly embraced that idea by insisting that their students only speak English and otherwise mimic white culture. To eradicate native identity was to change the habits of students, to strip them of their Indian ways of life, to devalue older practices and replace them with conventionally American sets of behaviors and beliefs. Policies to make Indian culture vanish did not entertain the notion of bicultural identities, which ultimately became the desire of many twentieth-century Indians. Instead, to stimulate the kind of cultural changes that would signal assimilation to the dominant society, Peairs adopted Pratt's stance of creating interventions to change the evolutionary path of Native American children. Therefore, he insisted on stern discipline, cropped hair, uniforms, and church attendance for his students. He rarely released students back to their parents before their term of enrollment expired and often persuaded students to stay away from the influence of their reservation homes for as long as possible. This version of citizenship training would eradicate affection for native traditions, Peairs claimed. "There never was a Haskell graduate who went back to the old customs," Peairs boasted, even though a few years later he reported to the *Kansas City Star* that the school considered their efforts successful if as much as 9 percent of the graduates did not do well "on the outside" and went "back to the blanket."[31]

What united reformers like Elizabeth Comstock, Laura Haviland, and Hervey Peairs was an optimistic hope in the power of education to help African Americans and Indians become better citizens. Throughout the country, highly influential white educators, religious leaders, and policy makers espoused their educational philosophies and referred to themselves as "Friends of the Indians" and "Friends of the Negroes." These friends were ideologically united by a sense of missionary fervor and a belief that their efforts reflected their duty to their God and nation. In 1891, when Merrill Gates stated the purpose of the Lake Mohonk Conference on the Indian Question, an ostensibly nonreligious meeting organized to influence Indian policy between 1883 and 1916, he declared, "This is essentially a philanthropic and Christian reform." During Gates's career, he held secular positions, including presiding over both Rutgers University and Amherst College and serving as secretary of the United States Board of Indian Commissioners, but his Christian motivations unmistakably drove his reform efforts: "Whatever may be our views, our slight differences of view or differences that may seem to us profound, we all gather here believing that the Lord of the world is the Lord Jesus Christ; believing that, ever since God himself became incarnate, for a man to see God truly, he must learn to see something of God in his fellow-man, and to work for his fellow-men."[32] For over thirty years, the Lake Mohonk meetings had no official standing within the government, but its membership grew to 250 guests and generated some of the most significant influence over federal Indian policy. Senator Henry Dawes, for example, told participants at the 1886 meeting that he "got valuable ideas" to incorporate into his bill that passed as the 1887 General Allotment Act (Dawes Act), which allowed for the division of tribal land into allotments for individual Indians. Thanking his supporters in 1887, he stated that without the conference, the Dawes Act would not have been put into law.[33]

In 1890, Albert Smiley, the Quaker philanthropist who originally founded the Lake Mohonk Conference on the Indian Question, invited reformers to talk about situations in African American communities at the Lake Mohonk Conference on the Negro Question. Smiley gave a special invitation to certain white southerners to ensure their participation even though he excluded black representatives from the discussions. The meetings closely resembled Smiley's first set of conferences, especially in their religious overtones. For example, W. H. Hickman, the president of Clark University, a school founded in 1869 by the Freedmen's Aid Society, stated at the second meeting, "If we turn to the word of God, we find the duties of the stronger race to the weaker race clearly and strongly set forth."[34]

The spirit of service that drove reformers from both religious and secular backgrounds was steeped in rhetoric that fused the meanings of Protestant Christianity and American citizenship. Although there was an evangelistic concern about saving the souls of children or preparing immortal souls for the next world, as Laura Haviland professed, something larger was at stake in the late nineteenth century. Christians, in particular Protestant Christians, and Americans were considered synonymous, and therefore, that notion allowed members of the white Protestant majority to imagine themselves as representative of the priorities for the entire nation. Christian principles guided the reformers' efforts, not only making them seem sympathetic and focusing on serving others, but also allowing them to feel that their own souls would be redeemed through their work on behalf of minority populations.[35]

In addition to feeling compelled to do their Christian duty, white reformers educated African Americans and Native Americans because they had concerns for the welfare of the United States. They believed that the fates of all inhabitants of the country were inseparable, and that if those who needed help were not uplifted, the entire nation would decline into industrial bankruptcy, social degradation, and political corruption. Unschooled communities could threaten the public welfare and might become an economic burden on the rest of society. Former president Rutherford B. Hayes, the unanimously elected chair of the Lake Mohonk Conference on the Negro Question, represented the concerns of the dominant society by stating, "These millions who have been so cruelly degraded must be lifted up, or we ourselves will be dragged down."[36] Albert Smiley agreed, stating that without citizenship education, "they will become a dangerous element to the community, liable to be thrown at any moment into the hands of demagogues who may use them for bad purposes. I believe that our only safety is to give the Negro a Christian education."[37]

Armed with a sense of duty to their God and their country, reformers attacked what Richard Henry Pratt called "the gross injustices to both races." Pratt argued that uplifting African Americans and Native Americans through education would enforce the safeguards of the Constitution and the Declaration of Independence, and white Americans would be less tempted to be unjust where both races were concerned.[38] Lydia Maria Child, the famous abolitionist turned Native American advocate, believed that, if nothing else, reformers' efforts to educate African Americans and Indians would help the country live up to its Revolutionary-era promises of equality, justice, and democracy. Cora Daniels Tappan envisioned that her efforts to ameliorate the situation of disenfranchised members of society would not only improve their plight but also aid the entire county. At an 1869 Universal Peace Society meeting, Tappan pointed out the inconsistencies in equality in the United States: "A government that has for nearly a century enslaved one race (African), that proscribes another (Chinese), proposes to exterminate another (Indians), and persistently refuses to recognize the rights of one-half of its citizens (women), cannot justly be called perfect."[39]

In the nineteenth century, the most important legislative attempt to address citizenship, the 1868 Fourteenth Amendment to the Constitution, was meant to guarantee legal citizenship to American-born blacks and to some Indians, depending on their tribal status. The nation's policy, however, did not include all Indians and de facto or de jure segregation prevented most members of both groups from enjoying the privileges of their nominal legal status.[40] In Kansas, specific efforts to legislate racial equality, especially between its white and black inhabitants, helped the state promote its legacy as the Free State. Senator Jacob Winter spoke most adamantly about equality and citizenship when he delivered a bill to the 1874 state legislature proposing to ensure civil rights to African Americans. He wanted the law to pass for the sake of blacks but also to expand the commitment to freedom that the state professed. Invoking sentiments about a particular claim to freedom, Winter implored, "Once more let me appeal to you in the name of this, our glorious young State of Kansas; this State that was born free; this State that stood in the front ranks in the great contest for freedom." Winter's civil rights bill would not only enfranchise African Americans but would allow "a person invested with all the rights and attributes essential to his humanity . . . [the freedom] to seek his own happiness in subserviency only to the rights of his fellow citizens." In the "name of American citizenship," Winter continued, "let the enfranchised slave, now an American citizen, have an equal chance in the race of life." Passing the bill, he argued, would enable African Americans and the rest of society to "forever cleanse the body politic from the last remains of the scum and dregs of slavery," allowing peace and order to prevail throughout the state. Even though Winter tried to appeal to a sense of self-preservation among his fellow legislators, the bill did not pass, and the struggle of minority populations to attain the kind of freedom that Kansas purported to offer continued.[41]

There were other attempts to ensure citizenship for blacks and Indians in Kansas, including proposals in the state senate for civil rights bills and an attempt by one state representative to eradicate the word "white" from the state constitution so that all Kansans would have access to constitutional rights. On a national level, the Dawes Act was intended to destroy the reservation system in an effort to transform Native Americans into landowners and subsequently grant them rights of citizenship. Individual landownership would gradually bring about independence for Native Americans without granting en masse privileges of suffrage or other significant political rights.[42] Despite attempts to legislate the expansion of citizenship rights to include African Americans and Native Americans, these two groups struggled to fit into American society well into the twentieth century, and reformers commonly referred to these struggles as the "Indian Problem" and the "Negro Problem."[43]

Attempts to Solve the Indian Problem and the Negro Problem

While legislative efforts to resolve the Indian Problem and the Negro Problem continued, reformers increasingly turned to citizenship training as the most effective way of addressing the needs of these two groups. They believed that by positioning themselves as white ambassadors to African American and Native American communities they could carry out educational campaigns that would transform students with racial or tribal identities into adults with an American one.

Children became the primary targets of citizenship training. Although born in the United States, Native American and African American children were nonetheless treated as immigrants, foreigners, or aliens because their cultural identities seemed incompatible with the dominant society. Some black schools did offer night classes for adults, but most reformers believed that youth held the greatest potential for new citizenship roles. Children were more malleable and less habituated to older traditions and behavioral patterns than adults. By focusing on youth and high-school-aged adolescents, reformers hoped to reverse what they thought of as the pernicious effects of the legacy of slavery on African American children and of savage beliefs and practices on Native Americans. They optimistically believed that with proper education, and in the case of Indian children, removal from their families, the condition of an entire race would experience radical improvement in just a single generation.[44]

Proper education meant suppression of black and Indian culture and adherence to white, middle-class, social and gender norms. Expected to mimic whites, students were only allowed to speak English, practice Christianity, wear uniforms, obey strict rules, develop specific skills, and adopt the ideology of hard work. Commissioner of Indian Affairs Thomas Jefferson Morgan thought that, in the case of Indians, such controlled educational environments would allow "race distinctions" to "give way to national characteristics," so that they could be absorbed "into our national life, not as Indians, but as American citizens."[45] Albert Smiley said that African Americans also needed elevation "in every direction" in order to "rise to the full stature of true American citizenship."[46] Rhetorically, reformers presented the Indian Problem and the Negro Problem as two sides of the same coin that could be addressed with one educational philosophy and similar approaches.

Perhaps reformers used similar rhetoric when speaking of the Indian Problem and the Negro Problem because so many of them had worked with both populations in the past. Elizabeth Comstock, a lifelong advocate for African Americans, had also ministered to the Oneida Indians of Wisconsin. Richard Henry Pratt had led African American troops, specifically former slaves, in Indian wars and had also commanded Native American scouts before starting Carlisle Institute. The American Missionary Association (AMA), a Protestant society committed to bringing about full and equal citizenship privileges to Native Americans, also partnered with the Freedmen's Bureau to expand educational opportunities for African Americans. In order to do so, the AMA redirected missionaries, who had been preaching to Native Americans in the West in the 1850s, to freedpeople's schools in the South in the late 1860s. Under President Ulysses S. Grant's 1868 Peace Policy, a program that shifted the government's early nineteenth-century extermination programs aimed at Indians to more compassionate efforts, some of the same missionaries were then moved out West to work with Native Americans again. Lobbyists, such as Grant's Commissioner of Indian Affairs Edward P. Smith, spent his career arguing for both Native Americans and African American freedpeople. Failing to see Native American and African American issues as divorced from each other, reformers strongly believed that education was the common solution to the "problem" of both Indians and blacks, who could be brought into active roles in American society through citizenship training.[47]

At the same time that reformers professed an ideology of equality and freedom, they were also largely responsible for reinforcing the existing racial hierarchies that would ultimately cause the dominant society to marginalize African Americans and Native Americans for decades to come. Reformers overlooked their own complicity in reinforcing the same racial hierarchies that they argued could be overcome through education. When they characterized Native American and African American identities as problematic, inferior, and intimately linked to the past, they reinforced their personal claims on normative American identities. Engaged in social uplift, reformers also invested in preserving racial hegemony in which they would maintain their dominant positions.[48] In fact, these friends of Native Americans and African Americans engaged in a large-scale colonization project that merged ideals of church and state, crossed racial boundaries, and cost millions of federal and private dollars.

Reformers' beliefs about citizenship and their strategies for reform rested on a set of assumptions about racial distinctions and hierarchy. Influenced by the late-nineteenth-century growth in the discipline of physical anthropology, most whites embraced a monolithic idea of civilization which held white Europeans and Americans as a standard against which all others would be measured. Cranial measurements and prevalent evolutionary race theory led many to believe that racial differences were permanent and hierarchical. End-of-the-century racial ideas were enhanced by social Darwinism and imperialist ideologies coinciding with a rise in racial violence throughout the nation. The 1896 *Plessy v. Ferguson* decision reinforced racial distinctions, making it legal to discriminate between the races.[49] This racialized climate made it easy for whites to think of themselves as a distinct and advanced race. As General Samuel Chapman Armstrong, the founder of Hampton Institute in Virginia, claimed, whites were at least two thousand years ahead of African Americans, and therefore, were naturally superior. Armstrong added that African Americans were biologically inferior and part of a "child-like race."[50] W. H. Hickman, president of Clark University, a Freedmen's Aid Society school, used similar language to describe blacks: "The Negro is weak. He is a grown up child." Hickman believed that millions of African Americans were "in a crude and unassimilated, ignorant state" that put the country in peril and made "race strife imminent and inevitable."[51] Elizabeth Comstock and Laura Haviland's KFRA reported the "extreme ignorance" of African Americans and the organization's plan to meet their "great desire for knowledge, both of books and of business."[52] Hervey Peairs thought that Indians were inherently behind white Americans in terms of evolutionary development because they were born into barbarism:

> Between the red man's baby and all others, there is an almost insurmountable wall; he is by birth an alien, separate from his fellows, shut off from opportunity, predetermined to degradation. He is an outcast, and although he is not taken and thrown into the river or destroyed, as were the male children among the Hebrews in Egypt, he is in many instances doomed to a living death. With generations of barbarism behind him, the iniquity of the fathers is visited upon the children, and the little papoose falls heir to many physical, mental and moral diseases and weaknesses.[53]

Believing that uplift of African American and Native Americans was completely dependent upon the influence of whites, Richard Henry Pratt frequently encouraged his Indian students to have close contacts with whites. He did not, however, want them to associate with blacks because he thought that existing and severe racial prejudices against African Americans would have negative consequences for his Native American students. A minority of reformers, like Reverend A. W. Pitzer, thought that citizenship campaigns had already succeeded in the South, where he credited whites with paying for the bulk of African Americans' education; but most reformers, including General O. O. Howard, argued that federal programs had failed and much more work still needed to be done. Others went a step further to argue that minorities would benefit from an extended period of domination by white Americans, so that by the twentieth century, as Frederick Hoxie argues, racial tensions throughout the country encouraged whites to turn from assimilation ideals toward societal hierarchies to make sense of the growing diversity in their communities.[54]

At the top of the evolutionary ladder, white Americans positioned themselves as caretakers of all of the rungs below them. "We believe that we have a duty to the less-favored races," said Merrill Gates at the 1899 Lake Mohonk meeting. Reverend Lyman Abbott referred to the "duty of Christians to govern inferior people." Reverend James M'Cosh stated that the greatest Christian responsibility rested with whites. Mother Katherine Drexel, a Catholic sister who founded an order of nuns dedicated specifically to the education of Native Americans and African Americans (Sisters of the

Blessed Sacrament of Indians and Colored People), claimed that both races were the direct responsibility of white Americans. Such sentiments were supported by Rutherford Hayes, who reminded attendees at the Lake Mohonk Conference on the Negro that white Americans were the "keepers" of their "brothers in black." He added that white Americans were responsible for blacks' condition because they had "deprived them of their labor, liberty, and manhood." Because whites had benefited from the labor of African Americans, Hayes declared that there was no excuse for ignoring their plight.[55]

Their reliance on racialist ideology led white reformers to reinforce notions about the very hierarchies that they wanted their own students to overcome. The racism that had justified overseas imperialism and the conquest and subjugation of Indians within the United States allowed reformers to expand their sense of superiority and to develop a sense of imperial consciousness. For example, when federal Indian agents were directed to stop the Sun Dance of the Plains Indians or other rituals that were considered "savage and barbarous," they engaged in activity comparable to the ways that other imperial powers subjugated native inhabitants.[56]

The kind of colonialism that took place in schools was what Margaret Jacobs refers to as "cultural imperialism," where Indian native languages, customs, and allegiance to tribal groups were forbidden; African Americans were taught more about how to be good laborers than about the history of their race; and it was assumed that whites would dominate over other races. Colonialism was not just a public activity that took place on battlegrounds or through political and economic structures. Rather, it existed in the "most intimate spaces of private homes, whether the home of the colonizers or the colonized."[57] This notion extended to the confines of schools as well. Whether private, religious, or public, schools provided a physical, intellectual, psychological, and emotional space where one group of empowered people (white reformers, teachers, missionaries) could impose their set of values on another group of disenfranchised people (African American and Native American students) and thus influence their appearance and behavior. If colonial projects defined racial classifications, as Ann Laura Stoler argues, then schools provided an environment "where relations between colonizer and colonized could powerfully confound or confirm the strictures of governance and the categories of rule." Such relationships are the "intimacies of empire" and "intimate frontiers" that Stoler and Albert Hurtado refer to in their work, respectively.[58] Although white Americans considered their educational campaigns generous and thought of themselves as guardians of blacks and Native Americans, their sense of guardianship, a mixture of paternalism and social control, implied control over lands, supervision of personal lives, and ongoing discrimination.[59] Even if reformers did not accept what they thought of as racist ideology, their complicity with paternalistic and ethnocentric policies provided a basis for the constant comparison between races in which whites served as a model and demanded what James McPherson calls a "one-way acculturation to white values and institutions."[60]

There was no question in the minds of whites that they stood at the top of the evolutionary scale, but ideologies of racial distinction and evolution remained confusing at the very bottom, where either Indians or blacks landed. In her study of nineteenth-century schoolbooks, Ruth Miller Elson only found one that placed African Americans ahead of Indians in terms of gaining citizenship, while most others ranked blacks at the bottom. Some whites compared Native Americans to European immigrants, who could more easily assimilate into white society than blacks and therefore were more evolved. Other reformers argued that African Americans had benefited from interaction with white Americans under the system of slavery and therefore they were more evolved than Native Americans. Randall Woods argues that long-standing prejudice against Native Americans might have particularly benefited African Americans in the West, where the fluidity of the frontier might have positively influenced whites' perceptions about blacks.[61] At Hampton Institute, where both blacks and Indians attended (although separately), a student ranked the "classes" of the "Human race" in order of superiority during an exam: "white people are the strongest . . . [then] Mongolians or yellows . . . Ethiopeans [sic] or blacks . . . Americans or reds." When the instructor requested, "Tell me something of the white people," the student replied, "The Caucasian is away ahead of all of the other races."[62]

A young Booker T. Washington taught at Hampton Institute in 1880 and experienced the advantages of racial ranking in which he held a position superior to Native Americans as the "house father" to seventy-five Indian male students and, at the same time, the liabilities of a lower ranking by the white public. Supporting existing beliefs in racial hierarchy, Washington noted that he was the only non-Indian in the building, and therefore, distinct from "wild" and "ignorant" Native Americans. While escorting one of his ill students, he found that the steamboat and hotel personnel had a different perception of his social ranking. "During my journey to Washington, on a steamboat, when the bell rang for dinner, I was careful to wait and not enter the dining room until after the greater part of the passengers had finished their meal. Then, with my charge, I went to the dining saloon. The man in charge politely informed me that the Indian could be served, but that I could not," he wrote. Later that day, when Washington and his student arrived at their hotel, "the clerk stated that he would be glad to receive the Indian into the house, but said that he could not accommodate me."[63]

Reformers' persistent endorsement of racial hierarchy certainly contributed to the shifting status that Washington experienced. Specifically, their notion that through education the Indian Problem, along with Native Americans themselves, would eventually disappear contributed to the larger problem of prejudice. Reformers eventually wanted to phase out segregated schools and require Native American students to attend public schools with white children.[64] Indian children would not only attend white schools, but the hope was that they would integrate and even marry into white society as well. "Many of our finest citizens are half or quarter Indian blood," a teacher from the state of Washington wrote to Hervey Peairs in a letter encouraging continued assimilation through intermarriage.[65] Reformers reasoned that if assimilation included intermarriage, racial distinctions would be muted in future generations. Some Native Americans found these discussions disturbing, including anthropologist and Society of American Indian member Arthur Parker (Seneca), who claimed, "The Indian through intermarriage is having his blood diffused through the veins of the white race and at the same time is becoming absorbed."[66] But white reformers continued to support educational programs that would diminish the "Indianness" that stood in the way of students' progress. Commissioner of Indian Affairs Francis Leupp likened Native Americans to tadpoles, which are born in the water with a tail, but without legs. "When the tadpole develops legs," he explained, "and is able to hop about on the land as a frog, its tail drops off of itself." Extending the metaphor, Leupp continued, "So the Indian will voluntarily drop his racial oddities as he becomes more and more of our common body politic, and learns to breathe the atmosphere of our civilization as his own."[67]

Whites who supported citizenship training for African Americans argued neither for the complete absorption of blacks into white society nor for intermarriage. Instead, reformers hoped that blacks would cultivate new roles in society by maintaining good behavior and becoming reliable, productive workers. Albert Smiley outlined a plan for citizenship in which blacks would be "practically educated; that they shall learn to be thrifty and taught industries; that they shall do away with all drinking habits, shall save money, accumulate property, be law-abiding citizens; that the family relations be well observed, and thus be a credit to our country."[68]

Although reformers consistently thought of themselves as the most benevolent advocates for both groups of people, their inability or unwillingness to understand the limitations of assimilation allowed them to ignore their own participation in reinforcing racial hierarchies and contributing to the emergence of racism in schools and federal policy.[69] Commissioner Thomas Morgan's 1890 address to a group of Native American students illustrates this point clearly. He told them, "As I sat here and listened with closed eyes to your singing, you were not Indians to me. You sing our songs, you speak our language. In the days that are coming there will be nothing save his color to distinguish the Indian from the white man."[70] Hervey Peairs used similar rhetoric when he reasoned that if the children of immigrants could meld into America, Native Americans could learn "our language, our industries [and] learn of the spirit and principles underlying American institutions and, as rapidly as possible, to prepare them to assume the full responsibility of citizenship in their adopted country."[71] The paradox in Morgan's and Peairs's imaginary visions was that the dominant culture did not grant Native Americans and blacks born in the United States the same level of inclusion that it afforded many European immigrant groups. Through the 1930s, racial distinctions trumped citizenship training in influencing the perceptions of people of color by white Americans. For example, when Robert D. Baldwin took his post as the superintendent of Haskell Institute in 1931, he declared to the entire student body and faculty, "We are all Americans," but he still noted in his speech the need to acknowledge a "distinction in races."[72] Alexandra Harmon explains the persistent references to racial distinctions by suggesting that "An Indian might leave his tribe, take up farming, convert to Christianity, speak English, and wear citizen's dress, but he could not discard his color or his history."[73] The same was even truer for African Americans. With the help of white reformers, African Americans could contribute to "national unity," but they would not be allowed to form social bonds with other races, according to W. H. Hickman. Talk of "social assimilation," he stated at an 1891 Lake Mohonk meeting, "is just as hateful to some of the representative Negroes as it is to the white people." Instead, Hickman believed that "Social equality will take care of itself." In the same breath, Hickman seemed to relinquish the very power that his peers claimed to have by stating that such changes in racial and social evolution would not be immediate and would ultimately be up to the "providence of God."[74] Racial hierarchies continued to be the ultimate barrier to full integration and assimilation regardless of students' adherence to the agenda that reformers set out for them.

Chapter Two

CURRICULUM

ACQUIRING THE
HABITS OF CITIZENSHIP

No white American ever thinks that any other race is wholly civilized
until he wears the white man's clothes, eats the white man's food, speaks
the white man's language, and professes the white man's religion.
— Booker T. Washington, *Up from Slavery*

Some men are born citizens; other must acquire the habit.
— *Civic Pride*, 1904

In 1896, Reverend Charles Monroe Sheldon wrote a series of sermons that
he delivered to his congregation at the Central Congregational Church in
Topeka. Each sermon challenged his congregants to consider their actions
toward each other and those less fortunate. Sheldon wanted to be clear
about the challenge that he had posed to his church members, so he stated,
"I will put my proposition very plainly, perhaps bluntly." He then asked for
volunteers who would pledge "earnestly and honestly" for the next year to
take action only after asking themselves a single question: "What would
Jesus do?"[1]

A year later, Sheldon collected his sermons into a book and published
them under the title *In His Steps: What Would Jesus Do?* A flaw in the original copyright allowed as many as twelve different publishers to reprint
his book in multiple languages for their own profit, estimated from ten to
thirty million dollars. The challenge to think about what Jesus would do
before determining one's own course of action proliferated throughout the
globe in the 1890s and saw a resurgence of popularity one hundred years
later. Although Sheldon never received the entire monetary benefit from

Tennesseetown Kindergarten. Charles Sheldon opened a kindergarten for African American
children and encouraged self-improvement programs in the black colony Tennesseetown.
(Courtesy of Kansas State Historical Society)

his book, he continually asked churchgoers, made up of white congregants,
to base their actions on the social gospel ethic that he preached. Sheldon
even included himself in the charge to "follow Jesus . . . exactly . . . no matter
what the results may be." His own response to the question, "What would
Jesus do?" included ministering to the hundreds of African Americans who
had migrated to Topeka during the exodus to establish an all-black neigh-
borhood called Tennesseetown in 1880. In 1892, Sheldon opened a school
for black children in a renovated dance-hall and speakeasy—it became the
first kindergarten west of the Mississippi River as well as Sheldon's platform
for social reform.[2]

Charles Sheldon's concern for the education of African Americans resembled the ethos that Elizabeth Comstock and Laura Haviland had expressed some fifteen years earlier. He believed in the importance of education as a vehicle to change an entire community, especially if individuals
could improve their moral character and ability to contribute to society.

"For, after all, if education does not result in better behavior," Sheldon claimed, "it is not true education." It was not enough for his students to acquire facts or knowledge; rather, he demanded an accumulation of virtues and habits that would improve the nation. Schools should serve as moral training grounds, so he wanted the Bible and Christian teachings to be central to citizenship training in public and private school. He even argued for engaging in prayer before commencing work at large factories.[3]

Charles Sheldon's desire to infuse religion into classroom teaching characterized nineteenth-century reformers' priorities regarding African American and Indian education. Schools offered an array of classical courses, including algebra, grammar, civics, geography, chemistry, history, botany, physics, composition, geometry, and teaching pedagogy, but students spent most of their time learning Christian principles and industrial skills to prepare for their futures. Educators married their students to nineteenth-century Victorian ideals even as the twentieth century brought a host of changes, including rapidly growing cities, increased urbanization, and shifts away from agrarian-based economies. The architects of Native American and black education acknowledged the importance of the traditional "three R's" (reading, writing, and arithmetic) and incorporated the basics into their curricula in both sets of schools. Traditional textbooks, however, did not provide the foundation for Indian and black education. It would be more accurate to point to two different R's (religion and rigorous work) which proved more important in the minds of reformers as they considered citizenship training for Indian and black students. Reflecting a colonialist agenda, they imposed Christian training and long hours of work to shape the minds, characters, and habits of their students. In fact, one reformer once stated that it "would be as strange to forget to work as to forget to read the Bible; their life would be incomplete with either."[4]

Similar schedules, classes, and adherence to middle-class, Christian, gender norms characterized both black and Indian schools. The intended outcomes of Native American and African American education, however, were vastly different. White reformers thought Native American education would prepare students to assimilate completely into white American society, while they designed African American education to prepare them for a permanently marginal station in society separate from whites. The 1880s and 1890s saw an expansion of educational opportunities for both Indians and blacks, but citizenship training also placed obvious limitations on minority students.

Religion, Patriotism, and Discipline

Religious fervor drove reformers' desire for a particularly Christian form of citizenship for African Americans and Native Americans. Christian citizenship would certainly save the souls of their students, but reformers also believed that religious training would contribute to a righteous empire in the United States. Post–Civil War Protestantism, described by Robert Handy as an "aggressive dynamic form of Christianity" or a "crusade for Christian America," meant to dominate both religious and secular aspects of American society.[5] Even in public schools, evangelical Protestantism infused the aim of moral character development, which often surpassed literacy and numeracy as educational goals.[6] When white reformers established Native American and African American schools, they prioritized religious indoctrination as an important venue for wielding influence over Indian and black communities.

If Indians and African Americans were to become righteous citizens, they would have to convert to Christianity and refine their religious practices. Lydia Maria Child, an abolitionist and activist for Indian and woman's suffrage, viewed this strategy as a panacea for many of the problems that Native Americans and African Americans faced. At Lake Mohonk meetings, Merrill Gates fused ideals of Christianity and citizenship to "break up these iniquitous masses of savagery" and to "immerse [students] in the strong currents of Christian life and Christian citizenship." Gates added that Christianity had "sanctifying" and redemptive qualities for Indians, but his larger concern was to bring Indians "under the sway of Christian thought and Christian life" so that, once properly indoctrinated, they would come under the jurisdiction of state and territorial laws rather than the rules of reservations.[7]

Although many blacks were already Christian—and most of them were indeed Protestant—white reformers still wanted to indoctrinate African Americans with a certain kind of religious practice. For Charles Sheldon, that meant Tennesseetown residents required supervision by white ministers rather than the black preachers who headed the four existing churches. Sheldon acknowledged that the black ministers exercised considerable influence in the community, but he thought that there was "not very much that could be called Christian influence."[8] Ednah Cheney, an abolitionist and an important figure in the Free Religious Association, expressed her desire to substitute controlled religious expressions for the shouting and noisy prayer meetings that she thought characterized the "religion of the Negro," which, she said, often ended in a "cataleptic fit."[9]

With no tolerance for superstition, alternative beliefs, or multivalent religious ideas in their curricula, reformers promoted conformity to a set of Protestant ideals and moral codes intended to govern behavior and encourage students' practices and piety. If students adopted such ideals, they would be transformed into productive, loyal citizens, guided by middle-class and gender norms. None of these values would last, however if "erected on sand" and not "built on the solid foundation of true Christianity." Therefore, schools required attendance in daily chapel, Sunday services, and additional Bible study or Christian instruction.[10] Reformers argued that to reach their aim of educating African Americans, they would have to transform the "*whole* child," as the Industrial and Educational Institute of Topeka noted. Therefore, schools organized themselves as "*nonsectarian*, but *thoroughly Christian*" and instructed students to bring along Bibles in addition to their toothbrushes, pillows, towels, and other basic necessities.[11] When Haskell Institute invited the inventor of basketball, James Naismith, to address the male students at the Indian boarding school, he presented them with a sermon titled "The Physical Advantages of Being a Christian." Teachers at Halstead Industrial Institute professed that through inculcation of Christian values and the preaching of the Gospel, "true salvation" would follow for their Native American students.[12]

Native American schools, whether run by religious or government leaders, did not delineate between church and state priorities and required their students to give strict attention to Christian beliefs and practices. For example, even though Halstead Industrial Institute gained financial support through a government contract, the school required students to ascribe to the Mennonite teachings that its founder, Reverend Christian Krehbiel, espoused. Halstead students learned their required Bible lessons and devotions each day and then attended Sunday school after a weekly worship service at the Mennonite church in town. Krehbiel himself baptized fourteen students during the school's ten-year existence between 1886 and 1896. At Haskell Institute, a federally funded and nondenominational boarding school, students could not refuse practicing Christianity, but could choose which denomination of Christianity they would practice. Once a decision was made, however, the school required students to attend weekly services, and students could not change their church without the consent of parents, guardians (who were often government-appointed Indian agents), or the superintendent of the school.[13]

At the federal level, the BIA kept a close watch on religious instruction and controlled students' exposure to religious practices by requiring attendance at services and Sunday school, yet forbidding any unchecked prose-lytizing by pastors, employees, or other pupils. At Haskell Institute, the BIA dictated six o'clock wake-up calls on Sunday mornings so that Catholic students could attend seven-thirty Mass either on campus or in the town of Lawrence. Protestant students attended churches in town at ten-thirty. Students seemed to have some choice about joining denominational meetings, Bible classes, and religious societies, but on Sunday afternoons, all students—Catholic or Protestant—were expected to attend General Assembly, when missionaries from Indian reservations and ministers from local Protestant churches spoke. Along with poetry and literary references, General Assembly speakers lectured on the Bible, instructions for living a Christian life, and methods for developing Christian citizenship. Christianity permeated so many lessons and activities at Haskell Institute that the school carried a "Religious Work Director" on its employment list.[14]

In the nineteenth century, a higher percentage of blacks than Indians practiced Protestant Christianity, but reformers still believed that African American students needed reinforcement of their Christian practices and values as a necessary step to prepare for their future citizenship roles. Christianity provided a model for "a true concept of duty, and . . . of altruism."[15] Embracing that philosophy, the Industrial and Educational Institute claimed that just by attending the school, black students developed "a Christian foundation where our young people are brought closer to Christ and influenced to lead better lives."[16] Even week-long summer sessions that promoted Christian leadership promised to "help leaders in a most practical way in rendering service to our people in their various fields."[17]

Charles Sheldon believed that part of the responsibility for developing African American Christian leadership resided with whites themselves. The kind of poverty that so many blacks had endured, he reasoned, resulted not solely from individual failure but from an "unchristian" nature within the larger society. After witnessing the poor conditions of his students, Sheldon's own response to inequality and labor exploitation included demanding Christian socialism among his white peers. Through Christian socialism, or what he thought of as the application of the teachings of Jesus, a change in the entire social life of humanity would take effect. Sheldon called for the expansion of Christian social teachings, as well as the application of principles of equality and love among all different races. Although at one point Sheldon himself had expressed discomfort with the presence of black—rather than white—preachers, he later charged those who expressed racial prejudice to conduct a serious reevaluation of their claim

"Wards of the Nation—Their First Vacation from School," Drawing by E. L. Blumenschein, *Harper's Weekly*, 17 June 1899. Federal Indian schools removed Native American students from their families for long periods of time and insisted on their adopting new ways of dressing, speaking, and behaving. (Courtesy of HarpWeek, LLC)

on Christianity. Albion Tourgée, judge and champion of African American civil rights, raised a point at the first Lake Mohonk Conference on the Negro Question that echoed Sheldon's: "So far as the peaceful and Christian solution of the race problem is concerned, indeed, I am inclined to think that the only education required is that of the *white* race."[18]

Although Sheldon and Tourgée held whites accountable for their own interest in African American economic deprivation and racial prejudice, Sheldon's reform efforts still included considerable attention to modifying the behaviors and beliefs of black students and their parents. In fact, he created programs that required even the youngest of students (kindergarteners) to develop skills and values that would help them rise out of poverty. Sheldon believed that poverty created a "bare and cheerless home" and diminished "all the sweet graces of life"; therefore, the first step was "to sow the first seeds that are to produce adults of sound mind and in a sound body,—good citizens and true Christians."[19] Sheldon's emphasis on Christian socialism among whites made his rhetoric somewhat different from the language of his contemporaries, but his willingness to hold whites accountable for their prejudice against blacks and his outreach into the Tennesseetown community earned him endorsements from black newspapers. For example, in 1913, when he invited the Fisk University Jubilee Singers to perform in a church-sponsored series, the *Topeka Plaindealer* praised the program as one that encouraged racial harmony: "The devil and Jim Crow were not visible. We are glad to know that there is in Topeka one congregation of white Christians which practices what it teaches and preaches."[20] Sheldon organized many of the church's social services in Tennesseetown, including medical and legal care and small, interest-free loans provided by his father-in-law and banker, E. B. Merriam. Sheldon himself took credit for the high literacy rate, 87 percent, in the community and also boasted that residents owned 5,306 books and 147 subscriptions to newspapers. Fifty-two percent of those who worked as laborers owned their homes, thus beating the state average of 33 percent. No doubt he was also proud of an alumnus of the kindergarten, Elisha Scott, whom Sheldon mentored, financially supported, and encouraged to attend law school at Washburn University. Scott became a lawyer arguing many civil rights cases including *Brown v. Board of Education* before the Supreme Court.[21]

Like most African Americans, many Indian students already practiced Christianity when they arrived at school, but reformers ignored that fact and blended conversion and American patriotism into a form of religious instruction that permeated the lives of their students. They frequently argued that Christianity would help Native Americans become better citizens, but their programs suggested that they also wanted to use Christianity to leverage a distinction between students and their unschooled family members. Hervey Peairs directly linked Christianity and "really civilized people," claiming that citizens could not be found "except where the Bible has been sent and the gospel taught."[22] Since reformers thought that Indians had been raised in uncivilized environments, the job of Christianity was to do more than provide spiritual sanctification for Indian students; it would provide a structure for all elements of character, including honesty, temperance, and other virtues.[23]

Reformers had a secondary agenda where Christian education for Native Americans was concerned. In addition to molding the character of their students, reformers hoped to develop ambassadors, or what Peggy Pascoe refers to as "native helpers," who would take their versions of Christianity to evangelize among their tribes.[24] Reformers hoped that males would eventually become missionaries in their own communities, and therefore older boys at Halstead Industrial Institute practiced religious leadership by directing nightly prayer services for the rest of the children. Although reformers had assigned that specific role to boys, girls had a stake in Christian citizenship, too. In fact, they were charged with the important responsibility of extending Christianity to future generations. As teachers and mothers, girls were to influence their children and, as A. B. Shelly, secretary of the Mennonite Mission Board, stated, "lead their tender hearts to the Savior." Shelly further explained the importance of women as anchors of Christianity within their families by saying that women's work was "necessarily of a private nature" because women's "most important field of labor" was the family. He added, "The church can never overestimate the influence the mother exerts, either for good or for evil, in the bringing up of her children. Give us good, pious mothers, whose aim it is to raise servants and handmaidens unto the Lord, and the church will reap the blessed fruits of their labors." Shelly's comments about Native American girls' education matched general beliefs about white girls' education. As the nineteenth-century common school proponent and school administrator Henry Barnard explained, girls needed education because "the great influence of the female sex, as daughters, sisters, wives, mothers, companions, and teachers, in determining the manners, morals, and intelligence of the whole community, leaves no room to question the necessity of providing for the girls the best means of intellectual and moral culture." Reformers impressed upon female students a sense of obligation and duty as they trained to manage their future households. Shelly also suggested that women use their roles to influence public opinion on issues such as temperance, as well as teach Sunday school, engage in mission work, nurse the sick, visit the poor, and perform other works of mercy.[25]

By training girls in housekeeping, child care, and Christian virtues, reformers planned to multiply their influence exponentially through the maternal influence of students over their future families and children. While boys would make particularly loyal and patriotic citizens, girls could be "suitable companions of the educated males" and provide a vitally important extension of citizenship training beyond the school into the home.[26] To work toward this end, schools reinforced existing gender norms and often provided residential cottages instead of dormitories for girls. In the cottages, older girls lived together with a matron in order to gain pragmatic experience taking care of younger children as well as maintaining the cottage, cooking meals, and conducting Bible studies. Peairs delighted in such practices because the training would produce "zealous christian women" able to reveal to youth of subsequent generations "the ideals of genuine Christian civilization."[27] Placing students in cottages also encouraged attachments and loyalties to new family units rather than old tribal alliances.[28]

If the fundamental purpose of education was character building and religious training in order to foster future leadership, domestic training of girls would contribute to that end. However, when such reformers placed value on girls' education, their emphasis on developing female helpmates and ambassadors ignored other possibilities for female citizenship. Reformers did not view their female students as potential participants in political processes, and although they sometimes made general references to Indian suffrage, they never acknowledged the specific campaign for woman suffrage that marched on during the same time that they established their coeducational schools. They also did not recognize how their version of citizenship training failed to prepare girls for lives as housewives because many African American and Native American women faced economic realities requiring them to seek paid employment outside of their homes. Glenda Gilmore calls this dilemma a "middle space" between gender spheres, where African American women would develop skills to work in a trade yet still be expected to retain a semblance of Victorian ladyhood. Education in domestic fields for girls of color reinforced the existing gender order but did not prepare them for a life of unpaid labor in their own homes as a Victorian model would dictate. In the end, black and Native American girls could only embody Victorian norms by making those ideals possible for others.

Ultimately, they sold their domestic skills and products in exchange for money rather than realizing their own domestic ideal.[29]

In addition to attending Christian church services, Sunday school, evening Bible studies, and schoolwide assemblies, both black and Native American boys and girls joined extracurricular associations to solidify their Christian foundations. The YMCA and the YWCA helped Industrial and Educational Institute students to bring their "redeemed souls to salvation" so that they could be better prepared for religious leadership as well as get "closer to Christ" and learn how to "live better lives."[30] Western University, an African American high school in Quindaro, also prioritized YMCA activities, and at Haskell Institute, Hervey Peairs asked the YMCA to open an official branch on campus to promote Christian leadership among boys while the YWCA promoted gender norms among girls or "revolutionize[d] Indian home life and communities."[31]

Military training, disciplinary rules, and uniforms further highlighted gender distinctions. Most notably, while girls lived in cottages and learned domestic skills, boys joined military companies and learned drills. Schools appreciated the disciplinary and patriotic components of such drilling, and when they organized military companies by age, they thought that they contributed to the future deterioration of tribal alliances. The watchful military supervisors also ensured strict discipline and issued sharp consequences for boys' infractions. For example, when two Haskell boys stole watermelons, it was their military company that had them arrested and punished. Another time, when complaints came to the school regarding boys "annoying people on the highway," it was the military company that forbade all its members from going off school grounds. The watchful eye of their leaders kept students in military companies in check, especially on Sundays when leaders conducted close inspections of their troops.[32]

The Industrial and Educational Institute of Topeka valued military training for its African American students for the same reasons that Haskell Institute did for its Native American students. In addition, the United States government offered the school financial grants to support its programs including an appropriation of $6,000 worth of equipment for improved instruction in military science in 1922. "Special attention is given to that kind of instruction which leads to the making of better citizens and the highest respect for the stars and stripes," administrators bragged. The financial incentives continued throughout the decade, and the Industrial and Educational Institute eventually expanded its military program in cooperation with the Veterans' Bureau. In the 1920s, the school offered industrial and vocational training to adults, including fifty ex-service men, so that the school could "serve our people and aid them in making [themselves] more useful and better citizens."[33]

Schools required their students to display their patriotism, but the privileges of citizenship that such displays might have earned did not necessarily come to African Americans and Native Americans. Even during World War I, when many boys of high school age left their respective schools to join the armed forces, black men still experienced widespread disenfranchisement; and many Indians, despite their service, would not acquire legal citizenship until 1924. Female students also experienced widespread prejudice, but school officials still expected them to participate in patriotic activities. Both boys and girls filed into the dining halls and classrooms in military order and recited the Pledge of Allegiance. As an added offering of patriotic display, the Industrial and Educational Institute offered classes for African American veterans in tailoring, agriculture, raising poultry, and other industries, while the school raised the flag each morning with reveille and lowered it in the evening with a military salute. To emphasize that his Indian students were as ready for citizenship as white students, Hervey Peairs rejected an alternative version of the Pledge of Allegiance and chose to have his students say the pledge used by white students in public schools throughout the country. Such displays of patriotism, reformers reasoned, did not necessarily prepare students for citizenship, but made them worthy of it.[34]

Discipline at boarding schools further reinforced notions of self-control, gender boundaries, and conformity. Schools strictly controlled all students in their movement and activities, and students found their activities closely supervised, including the inspection of incoming and outgoing mail. General inspection of dormitories took place as early as six o'clock in the morning, and students could not leave school their campus without explicit permission from a teacher. At the Industrial and Educational Institute, punishment for leaving school without a written excuse was expulsion and forfeiture of any credits that the student had saved in the school treasury. Demanding that students conform to the rigorous schedules and discipline, the school stressed *"unexceptionable deportment and strict attention to all school duties,"* adding, *"we conduct no asylum for the lazy, nor reformatory for the wayward."*[35]

Girls had even closer supervision resulting in less mobility than boys at boarding schools. Although both boys and girls needed permission to leave school grounds, only girls were obligated to have the additional protection of a chaperone. "*No young lady student permitted to leave the grounds un-less accompanied by a lady teacher,*" read the only italicized statement in the "Regulation" section of the Industrial and Educational Institute manual. Matrons accompanied female Haskell students into the town of Lawrence for church services and shopping on Saturday afternoons.[36] Esther Burnett Horne (Shoshone), a graduate of Haskell Institute, suggested that school officials feared that female students would get pregnant "without constant supervision," so by separating boys and girls for outings, reformers intended to add a layer of protection for girls, but also reiterated a gender hierarchy that required girls to have more help and less independence than boys.[37]

Uniforms symbolized discipline and conformity for all students. At the Industrial and Educational Institute, uniforms represented a "secure system" as well as "neatness and economy" while on campus. They also made students easily recognizable to school officials, the public, or the police.[38] Most Native American schools issued one or two uniforms for students at the beginning of the school year and had them sew additional clothes. At the Industrial and Educational Institute, African American girls wore a school or work uniform and had a special dress uniform for holidays. They were not allowed to incorporate silk or satin dresses into their wardrobe because the school thought that such a display of "expensive or elaborate apparel" would inhibit the recruitment of "poor but worthy girls and young women" to the school and take away from "the time and attention that the student should give to studies and trade."[39] On Thanksgiving, Christmas, and Easter, girls could wear dark blue skirts and white waist shirts, but the school reiterated the "no special attire" regulation even for these special holidays and prohibited fancy attire in general. Even on special days, uniforms maintained a utilitarian function that promoted stability, conformity, and frugality rather than stylistic fashion.[40]

Rigorous Work through Industrial Training

Christian indoctrination, strict discipline, and displays of patriotism structured the days and nights of both black and Native American students, but students also spent part of their days engaged in formal instruction. The industrial programs designed by Hampton Institute and Carlisle Institute emphasized training in farming, domestic work, and trades and became the models for Indian and black schools across the nation. Between 1890 and 1910 as many as twenty-five industrial schools opened for Indian students, and in 1888, Booker T. Washington's Tuskegee Institute opened for African

Americans and quickly became the most famous outgrowth of what was soon referred to as the Hampton Model. Schools founded with elaborate industrial programs, such as the Industrial and Educational Institute and Western University, proudly enjoyed the moniker, the "Western Tuskegee" or "Tuskegee of the West," even though they often modified the Hampton-Tuskegee Idea.[41]

Carlisle and Hampton's model of boarding school education required control over every hour of students' lives, including evenings, weekends, and summers. "Total institution," a term that sociologist Erving Goffman coined in 1968 to characterize a place that formally encloses a group of people, separating them from the wider society, has been employed by historians of Native American education to describe boarding schools such as Haskell Institute and Halstead Indian Industrial School. In a total institution, students arose early in the morning, cleaned their rooms and did chores, ate breakfast together, and then began classes. Standard schedules included mornings filled with traditional coursework such as reading, arithmetic, and history. Afternoons were dedicated to manual labor, including working the fields, preparing evening meals, sewing or repairing uniforms, ironing, doing laundry, building new buildings, and doing other work needed to expand, or at least maintain, the schools. Through the 1920s, students spent half the day in classes and the other half engaged in domestic work, farming, or school maintenance. A Halstead Industrial Institute student, Frank Sweesy, described a typical school day by explaining, "In the morning we work out in the fields, to plant corn and cut weeds. The corn and wheat, [and] oats are growing pretty good. What is planted and sown looks green."[42] Sweesy's description suggests that he took pride in his work, but it also reveals that the school unabashedly required student labor as an educational foundation.

When schools offered athletics or music activities, practice and rehearsals took place in the late afternoons. To reinforce Christian indoctrination, speakers, Bible studies, and YMCA and YWCA activities occupied the evening hours. Native American students worked for local white families during the summer outing programs. At black schools, the same pattern was followed; at the Industrial and Educational Institute, for example, students worked outside of school hours and during the summers to earn money for tuition or to learn a trade.[43]

Although schedules varied, the most important part of a student's day consisted of industrial training. Training in practical, industrial fields initially had a twofold purpose: preparing students to learn skills so that they could earn a living once they left school, and providing the much-needed labor to keep the school running. Training encouraged Native Americans to become more economically self-sustaining and, reformers believed, less likely to resume their tribal identities when they left school. Industrial education permeated most primary, secondary, and normal schools for African Americans and expanded significantly in the 1880s. Beginning in 1881, large contributions from the Peabody Fund and the John F. Slater Fund, as well as passage of the Blair Bills of the 1880s and 1890s and the Smith-Hughes Vocational Education Act of 1917, added incentives to expand industrial training at schools that were strapped for funds. Historians have viewed such funding as the sacrifice of racial equality in education in favor of priorities that were more consistent with white supremacy. But even black colleges, otherwise committed to racial uplift and strong, intellectual education, also offered some industrial training for both male and female students seeking degrees, especially for those working their way through school.[44]

Industrial education not only provided students with training for future work but also disproved the idea that Indians and blacks were predisposed to laziness, which many white reformers believed. Whites assumed that African Americans lacked an appreciation of the dignity of labor because work had been forced upon them as slaves; and they thought that Native Americans did not have enough work to do on reservations. At the Lake Mohonk Conference on the Negro Question, A. F. Beard, secretary of the AMA, expressed his concern about a lack of orderliness, understanding of time, accuracy, values, and proper home life among African Americans.[45] Samuel Armstrong declared that slavery had taught blacks how to labor, "but gave him no respect for labor."[46] The annual announcement for the Industrial and Educational Institute linked industrial education with a remedy for laziness even more explicitly: "*Every student must pursue regular work in the industrial department.* We have no room for the lazy or indolent."[47] Elizabeth Comstock thought that many African Americans had worked only in cotton fields and sugar plantations, and so they were "entirely unprepared" to make a living any other way. Therefore, she thought that they had to learn to face the challenge of work like "their more favored white brethren have been used to all their lives."[48] Helping them develop a love of work would make African Americans less dependent on charity, and therefore, at Comstock's school, industrial training became the primary curricular component to encourage that result. Leon Litwack suggests that the type of American identity that blacks had been promised was based on "a democracy of economic equality," ethics that Comstock and others encouraged. Schools reflected Litwack's assessment of nineteenth-century America "in which success came ultimately to the hardworking, the sober, the honest, and the educated—to those who adopted a work ethic of diligence, perseverance, and punctuality; served their employers faithfully and respected authority, property, and the sanctity of contract; cultivated habits of thrift, cleanliness, and temperance; and led moral, virtuous, Christian lives."[49]

With the immediate aim of preparing students for future employment, industrial education also had a larger goal of character development. Industrial education could not cure all human ills, but administrators at the Industrial and Educational Institute thought it might provide "the beckoning hand of promise" and "the illuminated path to practical, essential training" that would outfit all students for the duties of life, prepare them for more productive work, and help them to command higher wages.[50] It is not clear how reformers explicitly defined higher wages, but they thought that students who learned to love their work would then earn more money and become more self-sufficient as adults.

Industrial education included training in the trades, and each trade required advanced training as students got older. For example, male students learned how to use a printing press and how to care for an office in their first year, but later in their third year, printing students took advanced lessons in proofreading and typesetting. First-year female students learned how to thread a needle and practiced their sewing on scraps of cloth, but in their second year, they advanced to making dresses by pattern. Students who succeeded in the dressmaking courses could then advance to "making and finishing garments of every kind from different materials."[51] In the 1920s, the Industrial and Educational Institute shifted toward more professional areas, including teacher training.[52] During the Great Depression, however, the school returned to an emphasis on industrial training as a model for the education of black students.

The great quantity of goods produced and buildings repaired or built during this period suggests that students' work went beyond the purpose of teaching them skills. For example, by 1885, only a year after Haskell Institute opened, girls in the school bakery used 1,900 pounds of flour per week. In 1890, a baker and three student assistants made 335 loaves of bread per day. Five years later, both boys and girls not only prepared food for all of Haskell Institute's students, faculty, and staff, but also made uniforms, farm wagons, saddles, and other equipment that the school eventually sold for $10,000. In addition, students prepared 1,139 pairs of shoes, 2,590 bushels of corn, 658 bushels of wheat, 125 bushels of tomatoes, and 300 apples. Girls made 688 shirts, 526 dresses, and large amounts of canned vegetables and fruit. In 1894, students cultivated two hundred acres of land and tended to hundreds of cattle, pigs, and mules. In addition to large agricultural fields that boys tended, all students, including young children, grew vegetable gardens to raise food that would supplement limited government rations. Male students helped with the construction of their campus buildings, while female students maintained the day-to-day tasks, including laundry. Even young students in the primary grades at Haskell Institute and the kindergarten in Tennesseetown did their share by picking up litter on school grounds or tending to small gardens with cotton, watermelon, popcorn, and tulip crops. When Haskell Institute needed a new boys' dormitory, the boys themselves provided the labor after the contractor designed plans. When the Industrial and Educational Institute needed an athletic field, the administrators estimated that a sum of $1,000 would provide the funding for the field, if students would provide the labor. Haskell Institute's new gymnasium in 1915 and football stadium in 1926 were also constructed with student labor.[53]

Reformers did not hide the fact that their students spent considerable amounts of school time engaged in productive labor. Student work—farming, gardening, sewing, cooking, baking, repairing, and building—made up for shortfalls in government appropriations. In 1924, the BIA considered student work a mark of assimilation, and Commissioner Charles Burke claimed, "As a result of this practical training there are many hundreds of young men among the Indians who can, if necessary, shoe a horse and repair its harness, set a wagon tire, lay a concrete walk, and even build a house, and there are as many young Indian women who can do any kind of house work, care for children according to the hygienic methods and give to their homes a touch of art that makes them attractive."[54]

Critics expressed concerns about student labor. For example, in 1895, Superintendent of Indian Schools William Hailmann reminded officials that "the industrial work of the school should cease to be mere drudgery." Students should not be turned into "mere toilers or choremen or chorewomen," he added.[55] Despite this concern, students continued to toil as part of their school responsibilities. Estelle Reel, superintendent of Indian schools, emphasized industrial education over intellectual coursework in 1901, when she authored a guidebook for Indian schools that promoted the Native American student as a willing worker whose character warranted more attention than his or her intellect. As federal funding for Indian

Native American Young Men Farming. Indian boarding schools stressed agricultural training for boys and domestic lessons for girls throughout the late nineteenth century. (Courtesy of Kansas State Historical Society)

boarding schools declined in the twentieth century, student labor only continued to increase until the late 1920s when schools adopted labor-saving devices or made other changes in response to the harsh working conditions exposed in the 1928 Meriam Report, an investigation of federal schools.[56]

In addition to promoting a productive school day, industrial training kept some students from failing out of school when they performed poorly in scholastic courses. For example, when Winnie Rogers (Cherokee) transferred to Haskell Institute from Carlisle Institute, she was twenty-one years old. She was relatively well-behaved and tried to achieve the minimum standards in school, but having received little academic foundation in the primary grades, Rogers constantly struggled in her coursework and tested at a fourth-grade level. Her teachers advanced her to the seventh grade "to avoid humiliation and to keep respect of classmates," but her principal thought that Rogers was wasting her time in academic classes. To the delight of administrators, Rogers proved to be one of the best students in sewing and cooking classes, so they recommended that she advance to a dressmaking school so that she would get "*vocational* training for *life*." Mary Stanley, a matron at Haskell Institute, thought that Rogers's vocational training was her last hope for success and noted in the margin of her report, "At 21 a girl is too old to be getting nowhere."[57]

Despite the fact that white reformers used similar rhetoric and laid out nearly identical curricular and extracurricular plans at Indian schools and black schools, their final expectations of their students differed. They insisted on removing Indian children from their homes, constructing substitute families for them in dormitories and cottages, and placing them with white families during the summer months. With plans to integrate Native American students into public schools and encourage intermarriage, reformers created Indian schools as, according to Wilbert Ahern, a "temporary necessity on the way to immersion."[58]

The plan for African Americans, however, had much greater limits. By guiding African American students through industrial training, imposing rigorous schedules, forcing allegiance to Protestantism, and so on, reformers ultimately trained them to maintain a lower station in society. The curricular focus on character reform lacked what Adam Fairclough refers to as "substantial concern for economic or political causes of racism and African American oppression" and denied those students opportunities for considerable racial uplift.[59] Industrial training would never prepare African Americans for jobs with enough income to claim the privileges of the middle class, but eventually as adults, black students would uphold middle-class values and accommodate the dominant culture with their skilled labor and domestic work.[60]

Islands and Communities: Locations of Schools

By the turn of the twentieth century, critics certainly recognized that citizenship training for Indians had led to neither their complete disappearance into white society nor their economic uplift. But until that point, keeping students away from the influence of families was a cornerstone of Indian education. Boarding schools were often located away from reservations, or on the outskirts of their respective towns, so that they became islands unto themselves. Reformers deliberately limited students' interactions with anyone other than their peers and the school's staff and faculty, and they heeded warnings from other missionaries and educators that contact with reservations might lead to a reclamation of traditional practices and a repudiation of Christianity. Believing that reformers had to guard their students from undesirable exposure, Christian Krehbiel argued that if students "returned to their Indian ways," it would be a step backward in the evolutionary process.[61] Rejecting the notion that family life might contribute to an Indian student's development, Hervey Peairs argued, "He learns nothing of value at home; nobody there is competent to teach. He learns nothing from his neighbors; nobody with whom he associates does anything better than he finds in his own home."[62]

White community members supported separating Indian children from their families before they were old enough to become set in their habits and ways. Whites supported the work of boarding schools that cut "the cord which binds the Indian race to a Pagan life" and substituted "civilization in place of superstition, morality in place of vice, cleanliness in place of filth, industry in place of idleness, self-respect in place of servility—an elevated humanity instead of abject degradation." Critical of Indian parents whom whites considered "ignorant" and trapped in "barbarism," the *Topeka Capital* emphasized "the importance of detaching [children] from their parents and placing them in such an institution as Haskell Institute to be trained up during the formation periods of their lives into civilized habits and industries."[63]

There is no evidence that African American children were forced away from their families to attend boarding schools as Indian children were; however, there is substantial evidence that Native American children endured many pressures to attend schools founded by white reformers. If parents refused to release their children to Indian agents, for example, the government could stop their annuity payments and parents faced threats from police or soldiers sent by the BIA to show "that we mean business."[64] Speaking at the Indian Educational Convention in 1891, G. I. Harvey likened a boarding school superintendent to a "good rustler." A superintendent should possess multiple abilities, including being "able to arrange a school program, kill a hog, help at the singing, brand the calves, set window-glass, settle a boy, put a nail here, a screw there and a post somewhere else." With those skills "he can get children from the camps, and if he can *get* them, he will have the ingenuity to *keep* them."[65] Compulsory attendance laws reinforced the power of representatives of the United States government to force tribal children from their homes and place them in schools. Therefore, when boarding school recruiters went to reservations to enroll children in school, parents often felt threatened if they appeared hesitant or unwilling. Although reformers repeatedly argued that Indian children should attend boarding schools to learn about citizenship, which included modeling an American family ideal, they failed to see the irony that their own forceful methods threatened to dismantle existing Indian families.[66]

Once Native American students arrived at a school like Halstead Institute or Haskell Institute—either by choice or force—administrators kept them enrolled for as long as possible, and sometimes beyond their original term. Christian Krehbiel argued that Indian students had to go to school until they could "stand for themselves against the many temptations which they will meet when they go back to their relatives."[67] Hervey Peairs believed that, even when Indian agents forced children away from their parents, their actions were justified in the name of citizenship development. Children "taken from homes of ignorance and superstition" had greater potential to progress than those who remained.[68] The *Topeka Daily Capital* echoed administrators when the editors told their readers, "The idea is to keep him away from his uncivilized relatives and friends until his habits become fixed."[69]

With the goal of "fixing" Native Americans in mind, reformers herded their students into an environment filled with strangers, including white teachers, matrons, administrators, and a host of students from a variety of tribes from the Dakotas, Nebraska, Kansas, Indian Territory, and other states. Conversely, most African American students went to school in their own neighborhoods, with other children from their communities, and were taught by white teachers and ministers who had some familiarity or contact with their home environments. Black students would not have to learn a new language or make the kind of drastic alterations to their dress that many Native Americans had, therefore, separation from parents did not seem as crucial. With the specter of slavery still lurking in all Americans' minds and without the threat of withholding government rations (as in the case of Native Americans) forcing black children away from their parents would have been virtually impossible.

In the 1880s and 1890s, an era of heightened racial violence and Jim Crow segregation, blacks moved to the North and to western states in large groups and established black towns with strong community ties. While Indian communities felt a constant threat of fragmentation by allotment acts and other government pressure that insisted on individualization rather than community building, African Americans were actually bound to the communities in which they lived—sometimes by choice and sometimes because of forced segregation. Locating schools within African American communities allowed reformers to reinforce the existing separation of blacks and whites and also allowed reformers to use children's educational programs as a vehicle to influence African American adults. Night schools, for example, helped to increase adult literacy as well as created a platform for community outreach. Through courses in carpentry, stone masonry, auto mechanics, agriculture, and home economics, schools meant to "serve more people and serve them in a much larger way than we do now." For example, during its tenure in Topeka, the Industrial and Educational Institute taught school-aged blacks during the daytime, but when classes ended, the building functioned as a community center where African American organizations, such as the Inter-State Literary Society, the Kansas Women's Club, and the Lincoln-Douglass Club, held conventions.[70]

The Tennesseetown Kindergarten provides the most vivid example of a reform effort that expanded into the community beyond the original school. In 1893, when Charles Sheldon opened his school for young children, he hoped to use the kindergarten as a portal through which he could influence the other 700 to 800 residents living in the Exoduster colony. Sheldon's plan succeeded, and since the City of Topeka did not provide a public school for its African American residents, Sheldon's school added evening industrial training classes for older students before the end of its first year. Three years later, the school introduced sewing classes for girls and basket weaving for boys. Sheldon tried to form a "Boys' Brigade" consisting of military marching and drilling activities, but interest waned.[71] By 1904, the Tennesseetown library had better success accumulating 1,200 volumes and staying open every night of the week during the winter season. Additionally, the kindergarten's Mothers' League met weekly, the school consistently provided training for older students, and students and their families attended Sheldon's Sunday school and church socials. Sheldon invited black families to picnics at his church, at his home, and at nearby Garfield Park, and he also routinely visited Tennesseetown, offering lectures against drinking and lawlessness and promoting economic responsibility. The kindergarten operated this way for eighteen years until Topeka incorporated the school into its school system.[72]

In black neighborhoods, white reformers did not try to create new family structures for their students as they had in Indian schools. Instead, they used education as a means to connect with larger black communities. Sheldon and kindergarten teacher June Chapman visited the homes of their African American students, and Sheldon also established a Village Improvement Society, which hosted contests for residents. Families won prizes for the best lawns, neatest homes, best gardens, and best poultry raised. In 1901, Sheldon had leadership roles in the society transferred from white volunteers to black community members, although the white volunteers continued their involvement. Students also entered contests including such national competitions as the 1904 St. Louis World's Fair and the 1907 Jamestown Tercentennial Exposition, where they won awards for their arts and crafts. Mothers volunteered in the community and raised funds for projects through the Sheldon Congress of Mothers and the Kindergarten Auxiliary. Tennesseetown residents enthusiastically involved themselves in Sheldon's outreach activities, but his education and outreach efforts perpetuated African Americans' isolation in their segregated settlement without providing encouragement to integrate themselves into the dominant society.[73]

At the same time that reformers' efforts among African Americans reinforced segregation, they encouraged integration among Indian students. Absorption into white society began with the creation of substitute families headed by male teachers in paternal roles and female teachers assuming maternal roles. In 1886, at Halstead Industrial Institute, Christian Krehbiel went to added lengths to create a familial atmosphere. First, he moved his school from the town limits to his own farm and then enlarged his house to accommodate his students along with the Krehbiel children. He made himself superintendent and hired his wife and sons to serve as teachers and surrogate family members. To add to the feeling of family unity, the students and Krehbiel family members ate together at one long table in the basement of the home. The school continued to operate this way through 1896, during which time, students (most of whom were from Indian Territory) stayed for an average of three years. Eventually Krehbiel's farm and the land around it became known as Krehbieltown.[74]

The outing program also encouraged Indians to assimilate and be absorbed into white families. Originally designed by Richard Henry Pratt at Carlisle Institute, outing programs placed students into the homes of Christian, white families, where they practiced their domestic and industrial skills, earned small wages, and experienced complete immersion into white, middle-class life. Pratt believed that through outing, students would complete their acquisition of English language skills, including the nuances of the language, gain goodwill and appreciation from white patrons, and finish the final stages of citizenship training. The outing program, a popular standard at boarding schools in the 1880s and 1890s, provided an important element in the assimilation process, so Congress made appropriations to place Indian children in white families and even allocated funds specifically for transportation, medical, and clothing costs of outing students.[75]

Boarding school curricula segregated boys and girls in their studies, and the outing program continued that trend by assigning girls to domestic work within the confines of patrons' homes and boys to farming, harvesting, or trade assignments on farms or in nearby cities. Esther Horne Burnett remembered that Haskell Institute sent her to work in Kansas City, Missouri, for two years. During the first summer, she helped a family take care of two infants, and the next summer she served as a downstairs maid for a doctor and his wife.[76] If boys did not work on family farms during the summer months, their own schools often hired them to spend their summers repairing old buildings or constructing new ones.

The outing program encouraged students to learn how to earn and save wages, so school officials and BIA commissioners made some effort to ensure that their students received fair wages, or at the very least, a minimum wage of fifty cents per week, but wages varied with a maximum of fifteen or twenty dollars per month. Students often kept less than half of their earned wages and the rest went into school accounts as a step on the path to self-reliance.[77] At Haskell Institute only one-third of a student's income was paid directly to the pupils, and officials guarded their judicious spending. Patrons sent the majority of students' wages to the school along with their monthly reports on the students' performance at their homes. Girls' rates of pay varied from as little as two to ten dollars per month for being a "general helper" in charge of washing, ironing, cleaning, and cooking. Other girls could earn three to five dollars per week working in a family's home. From 1920 to 1921, girls could earn nine dollars per week doing housework in a family's home, but the average wage was much lower, and there was no guarantee that any student would ever receive all the wages earned.[78]

School officials took some care in placing their students with patrons, including checking each patron's home "from kitchen to attic," inspecting a student's room, and inquiring about the business and the religious practices of each family. Patrons were charged with students' moral and physical safety, and therefore, outing matrons routinely inspected homes during students' assignments and reinforced rules ensuring their safety. In 1919, Mary Stanley, Haskell's outing matron, sent a circular to all patrons "laying down new and very strict rules—the first violation of same to cause removal of the girl." Both students and their patrons had to sign contracts promising regular attendance at church and Sunday school. Additionally, students had to dress and conduct themselves properly at all times, bathe at least once a week, and be "kind, courteous, helpful, and agreeable to those about them, in order to obtain the greatest benefit of their outing." Boys were forbidden from gambling and the use of tobacco or liquor, and the rules required all students to be honest, industrious, and helpful to their employers.[79]

Because the safety of girls was of particular concern for school officials and patrons, they did not allow female students to leave their patrons' homes without the accompaniment of the patron or another responsible member of the family. Rules forbade girls from receiving visits from boys without "direct permission from the superintendent." When Mildred Jandreau received letters and cards from Morgan French, a Haskell boy who also spent the summer in an outing assignment, Jandreau's patron nervously forbade her to leave the house—even for church with the family. Her patron reported the communications to the outing matron, who then alerted the superintendent, urging him to discipline the boy "before any trouble arises."[80]

It is hard to measure the range of experiences that students had within the outing program because much of the archived documentation was controlled by the outing matrons, school officials, and the BIA rather than the students themselves. Some girls expressed happiness about their assignments and even greeted the outing matron with kisses upon her arrival. Dallas Whipple told other girls how pleased she was with her patron's home, and those girls told the outing matron that they wanted to live there after Whipple left. Still there were others who protested their outing assignments, defied their surrogate parents, and ran away from their hosts' homes. Despite the enthusiasm of girls like Dallas Whipple, evidence suggests that the outing program benefited patron families more than the students themselves as a number of patrons failed to ever embrace students as family members, and simply viewed them as employees whom they wished could work beyond the summer months.[81] The constant demand for students in boarding schools—Haskell Institute often received up to twice as many requests for student workers as they could provide—suggests that the program minimized its educational components and reduced into an inexpensive work program. Even Richard Henry Pratt himself became critical of the outing program by the time he retired in 1904; later the Meriam Report corroborated Pratt's suspicions that some schools had created more of an Indian child labor system than an avenue for their full absorption into white society. Scholars have also argued that the outing program ultimately made Native American students common laborers and domestic servants, a conclusion that the BIA recognized in the 1920s. By 1930, the Indian outing program had ended.[82]

The fact that African American students did not engage in an outing program as elaborately designed as the one that engaged Native Americans reflected reformers' beliefs about the limited roles of blacks in society. African American students, although sometimes hired out to white employers to do work, were never part of a program that incorporated them into white families for months at a time. Instead of sending black students to work in

white families' homes, schools provided opportunities for students to improve their trade skills. Male students at the Industrial and Educational Institute learned how to work at a quarry so that they could "earn part of
their expenses." Female students worked in the school laundry and garden
to reduce theirs. Emphasizing the value of work, the school presented opportunities to take a job as a privilege that only a *few worthy students*" were
given.[83] Employment for African American students also freed parents from
the burden of supervising them during the summer so that they could "go
every day to a useful occupation and at the same time have their children
protected and under proper environment and good influences during the
vacation." While students continued to develop trades during the summer
months, parents tended to their own jobs and schools benefited from productive summer labor.[84]

With an emphasis on Christianity and work, schools adopted mottos
that would remind their students of the real purpose of their educations.
Halstead Indian Industrial School declared that its aim was "To win fol-
lowers of Christ who would make an honest living as good citizens." Haskell Indian Institute's motto was more succinct, "Learn to Earn," which emphasized Indian students' responsibility to learn skills that would prevent
them from relying on the federal government for support. The Industrial
and Educational Institute promoted the motto, "How to Live and How to
Make a Living." The Sheldon Congress of Mothers of the Tennesseetown
Kindergarten for black children simply proclaimed, "Onward."[85] Reformers may have achieved their goals of indoctrinating students in Protestant
Christian principles and imposing long hours of work on their students,
but the ways in which African American and Native American students
and adults negotiated and struggled with such demands eventually helped
them fully develop their identities as Americans.

Part II

STRATEGIES OF NEGOTIATION

Chapter Three

STUDENTS

NATIVE AMERICAN NEGOTIATIONS
AT HASKELL INSTITUTE

I was grief-stricken and frightened, and I can still visualize myself standing there,
feeling lost and alone. I was surrounded by images that transported me back
to the last time I saw my dad before he died, and I thought, "I hate this place;
I will never be happy here." I wondered which direction my home was.
—Esther Burnett Horne, *Essie's Story*

Dear old H. I., how I too love her.
—Ralph Revere, 1910

On a Thursday evening in October 1919, Native American students at Haskell Institute gathered together for an evening program. An unpopular matron, known as Mrs. Douglas, had ordered male and female students to sit separately during the presentation. Many boys protested Douglas's demand by refusing to walk into the school's chapel. Consequently, the school disciplinarian sent them to their rooms for a study period. Just when the program speaker started to walk onto the stage, all of the lights in the building suddenly turned off. At first, school officials thought that a fuse had blown, but when Assistant Superintendent C. E. Birch went outside of the building, he found a large group of male students lined up on the road. At that point, Birch realized that the auditorium was not the only building that had lost its power—the entire campus was dark. Birch would soon learn that a group of "criminally and viciously" inclined boys had obtained a ladder to climb a pole and tear loose the electrical connection.[1]

With the campus darkened, Haskell students revolted, smashing light fixtures, looting the food supply, and ringing the school bell. Some boys reportedly yelled to girls, "Are you with us?" and "Let's have a social." Another student threatened Birch by yelling, "Let's string him up!" The uproar continued for the entire evening. Teachers and administrators finally restored order, and eventually they decided to expel nine students—four boys and five girls—for insubordination and destruction of school property. Birch reported that "after considerable damage and commotion of a pretty disgraceful character had gone on, I succeeded in getting hold of the boys and persuaded the most of them to go to bed." He also noted in his report that many students had been taken aside for a "heart to heart talk" in hopes of persuading the calmer students to help maintain order among the rest of the student body.[2]

Although Birch wanted his supervisors to rest assured that he had quickly restored order after the blackout and that school employees were "in good spirits, not discouraged, and ready to fight it out," the story of the 1919 Haskell Institute protest reveals an important episode in student determination in an otherwise controlled educational environment.[3] For nearly four decades, white reformers had endorsed a strict curriculum for Native American students that demanded complete submission, and Indian students had demonstrated a range of responses to the expectations that their schools placed on them. In the end, they did not necessarily create a revolution that would suddenly alter the course of curriculum. Instead, when students challenged the intrusive, oppressive, traumatic environment of their schools, they engaged in a process of defining citizenship for themselves.

Many students agreed that assimilation into the dominant society would lead to their financial and social success, but to them assimilation did not necessarily require the passivity or complete surrender that reformers demanded. Instead, students showed that they could employ a wide spectrum of strategies. They could take advantage of, tolerate, or remove themselves from the parameters that white reformers had imposed with the founding of Haskell Institute in 1884. As a consequence, many Haskell students demonstrated that to become American did not mean a complete erasure of Indian cultural attributes. In fact, an unintended outcome of the boarding school experience was that students used their school environments to refine their own definitions of citizenship to include self-determination and cultural preservation.

Although students exhibited a variety of reactions to their school environment, it is important to note that a growing distrust of the federal system developed among most students during the height of the boarding school era.[4] The entire nineteenth century had been marked by Indian removal, white conquest for land, and interference with tribal self-government and control of family life and home. After a long history of Indian wars, forced removal, and containment, if government policy makers no longer thought of Native Americans as military enemies, they thought of them as wards in need of management and unable to make independent decisions. Between 1881 and 1900, Indian land holdings had declined from 155,632,312 acres to 77,865,373, and in the twentieth century, land restrictions changed, making it even easier for white settlers to gain ownership of land occupied by Indians. The 1887 Dawes Act had broken up reservation land but had largely failed to support Native Americans in their efforts to become farmers or to exercise what few rights they possessed. The 1906 Burke Act also failed in its purpose to grant land to Native Americans and keep whites from taking such land, so a legacy of illegal withholding or seizure of land continued through the early 1900s and contributed to diminishing faith in federal programs.[5]

Students' strategies of negotiation ranged from accommodation to outright rejection of school policies, including breaking rules, misbehaving in class, and working very slowly when assigned chores. Most notably, boys ran away or acted out publicly and girls started fires or stole from the supply closets. Both girls and boys used tobacco and alcohol, stole extra food from the kitchen, or left their dormitories without authorization. They used the native languages that their teachers had ordered them to forget, and they sometimes taught their friends forbidden tribal customs. Henry Roe Cloud remembered being punished for speaking his native language when he attended government schools, and Esther Burnett Horne remembered that during her Haskell days she secretly shared customs and traditions with other students. Such cultural exchanges, according to Horne, helped students develop a sense of community with each other and provided an important sense of autonomy that enabled them to resist complete assimilation: "Traditional values, such as sharing and cooperation, helped us to survive culturally at Haskell, even though the schools were designed to erase our Indian culture, values, and identities." Desire for independence manifested in adolescent rebellions, such as the time when Horne and a group of girls tried to get intoxicated by mixing ginger with water. She recalled, "One time, though, the brother of a friend of mine from Oklahoma got us a bottle of beer, and so we stayed home from dinner one evening, and divided that bottle of beer. We felt quite wicked and worldly drinking beer."[6]

Other students might have experienced the "worldly" or "ashamed" feelings that Horne described by pushing against the boundaries of institutional rules and taking advantage of opportunities that would help them determine their own futures. In the early twentieth century, these strategies included trying to gain admission into Haskell Institute's new extracurricular and academic programs, in particular athletic teams and business preparation courses. When students made special requests, such as seeking placement on a baseball team, they demonstrated that self-determination stood at the center of their understanding of citizenship.

From Protest to Arson

Scholars have sorted through the motivations of Indian students to try to make sense of their resistance patterns. Many of these students felt deep resentment because they were forced to separate from their families and traditions, or they felt stress because of the rigidity of their school environments, or they were angry about what David Adams calls the "uncompromising hegemonic assault on their cultural identity."[7] Trying to maintain a sense of individual or tribal identity contributed to the anxiety of boarding school students. Although cutting the electrical supply to their school buildings in 1919 was a dramatic (and exceptional) moment in Indian boarding school student resistance, the most common forms of protest can be characterized as what Kenneth Stampp and Deborah Gray White call "day-to-day resistance," a form of conscious action used to confront and survive oppression.[8] Students were not as likely to coordinate an outright rebellion as they were to feign illness, steal food, break equipment, mock teachers, drift among different schools, or even ingest hallucinogens. Some acted defiantly, were slow in doing their work, or were generally inattentive to their teachers' requests. Still others argued with their teachers or wrote letters of protest to superintendents about policies that seemed unfair or dangerous. Despite repeated assaults on their cultures, values, and traditions, students showed considerable adaptability and dexterity as they navigated through their boarding school experiences without much aid from parents or other adults.[9]

Resistance strategies also included incorporating forbidden Indian culture into their daily lives. Both male and female students plucked their eyebrows and braided their hair in traditional fashions. In addition to acting out individually, boarding school students formed protective and nurturing support groups, in which they would develop friendships and subcultures to help them tolerate their isolation and constriction. Haskell students secretly taught each other about tribal regalia, dances, languages, and legends, and Esther Horne Burnett confessed that she and her friends even had a set of phonograph records of Indian music that they played for each other when "we got lonesome for home." Knowing that the school would punish the sharing of traditional information, students learned how to hide such covert activities. "When BIA supervisors came along, I was very adept at sweeping the Indian components under the table," Horne claimed.[10] Much of the behavior she described could be characterized as typically adolescent in nature. However, since resistance patterns included preserving specific parts of their tribal experiences, such day-to-day strategies also point to a larger agenda of preserving the very cultures teachers tried to eradicate. As scholars have noted, it was the very attempt to break up tribal alliances and suppress the sharing of Native American culture that ironically prompted students to embrace a variety of traditional cultures and develop cross-tribal unity.[11]

On occasion, students formally protested their treatment, but even these complaints were sternly rebuked, as in the case of students who asked for more clothes since their government-issued clothing proved insufficient.[12] In a few instances, though, students' words did influence outcomes that directly affected them. For example, in 1917, a group of girls thought their matron treated them unfairly, so they bypassed their own teachers by writing directly to the commissioner of Indian Affairs in Washington to complain. They wrote, "The girls of Haskell are being mistreated by the head matron, Miss Keck, and we wish you would look into the matter as soon as you can. There has been more trouble with the girls this year than ever and we all dislike the matron very much. Girls have run away because of her meanness and strict rules . . . We await your reply with the wish that Miss Keck would resign." Upon learning of this complaint letter about Katherine Keck, Superintendent Hervey Peairs also wrote to the commissioner, suggesting that the girls were only protesting in retaliation for a recent punishment. While he dismissed their claim, he admitted in his letter that Keck had had a difficult year and that she had, in fact, made some poor decisions that year. "She has reached an age where it will be very hard for her to change her disposition and manner," he wrote, "and therefore I fear that it may not be pleasant for her or for the girls if she remains here, and the results may not be the best." Still, Peairs was reluctant to let it appear that he had fired a teacher in response to student complaints: "To do so would ruin discipline and the successor would find it impossible to control the situation." Although Peairs did not initially fire Keck, because the students had the audacity to write directly to Washington rather than to their own teachers they certainly raised awareness about both the matron's performance and their fellow students' dissatisfaction. It is not clear whether the protest directly led to Keck's firing, but the *Indian Leader*, Haskell Institute's school newspaper and yearbook, later reported that Keck had "retired" sometime that same year. By 1920, Keck had left Haskell Institute and was teaching domestic science at Flandreau Indian Boarding School in South Dakota. In this case, not only had students asserted their own ideas about how they should be treated, but their actions had made some impact on their teacher's tenure.[13]

Students without the patience to engage in day-to-day resistance or to move through the channels of the BIA in order to change their environments employed more drastic strategies, such as setting a school building on fire, a fairly common event in the boarding school era. All potential arsonists were not thwarted, but those who were caught suffered severe punishments as a deterrent to other rebellious students. For example, in 1908, three girls tried to burn down the school on the Potawatomi Reservation simply because, reportedly, they wanted to "stop school" in order to go home. They saturated the floor and clothing in the sewing room with kerosene, but before they were able to light the matches that they had hidden in their pillows, teachers detected the odor of kerosene and caught them. School officials had the girls arrested by the county sheriff, and they were transferred to a state reform school.[14]

Although this arson attempt did not occur at Haskell Institute, it certainly became well known to Haskell students; by order of the BIA, the *Indian Leader* reported in detail the Potawatomi girls' arrest as a cautionary tale. Publishing stories about Indian students' punishments became standard practice in school newspapers because reformers believed that published news would prevent further acts of arson. The *Indian Leader*, quoting a BIA official, highlighted the consequences of the act: "The punishment for the crime was very severe, but it should be a warning to all pupils in Indian schools throughout the United States that this Office will not tolerate crimes of this character."[15] News of two Menomini girls who burned down the reservation boarding school in 1905 also circulated widely. In this case, the punishment for the primary arsonist was a severe sentence in the federal penitentiary in Fort Leavenworth, Kansas, as a means of issuing a "warning to all pupils in Indian schools throughout the United States."[16]

Despite reformers' efforts, fires continued to play a role in boarding school history. At Haskell Institute, some fires resulted from uncontrollable forces, such as on two occasions in 1907, once when lightning caused $35,000 worth of building damage and another time when spontaneous combustion started a fire that burned a building to the ground. Other fires, such as the 1905 burning of the dairy barn, unmistakably started from human hands. However, when school officials investigated the cause of the blaze and interviewed employees and male students (female students were not suspected of causing this fire), they could not find enough evidence to make a specific charge. They could only speculate that wandering tramps had accidentally set the fire. From then on, Haskell Institute conducted twice-monthly fire drills that they hoped would help to prevent future losses, but concerns persisted for at least two more decades, and fire safety warnings routinely arrived on the desks of school officials through the 1940s.[17]

Both boys and girls suffered punishment for setting fires at boarding schools, but evidence suggests that girls more frequently started fires than boys. Female students' use of fire as a medium of resistance may have been linked to their access to laundry and sewing rooms, the reported point of origin for many fires. Destroying their own schools rather than running away from them may have been a more feasible option for female students because they knew that an unchaperoned girl would cause suspicion among townspeople. In general, girls did not view running away as an easily managed strategy of negotiation with school administrators, but boys frequently employed this strategy, and the number of runaways only rose after the turn of the century. Compared to the 45 students who ran away in 1885, in 1910, 53 ran away in the month of September alone. During a three-month period between September and November, runaways numbered 109 in total. Granted, this total includes repeat runaways but the high number still suggests that running away was a frequent strategy. In letters referring to "desertions" and arrests written between 1910 and 1918, 31 Haskell boys were counted compared to only a single girl. A similar pattern appeared at Chilocco Indian Agricultural School, Oklahoma's federal boarding school, over a four-month period when 111 boys but only 18 girls ran away. Still, an occasional female student did run away, and in the case of Ida John, she saved authorities the trouble of looking for her by refusing to go to Haskell Institute in the first place. Rebuffing pressure to enroll, she mentioned that she thought she was too old to attend an "indian school."[18]

When escapes did happen, reformers vigorously sought runaway students, issuing alerts to authorities in the nearby towns of Kansas City and Topeka or asking various sheriff departments to issue arrest warrants. Otherwise, Haskell Institute sent its own employees to capture students.

For instance, in 1909, when Margaret Miller (Chippewa) left the school for Kansas City, the superintendent had reason to believe that she would stop at the Victoria Hotel. Therefore, he ordered J. L. Smoot, superintendent of industries, to proceed to Kansas City to catch Miller. He charged, "Make a thorough search for her and if you find her arrest her and bring her back to Haskell Institute." In addition to issuing warrants, reformers also offered rewards for the return of runaways. In 1918, a reward was three dollars, and the school paid the travel expenses of the person who returned the roving student. Harsh punishment for runaways included lockup in the school jail for two nights to prevent a repeat offense and to deter others from running away.[19]

Despite such threatening consequences, unhappy and homesick students determined to leave would do just that. When students ran away, school officials often tried to engage parents in their children's capture. Reformers believed that returning to Haskell Institute (rather than their homes) was always the best option for a child's welfare. For example, when Carl Downing left without permission in April 1924, Hervey Peairs wrote to Downing's father and suggested that if the boy made it home, the father should examine the child for injuries and, if Downing was healthy, return him to Haskell Institute immediately.[20] Pleas made to parents combined with threats of student arrest did not always prevent successful desertions. In at least one case—and probably many others that went undocumented—when a Haskell boy made his way home to the Potawatomi Reservation, his father refused to return him. Despite appeals and threats of warrants, his father still refused to return the boy, so Peairs ordered a local Indian agent, Edson Watson, to capture him. He reminded Watson that the BIA not only expected him to have runaways escorted back to Haskell Institute, but required "subvouchers" documenting the arrest. To be sure that his orders were clear, he even enclosed the subvoucher forms for Watson to complete.[21] In this case and many others, school officials felt they had to pursue those who fled, severely punish offenders who were caught, and threaten those who would consider running away a strategy for self-determination.

Commercial Girls and Athletic Boys

Whether there were as many, or there were fewer, students who actually enjoyed attending school at Haskell Institute as there were students who did not will never be known, because the voices of students who disliked their boarding school experiences are generally lost without documentation. David Adams and Brenda Child have referred to students' willingness to attend boarding schools as a form of accommodation stemming from a variety of factors, including their fear of punishment, adoption of reformers' belief in civilized-savage paradigms, and desire for formal education, training, or inclusion on sports teams. For some students, a school like Haskell Institute provided opportunities that their home environment could not. Child specifically points to orphaned children who were sent to schools when their family networks failed to support them. She also notes that poverty influenced the decisions of families who could not afford to feed their children. Occasionally, Native American children preferred to enroll in segregated boarding schools rather than suffer the prejudice they experienced while attending public schools with white students. Parents might simply want to have a child join siblings at a specific school or, as in the case of Harriet Fairchild, have a grandchild attend a school that was closer to her home. Child describes the complexity of motivations for attending boarding schools by arguing that students could simultaneously resent their schools and find them useful.[22]

School environments could be demeaning and hostile, and yet there were some students who simply enjoyed being with their peers or saw education as a pathway to gainful employment and economic mobility. When they wrote letters to their former teachers and administrators about their own progress, they sang the school's praises and expressed gratitude for the education that they considered enriching. In most letters, they fondly remembered Haskell Institute and declared that their school days were the best of their lives. As Ralph Revere (Arapaho) wrote, "We were always so anxious to leave school and go out for ourselves little thinking of what a world of troubles there were and that the happiest days we knew were our school days." Tennie Lumby echoed Revere's sentiment when writing to Superintendent H. H. Fiske in 1910 that "Haskell is the best place yet in schooling." She continued by telling him that she had been lonesome since returning home from school, but happily reported to everyone she could that she had gotten her education at Haskell Institute. She even boasted that upon her return to her home on the reservation she had taken up cooking "like the ways I have been learning at Haskell."[23] Lumby's case might be exceptional, according to the view of Robert Trennert, who argues that the general outcome for female students was inclusion in neither white nor native culture and feeling trapped between them. However, students who found offerings in high school and college-level courses particularly attrac-

Native American Female Students Practicing Shorthand. Business courses attracted female students interested in living and working outside the prescriptions of Victorian gender norms. (Courtesy of National Archives and Records Administration, photo no. 75-EX-1DA)

tive gained training in business and teaching that helped them to avoid such traps.[24]

The first commercial course at Haskell Institute began in 1897, and by the 1910s, the Business Department was drawing many students, in particular young women, who found that if they acquired commercial skills that would lead to steady jobs, they could postpone marriage. Even administrators recognized that some girls needed protection from early marriage or pressure-filled proposals, so they helped facilitate their admission. For example, Florence Boyce (Winnebago) was seventeen when she expressed her desire to enter Haskell Institute. On Boyce's behalf, Lenore Bost (presumably an agent at a reservation in Wisconsin) endorsed her request by writing, "She is a very good girl, healthy, bright and in every way suitable for school, and we fear that her people will try to get her to marry if she does not soon go away. She is anxious to go now, but if she does not go soon she is likely to be influenced by her people and will not go later." Bost's reasoning must have convinced administrators because they admitted Boyce right away.[25]

To help graduates secure employment, Haskell Institute offered the civil service examination to male and female students of the Business Department. Since the federal government had made the dramatic transition from funding religious organizations to hiring civil servants to run government organizations and schools in the 1890s, anyone who wanted to work for the BIA had to become an official civil servant of the United States government. Passing the examination made graduates eligible for appointment to clerical positions in the BIA, the government department that employed a large number of Native Americans.[26] A preference to hire Indian employees had been implemented as early as 1834 with a federal Reorganization Act that encouraged assignment of interpretation, blacksmithing, teaching, and other agency personnel jobs to people of Indian descent. By the late 1890s, there were already 1,160 Native Americans employed by the Indian school service, representing 45 percent of the work force. Between 1888 and 1899, when the BIA more than tripled in size, so did the proportion of Native American employees. In 1896, President Grover Cleveland amended civil service rules to expand the hiring of Indians, particularly graduates of boarding schools. Although there were secure employment rates for Native Americans, the civil service exam did prove challenging for some graduates, and those who passed often stayed in blue-collar positions rather than moving up to professional positions. Compared to white employees, Indian employees received lower wages, but the school still boasted of its success in placing graduates of the business course in positions with the BIA and helping graduates earn wages that were generally higher than in jobs outside of the government. The ability of many students to obtain steady employment after their business training allowed the *Indian Leader* to declare in 1908 that "the Business Department at Haskell Institute is no longer an experiment."[27]

Women's BIA wages were more meager than men's, but female students still seemed to view the commercial course as an optimal route and entered this track in higher numbers than males. In 1908, for example, 61 percent of girls who graduated that year finished in business. These girls made up 74 percent of the entire group of students who graduated from the Business Department. Even if the jobs they would find were low paying, girls who took business courses attained a certain level of mobility, allowing them to seek jobs in new towns and cities rather than submit to traditional roles as wives, mothers, and domestics. When Mary Nash (Winnebago) reported that she was working in a law office in Nebraska, she declared that it was "a fine place to work" and admitted her sadness because her sister, Florence, had not received the same education that she had received. Evangeline Johnson-Gover (Winnebago) echoed Nash's enthusiasm for her education by pointing out that her experience had shown her that either business or nursing could be useful, particularly to single women.[28] Female students' strong attraction to the commercial course and their ability to find jobs in the BIA or in the private sector motivated them to expand their gender roles beyond the prescriptions of industrial education. Haskell Institute proudly boasted of its graduates' success. For example, in 1925, the school quoted the *New York Telegram and Evening Mail*, which had written that "Indian maiden graduates from the Haskell Institute make the most accurate highly efficient shorthanders and typists in the world."[29]

Male students also found the commercial course attractive, and several specifically sought admission to that track. Ernest Goforthe, a recent graduate of Hampton Institute, wrote to Haskell Institute to inquire about taking upper-level classes: "Would it be possible for an outsider, like me, to enter your school and take up that course?" To bolster his request, he offered references from Hampton and enclosed a dollar's worth of postage so that he could receive the particular details. The administrator replied that he would be glad to enroll Goforthe, reassuring him that the Business Department was not only thorough, offering stenography, typewriting, and bookkeeping, but that "there is now [q]uite a [demand] for graduates of this department."[30] The success of the program was made manifest in its innovations—it was the first school to offer a touch-typing class in the state of Kansas, for example—and in its ability to train graduates for positions that earned decent salaries, ranging in 1908 from a livable $600 annual salary to a substantial $2,400 annual income. Males admitted to the Business Department could choose from three options for their curriculum: entering only the business course, taking a partial business course along with a trade, or completing a trade course through the night school.[31]

Although students like Goforthe enthusiastically entered the Business Department, male students more frequently asked about the possibility of playing sports in their letters to school administrators. In the same way that the Business Department offered girls a chance to develop new professional roles for themselves, athletics offered boys opportunities to develop new versions of masculine citizenship. Along with a place on an athletic team, boys gained a certain amount of autonomy through sports. With the expansion of athletic programs at Indian boarding schools in the early 1900s, sports became increasingly important to such schools, many of which competed against college-level teams. In the 1920s, the size and success of Haskell Institute's program eventually surpassed Carlisle Institute's lead and recruited a host of talented athletes in football and baseball,

Native American Male Students at Football Practice. Participation in athletics at Indian boarding schools in the early twentieth century provided a way for many male students to define their own version of masculine citizenship. (Courtesy of National Archives and Records Administration, photo no. 75-L-3D)

as well as basketball, wrestling, boxing, and track. Many boarding school athletes went on to compete on college, professional, and even Olympic teams. Most notably, the legendary Jim Thorpe (Sac and Fox) played on Haskell and Carlisle teams before competing in 1912 Olympic track events and joining professional baseball and football teams. Because of the growth and prestige of sports programs, athletes often had more privileges than other students, including opportunities to go home more frequently; they also gained certain leniencies and even had more food choices than other students. There is some speculation that in the 1920s some athletes were ringers, called on to play in games but not responsible for completing regular classes.[32]

The admission of Amos Duggan provides an example of a student who used athletics as a way to assert his own terms for entry into Haskell Institute. Even before the height of athletic fervor at boarding schools, in 1907 Duggan knew that if he made it clear that his only reason for transferring from Carlisle Institute to Haskell Institute was to play football and baseball, he might be able to negotiate the terms of his enrollment. Instead of arriving at Haskell Institute in the summer as the school wanted, Duggan refused, claiming that he had a more desirable offer to play baseball on a summer team. Duggan stated that he would be available in the fall rather than in the summer and that he would eventually enroll to "help out" at Haskell. The school acquiesced, guaranteeing Duggan's spot on the football and baseball teams whenever he decided to arrive.[33]

Although very few female students made pre-enrollment demands such as the one that Duggan made, there are a few instances when female students asserted their wishes with school officials. For example, Sophia La-Pointe asked the superintendent if she and her friend Margaret Beauregard could be admitted together to Haskell Institute on the condition that they would take the sewing course without additional school studies. She also boldly requested a guarantee that they be allowed to return home the following summer if they paid their own transportation fares. Hervey Peairs sent applications for LaPointe and Beauregard with a letter indicating that he could make arrangements for them to take only the sewing course, provided both students were not young children but "of advanced ages." Through this negotiation, he also offered to pay the standard fare for them to travel to Haskell Institute, but told them that if they wanted to pay their own fares to return home during the summer, he would not object.[34]

Parents' Negotiations through Letters

Reformers who established Indian boarding schools focused their efforts on children's education because they believed that adults were lost causes and too heavily influenced by reservation life. Native American students, removed from their families and reservations and taken far away to schools like Haskell Institute by Indian agents or school representatives, found that they had to act on their own judgment, without the aid and advice of trusted adults. Unlike African American parents, whose children remained with them during their school years, parents of Native American children in boarding schools rarely visited their children, and within the context of their children's educational experiences, Indian parents were ultimately disenfranchised, ignored, or silenced.[35] The stories of boarding school parents are largely lost from the historical record, which consists primarily of the accounts written by BIA agents and school officials. When their children enrolled in boarding schools (by choice or by force), parents lost control of them and found it very difficult to exercise their own rights as parents or as citizens.

With the balance of power weighed heavily on the side of schools, reformers did not feel generally obliged to acquiesce to the requests that some parents managed to make. They believed that Indian parents relinquished the right to make such demands of school officials once their children had been committed to a term of attendance (typically a minimum of three years with a thirty-day vacation after two years), and their willingness to make exceptions to attendance rules proved quite rare. When reformers did grant a student's release in response to a parental request, it was only after that parent proved his or her intention to return the child by purchasing a prepaid, roundtrip fare from the school and back. If a student had a balance of unpaid fees on any account, however, the school refused to release the student. There were also many times when transportation tickets and accounts had been paid in full, but officials still refused to release students to their parents, and often they tried to keep students beyond their original terms of enrollment. The decision rested squarely in the hands of school officials who could easily void their own promises to release students even if the parents and children had fulfilled all of their original obligations.[36]

Like their children, Native American parents who protested against or negotiated with school administrators did so for their own, individual sake, not with the intent of making systematic, legal, or institutional changes. In general, Indian parents did not organize collectively to influence their children's educational experiences, but their letters reflected common feelings and strategies. Respectful and courteous in their tone, the letters' cursive penmanship suggests that the parents—or at least their amanuenses—had been formally educated at some point. If parents asked for the return of their children, they often turned to pleas rather than demands, and they often gave reasons to justify their requests, including needing a child's help to care for a sick relative, wanting a sick child to be in the care of a family member, hoping a child could work on the family farm or care for livestock, or wanting the school to honor its original promises. Parents typically reminded administrators of the number of years that had passed since they had seen their children, hoping either to elicit sympathy or to demonstrate that they had fulfilled their part of the enrollment agreement. If they had the financial resources, parents offered to pay for their children's transportation from school to home and back again to preempt the school from using a financial excuse to deny permission to travel. Many emphasized how much their children liked attending Haskell Institute, as if to assure an administrator that they were not asking for a return to permanent custody but just a chance to have them at home for a visit. Despite such rhetorical strategies, most requests from parents were simply denied. Within the context of what Frederick Hoxie refers to as the "guardianship doctrine," where reformers believed that the government's role in the lives of Indians was to protect and supervise them, and not necessarily to ensure their equality, it is not surprising that school officials wanted parents to relinquish control over their own children for as long as possible.[37] The conventional rules of the boarding school program demanded that students divorce themselves from their parents and traditional cultures, and reformers had the full support of a powerful federal bureaucracy behind them. Conversely, Native American parents had little support for their individual efforts. Reformers maintained that students were their wards and that parents were ill prepared for raising future Americans, which is why it is surprising to find any cases where a superintendent, like Hervey Peairs, accommodated a parental request. During the course of his tenure at Haskell Institute, Peairs wrote hundreds of letters to parents, most of them responding to a request to return a child and most of them firmly refusing such requests. Brief and unsympathetic in tone, Peairs's letters frequently consist of two or three sternly crafted paragraphs expressing his reluctance to make exceptions to strict school policies. In a few cases, however, especially when a parent persisted, Peairs acquiesced.

A series of letter exchanges between T. B. LeSieur and Hervey Peairs illustrates the struggle of parents to assert themselves against the stubborn bureaucracy of a federal Indian school and the superintendent who stood at the helm. LeSieur initially wrote from Rossfork, Idaho, to instruct Peairs to deposit money into his daughters' accounts and to inform him that since Lillian and Althea had already been at Haskell Institute for five years, LeSieur would let them decide whether or not they would stay at the school for another year's term. The implication was that Peairs could not force the girls to stay because they had fulfilled their original term of enrollment. Peairs expressed his reluctance to release the girls, and this frustrated LeSieur. Although he had originally asked the school to pay for Lillian and Althea's travel expenses, as an exchange of letters flew back and forth over a three-month period, LeSieur became more demanding about his children's return and less concerned about who would pay for their travel expenses.

When Peairs suggested to LeSieur that returning the children to Idaho would not be in the best interest of the girls, LeSieur took offense and immediately wrote back declaring that his children should leave school without further delay. Although he had originally wanted them to graduate from Haskell Institute, his frustration with Peairs had grown to the point that he had decided that Lillian and Althea could either finish their educations at the nearby public school or the Fort Hall Indian School. LeSieur felt that the girls' return would give him the chance to know his daughters better. He also wanted them to learn more about their traditional culture, which must have irritated the superintendent, who had promoted policies of total assimilation throughout his career. LeSieur insisted that he wanted his daughters to learn more about their home culture "as they do not know much about home or home ties." In this parent's mind, citizenship did not put education and native culture in opposition to each other. He believed that he could enroll his daughters in school—even the Fort Hall Indian School, where the curriculum surely would have encouraged assimilation— without denying their embrace of family and community histories.

T. B. LeSieur's desire to teach Lillian and Althea the very traditions that white reformers had worked so hard to make them forget undoubtedly upset the superintendent, but Peairs did not cite this concern as a reason for his reluctance to return the girls. Instead, he argued that both girls maintained good health, were "doing well here," and therefore should not be taken from Haskell Institute. Peairs implored LeSieur to keep the children in school for another year or two and suggested that Lillian and Althea's opinions should not factor into decisions about their schooling: "Children must understand that there are stronger wills than theirs, and parents cannot do anything else that is of greater benefit to their children than to keep them in school." Peairs tried to appeal to LeSieur's desire to see his children succeed in society by writing, "I know you appreciate education and its value to young people, and I believe that when you consider the matter more carefully you will realize that the next year or two will be of greater value to the girls if they are kept at Haskell than anywhere else."

LeSieur was not flattered, and in fact became quite angry, reporting that he did not understand why Peairs would "insist on detaining my children." He reported that the children had written about their desire to go home in letters to him and that they had more than fulfilled their enrollment obligation by attending Haskell Institute for five years. He suggested that Peairs's reluctance to pay for his daughters' return might represent his attempt to "hoodwink" him, but he gave Peairs the benefit of the doubt because he "would be sorry indeed to think that the management at Haskell should resort to concupiscent subterfuge to gain or retain pupils." In closing, LeSieur reminded Peairs that he had always been a "friend to Haskell" and was insulted by the obstructions that Peairs had created to delay his children's return. LeSieur concluded that he was "getting anxious about the matter" and advised Peairs to "do something."

Peairs finally acquiesced, but not without rebutting several points that LeSieur had made in his letters. He argued that the school's refusal to pay for the girls' travel was not "subterfuge or anything of that kind" but rather government policy to pay only for travel expenses once in three years for students. He scorned LeSieur for not accepting that policy and accused him of being "entirely governed in your decision by the wishes of the little girls, who are not old enough to really appreciate what an education may mean to them." Peairs added that he still believed that the girls should stay in school and that their desire to return was based on nothing more than juvenile anxiety because they were "just at the age when girls are apt to become restless." Finally, he stated that he would release them at LeSieur's expense of fifty-five dollars plus some money for incidentals. "This is really doing more than I should," he concluded.

LeSieur's children did return home, and records suggest that his demands were met (with the exception of paying for Althea and Lillian's fares himself). Perhaps more importantly, LeSieur also got the last word in his angry exchange of letters with Peairs. On 15 July, LeSieur sent a letter to Peairs along with sixty-two dollars to cover the traveling expenses for his daughters. He told Peairs that having to pay the fees created financial hardship for him and suggested that Peairs should feel bad for forcing him to submit to such requirements. LeSieur also made it clear that he thought that he himself had been a good citizen during his daughters' enrollment. For example, when the girls came home for a standard summer vacation, he had returned them to the school as promised. "I did my part in good faith," he declared, and then he accused Peairs of being dishonest by concluding, "You have not treated me fairly and I know it."[38]

In the end, T. B. LeSieur won his battle with Hervey Peairs. The girls went home, but not because of any generosity or sympathy on Peairs's part. LeSieur's determination, persistence, and belief that he had the right to negotiate with a school administrator for his children's return made the situation turn in his favor. Peairs, who rarely had his decisions about students' enrollment challenged, was probably not used to such a vigorous exchange of letters and was likely worn down by LeSieur's insistence and his refusal to be persuaded by long discussions of government policy and school rules. Peairs knew that the girls had fulfilled their original term of enrollment but was unaccustomed to a parent calling into question his integrity or power as a school administrator. That strategy may have tipped the argument for LeSieur. Certainly his vehement expression of his rights as a parent and his ability to pay for his daughters' travel helped him win his case in the end.

That same summer of 1907, Hervey Peairs engaged in another tense battle of wills through letters. Annie Pryor probably anticipated that her request for the return of her daughter would be met with a struggle, so she had Cora Taber, a white woman, write to Peairs on her behalf. Pryor, the mother of Maud and Mamie Valley (Shoshone), was "much alarmed" about the fate of her daughter Maud because her sister, Mamie, had already had been sent home due to a failing battle with consumption. Taber noted that the local doctor had examined Mamie, concluding that she was "very badly off indeed and [the doctor] could not understand how the case had been let go so long, and how she could have been kept at the school when she was unfit for study." She added that the doctor wondered why Mamie had not "been sent home long ago."

Annie Pryor's primary worry was for the welfare of her daughter, so she might not have had a broader concern for the rampant outbreaks of communicable diseases and serious illnesses at Indian boarding schools. Seven of the first eighteen students who attended Halstead Institute died from tuberculosis in 1889; outbreaks of measles, mumps, meningitis, and trachoma frequently threatened school communities; and an influenza pandemic made over three hundred students at Haskell Institute critically ill during 1918 and 1919. Pryor certainly would not have known that because of such illnesses the school maintained its own cemetery, interring students ranging in age from six to twenty-six.[39] What she did know was that Mamie was so ill that she barely made it home alive. The conductor of the train on which Mamie traveled from Kansas to Idaho called the doctor upon their arrival in town, and the doctor would not allow her to travel from the train depot to the reservation by stagecoach for fear that she would die on the road. Pryor feared that her other daughter, Maud, might be suffering from the same condition and she wished that "Mr. McCain [McKoin, the Haskell Institute recruiter] had never taken the girls away."

Peairs's response adamantly defended the decisions of the Haskell administration and physician to send the ill Mamie Valley home by train. He took no responsibility for Mamie's illness and repeatedly stated that she had arrived home in poor health because she had contracted her disease before she even started school. He declared that the school should be blamed neither for her disease nor for the kind of care that she had received. He explained that although Mamie was obviously ill, the school did not send her home immediately because "the distance being so great and the expense so heavy, we thought that we would be justified in keeping her for a time, putting her under treatment and making an attempt to build her up." After failed attempts to improve Mamie's health, reformers finally decided to send Mamie home because Peairs "felt sure that her mother would rather have her come home than to stay here and die." In a tone that was more declaratory than sympathetic, Peairs stated, "My experience has been that parents almost invariably prefer to have their children sent home when their health fails, although they may be in a very weak condition and are very poorly when they reach home." Before closing his letter, Peairs urged Taber to convince Mamie and Maud Valley's mother to leave Maud enrolled because her sister had not, according to Peairs and the doctors, contracted her consumption at school. Additionally, he wrote, "Such cases as this often prejudice Indian people against the schools, and the friends of education who are on the grounds, and know more about such matters than Indian people do, ought to be willing to explain matters. If you are really a friend to the mother and to Indian education I hope you will explain this matter to her."

Taber wrote again to Peairs to explain that, while the place where Mamie had contracted consumption was debatable, she still held Peairs responsible for keeping Mamie at Haskell Institute until the disease "had reached the last stages and she had very little chance for life." She also wrote that Mamie's mother had made two previous requests for her daughter's return during the autumn of 1906 and was not likely to give up. Taber added, "There is no certainty that [Maud] may not contract the disease, and with Mamie in her present condition you cannot blame the mother for a certain prejudice, as you call it, in the matter. It seems to me that it is not a question for you and me to decide as to whether it is best for Maud to come. Her mother wants her and she keeps asking me to write for her." Approximately six weeks after Taber's initial request, Peairs finally agreed to release Maud Valley, under the condition that Maud's mother pay for her transportation. Taber told Peairs that Annie Pryor was so determined to have her daughter home that the issue of payment was unimportant—she had already decided to raise the money for a ticket for her daughter if the government would not pay for Maud to return home.[40]

Both T. B. LeSieur's and Annie Pryor's lengthy and argumentative exchanges illustrate parents' resolve to recover their children despite the initial opposition of superintendents. While most other parents relented after making one or two requests to have their children returned, LeSieur and Pryor continued to argue for their children until they won. Although such lengthy exchanges appeared less frequently than the one- or two-letter exchanges between parents and administrators, they are important pieces of evidence demonstrating parents' own sense of citizenship rights despite the stern opposition of a school that frequently denied parents authority over their own children.

The most remarkable strategy that a parent of students employed was a lawsuit waged against Haskell Institute in 1909 by Olive Burson (Cherokee), a mother of four children. Burson had directed earlier requests regarding the release of her three daughters to Peairs, claiming that her children, Rachael, Blanche, and Unida Burson (all listed in the records as Ute), had attended Haskell Institute for five years—two years beyond her original agreement with the school. Burson had made frequent requests between 1907 and 1909 to have her children released from Haskell Institute, but Peairs flatly refused to release the children because he believed Burson to be an unfit mother. Feeling that she had reached an impasse with school officials, Burson moved to Lawrence to live closer to the school and then resorted to legal action.[41]

In October 1909, on behalf of Olive Burson, a writ of habeas corpus was issued in the United States District Court of Kansas against the administration of Haskell Institute, demanding the discharge of her daughters. In the face of this charge, Peairs and the other respondents, Bertha Macy and J. O. Milligan, issued a countersuit, arguing that as the girls were "bright, intelligent Indian girls" they should not be returned to their mother; rather, they should be secured into "good families." The countersuit stated that Burson had not provided a proper home for her daughters. In the Haskell affidavit, there is no mention of Burson's inability to provide financial or religious support for her children. Rather, the main contention is that Burson, a widow who "appears to be a white woman," had been living in the same house in Lawrence with Bill Fry, "a Negro, who is an ex-convict from the State Penitentiary" and "of exceedingly bad reputation in the City of Lawrence."[42] Peairs contended that Burson and Fry were unmarried and that they lived with other African American adults. In a sworn affidavit supporting the countersuit, A. J. Anderson, a doctor who had visited Burson's home, charged that the house "was in an unwholesome condition."[43]

This living arrangement, or more specifically, Burson's liaison with a black man who was also an ex-convict, prompted Peairs to keep the Burson girls at Haskell Institute until they could be transferred into homes that he considered better suited for them. Peairs proposed in the countersuit to find alternative families, "where proper influence and surroundings will be assured" for the girls instead of sending them back to their mother. He believed that placing the girls in a new home would be in their best interest and that returning them to their mother would be "vicious in the extreme."[44]

A few months before Olive Burson had initiated her suit, Peairs sent a letter to one of the girls, Blanche, to explain why her request to go to town to see her mother had been denied. "I shall have no objections if your mother comes to the school to visit you, but I do not want you to go to visit her so long as she lives where she does," he ordered. Peairs's primary objection was not that Burson and Fry were unmarried or that Fry was an ex-convict, but that they were a mixed-race couple. Antimiscegenation laws in Kansas had been repealed before the territory became a state, but Peairs reflected the sentiments of his times: during Jim Crow, many whites vehemently opposed blacks living with whites. In reply to Blanche's request "to know the reason why we Burson girls are not allowed to visit with our mother a little," Peairs bluntly stated his racialized belief that "you know as well as I do that the fact that your mother is now living with Negroes, whose reputation is not good is sufficient reason for you not spending much time with her."[45] A subsequent superintendent, John Wise, continued Peairs's line of argument four years later when he considered sending Unida away from Kansas through the outing program rather than let her live in such close proximity to her mother. In 1916, seven years after the initial case, when he made plans for Unida's graduation, Wise still considered Olive Burson's home undesirable, but he did not find a permanent replacement home for Unida or any of the other Burson children.[46]

The collection of documents regarding the Burson children contains neither a judge's ruling on her case nor a settlement. A document dated 11 October 1909 states that Olive Burson gained authorization to transfer the youngest daughter, Unida, from Haskell Institute to Sherman Institute, Indian Industrial Training School, Riverside, California, for a term of four years, but she did not ultimately make the transfer. School records list Rachael as leaving in 1910, although it is not clear if her departure resulted from the suit or if she had run out of coursework after attending Haskell Institute for the exceptionally long term of ten years.[47]

Despite these gains for Burson, in a quick turn of events, her children were back at Haskell Institute—and, it seems, with her permission. After learning that Unida could be transferred to a California school, but a younger brother, Weldon (Ute/Cherokee), was too young to be admitted with her, Olive Burson concluded that they should stay together and asked for both children to be admitted to Haskell Institute "unlless [*sic*] they both can go to some other close school by."[48] Weldon would not be admitted for a five-year term until 1912, but Unida must have returned to Haskell Institute immediately following the suit because by 1913, she appeared on a list of outing program students sent to Washington, D.C., to spend a summer working for families there.[49]

The significance of Olive Burson's case is not in the final outcome. Rather, it was her ability to work through legal channels to recover her children (albeit briefly) that demonstrates her persistence and ingenuity despite the strength of her opponent. Although Olive Burson had probably not been formally educated—she only made a mark where she needed to sign documents—she understood that her best chance of recovering her children was through official, legal channels. Like T. B. LeSieur and Annie Pryor, Olive Burson realized that the best way to challenge Haskell Institute was to use language and systems of communication that the school officials would respect and that would force a response from them.

Although the cases of LeSieur, Pryor, and Burson illustrate that parents could aid their children, the majority of students had to rely on themselves to negotiate with reformers over the constraints of their schools. "Without parents around," Esther Burnett Horne recalled, "we learned to work hard and be responsible for our decisions and actions."[50] Unlike the movements that black parents formed to campaign for their children's improved education and integration, Native American parents did not form organized collectives to dramatically change the nature of Indian education. With growing reluctance to rely on the federal government to ensure the rights that accompanied their roles as citizens, Native Americans instead employed strategies of negotiation to express their individual concerns. In the 1920s, when pan-Indian movements did emerge, they bolstered activism focused on sovereignty and cultural renewal rather than integration and inclusion.

There is no doubt that African American students could speak up for themselves, too; black students initially objected to the admission of Indian students at Hampton Institute in the 1880s, for example.[51] Additionally, in 1928, at Western University, an African American high school in Quindaro, students staged a strike when three female classmates broke rules of propriety by allowing male visitors to enter their dormitory rooms after curfew. The students did not protest the punishment that their classmates received but instead argued that their consequences were too light and not stern enough to honor their own sense of respectability.[52] Other than these incidents, evidence suggests that African American parents (not students themselves) led the charge for educational change and eventual integration. Although individual black parents petitioned school boards to have their children admitted to white schools or request more money for the upkeep at black schools, the most significant forms of agitation happened in groups. Because of their close proximity to each other and because of a long-standing tradition of African American reliance on local and federal law to make good on Reconstruction-era promises for equality, black parents were more likely to agitate for systematic changes to the segregation that disadvantaged their children.

Chapter Four
PARENTS

AFRICAN AMERICAN INTEGRATION ON THE "PLATEAU OF UNCERTAINTY"

Knowledge is power, therefore we must get education for ourselves and our children. Each of us ought to consider the character and elevation of the colored people of Kansas as in his own keeping and labor with that view.
—Reverend John Turner, 1863

When Gordon Parks, the noted photographer, director, and writer, received the Kansan of the Year award in 1985 from the Native Sons and Daughters of Kansas, the president of the organization, Clarence Rupp, read one of Parks's poems that reflected his childhood days in Fort Scott. The poem, "Kansas Land," started with his fond memories of youth:

> I would miss this Kansas land that I was leaving.
> Wide Prairie filled with green and cornstalk;
> the flowering apple,
> Tall elms and oaks beside glinting streams,
> rivers rolling quiet in long summers of sleepy days
> for fishing, for swimming, for catching crawdad
> beneath the rock.

Rupp continued reading the poem that affectionately conjured up images of Parks's memories of blue skies and billowy clouds, the sounds of insects and birds, the sights of autumn-turning leaves, and the smells of a smokehouse full of meats preparing for a feast.

As Parks waited to accept his award, he quickly realized that Rupp had intentionally omitted the last lines of his poem that portrayed Kansas as both a joyful place to miss and a detested place that Parks wished to forget.

Those who were familiar with the poem in its entirety gasped at the omission as Governor John Carlin handed over the plaque. When Parks walked to the podium to receive his award, he thanked Rupp and then finished the poem for his audience, stating:

> Yes, all this I would miss—along with the fear,
> > hatred and violence
> we blacks had suffered upon this beautiful land.

For a moment, the audience sat still in a chilling silence while Rupp paled. Then they rose with applause in a standing ovation.[1]

Gordon Parks did not spend his entire childhood in Fort Scott, but he frequently reflected on his early years in the 1910s and 1920s in Kansas in autobiographies and novels. In those writings, Parks captured the contradictions that have been imbedded in the state since its territorial days. Recalling Kansas as a state ripe with both northern freedom and progress and southern prejudices and Jim Crow, Parks remembered, "Clumped in the vastness of the prairie, [Fort Scott] was proud of its posture as part of a free state, while clinging grimly to the ways of the Deep South." For Parks, the Kansan of the Year award would "help proclaim our truce." He wanted to use the opportunity to grant amnesty to those who engaged in the kind of bigotry and abuse that had flooded his childhood memories. But instead, the award represented a long legacy of conflict that African Americans had experienced in a state that promised freedom, yet failed to guarantee full citizenship for all members of its population.[2]

African American Populations

By the 1910s, most African Americans in Kansas had migrated to the state from the South or were born from parents who had. Unlike Native Americans, many of whom had been forced from the East to live near indigenous Kansas tribes in the 1830s or Native American students whom Indian agents put in Kansas schools from across the Plains, many African Americans had migrated during the exodus of the 1870s and 1880s, making the black population in Kansas slightly higher than in most northern states including Iowa, Minnesota, and Ohio.[3] A small number had migrated even earlier during the Civil War as members of the First Colored Infantry stationed at Fort Scott. The majority of blacks who went to Kansas did so with the belief that they would find freedom there that they could not claim in other regions of the country. Upon arrival, they found that the overall quality of life for African Americans was incomparable to their experience in the South. "We are better satisfied and contented here than we were in the South, principally on account of our improved social condition," a laborer observed.[4] Against the backdrop of a southern social system that denied African Americans the right to vote, control over their work, and freedom of movement, blacks streamed into the state with new hopes and high expectations. Black newspapers reported to Southerners that they could seek refuge in the region: "Leave the south if you have to crawl, come where you can have some protection. In Kansas and Oklahoma, you can enjoy the right of free speech and fair trial by jury, and your wives and helpless children will have your support." Blacks thought of Kansas as a place to start anew, where the possibility of "growing up with the country" reflected their optimistic hope for progress toward full citizenship.[5] Following the advice of earlier migrants, African Americans wedded their expectations of better lives to their movement. The white population stayed considerably larger than the black population in Kansas during the nineteenth century, hovering close to 95 percent, but migrants increased the overall population of African Americans to 43,000 in 1880, 52,000 in 1900, 54,000 in 1910, and 58,000 in 1920, giving the state the distinction of having the highest percentage of African Americans except for former slave states.[6]

Compared to the South, Kansas did offer better social conditions for blacks, but the state did not provide the shelter of equality that African Americans had hoped it would. On a national level, education for African Americans in the late nineteenth century was denied the kind of funding and local support that education for whites had. The South notoriously segregated its schools, and even proponents of black education often maintained that it should lead an African American to "be the best possible Negro and not a bad imitation of a white man."[7] Blacks and sympathetic whites populated the teaching ranks in African American schools, sometimes making due with shacks that served as schoolrooms, charred splinters that served as pencils, and Bibles that served as their only books. Fearing violence, African American students learned to hide their books when walking past whites in their communities.[8]

Similarities existed in the North, where school districts segregated black and white children from each other, sometimes as a result of existing or imagined geographic borders and residential segregation, but also in deliberate ways that violated state laws. As Davison Douglas argues, most northern states had engaged in school segregation throughout the eighteenth and nineteenth centuries even though many state officials denied its existence. The dramatic campaign to end segregation in the South has received more attention than the NAACP's concurrent campaign to end segregation in the North, but examining the latter struggle is just as important for understanding the kind of political and cultural barriers that prevented black children from attending school with white children. Whereas a set of laws established and reinforced segregation in the South through the first half of the twentieth century, northern states often prohibited school segregation by writing it into statutes that might or might not be enforced at the local level. Frequently school boards separated children by race with the support of white communities and even some black families who thought that their children would have a better chance at succeeding in all-black schools with black teachers.[9]

Kansas was not immune to such treatment of African American students and allowed legal ambiguity to dictate educational segregation. In 1868, for example, the law neither required separate schools for black and white children nor prevented such segregation. As the population of blacks increased, more laws encouraged segregation, such as the 1877 statute that permitted larger cities to create separate elementary schools. When black farmers started having difficulty finding white landowners willing to sell them enough property to build sustainable farms, many of them moved from the countryside to the growing urban centers to find wage labor, causing more concern among whites. Therefore, discrimination in public accommodations and schools became increasingly obvious and more widespread in Kansas just as in the rest of the country where Jim Crow had taken root. Many hotels barred African Americans, even prominent leaders like Frederick Douglass, who once tried to register at a hotel in Leavenworth. Douglass managed to stay at a hotel in Topeka instead, but he found that the capital city also practiced segregation in most public places, including hospitals, restaurants, and theaters. In residential communities, African Americans may have found tolerance in some mixed neighborhoods, but they were excluded from many others; they even had their lives threatened in some places. Potholes riddled the streets in predominantly black neighborhoods, and many towns had separate water fountains and trolley cars. Reflecting on his own experience, Gordon Parks described the segregated section of Fort Scott's movie theaters as the "buzzard's roost" and noted that while many restaurants had segregated sections, others completely barred blacks from entering "or there would be trouble." The town's two drugstores would not serve sodas to African American customers. Even the graveyards segregated Fort Scott's deceased black townspeople from whites.[10]

Gordon Parks fictionalized the town of Fort Scott as Cherokee Flats in his 1963 novel, *The Learning Tree*. Jack Winger, the father of the novel's protagonist, views Cherokee Flats as a place like "all other Kansas towns" in that it "wallowed in the social complexities of a borderline state. Here, for the black man, freedom loosed one hand while custom restrained the other. The law books stood for equal rights, but the law . . . never bothered to enforce such laws in such books." Capturing the complex contradictions between the promises and the realities of living in Kansas, Winger characterizes these conditions for African Americans as a "plateau of uncertainty."[11]

In the late nineteenth century, while whites pressured Native Americans to immerse themselves in the dominant society, they increased their desire to separate whites and blacks. Although racial violence did not occur as frequently in Kansas as it did in the South, blacks still experienced humiliating discrimination and frequently feared the possibility of hostility. African American newspapers reported incidents of prejudice ranging from racist jeers in restaurants and elevators to more violent outbreaks, such as the lynching that took place in Fort Scott in 1881, the attack on an African American youth held in a Leavenworth jail in 1887, and the mob attack on a black man who had been accused of burglarizing and killing members of a white family in Topeka in 1889. Newspapers often reminded their readers of the ever-present possibility of harm in their western New Canaan and provided details of brutal violence committed by whites against blacks in both the South and the North.[12] Newspaper editors expressed their sympathy and their outrage, if only in long, dramatic headlines, such as: "It Was Sickening; The Fate Of The Negro Ravisher, Henry Smith, Tortured And Burned To Death, His Eyes Put Out With Hot Irons, His Body Seared From Head To Foot Then Cremated With The Aid Of Coal Oil—A Display Of Demonical Cruelty With Hardly A Parallel In History."[13]

Across the nation, between 1880 and 1930, there were 3,320 lynchings of black people with a high point of approximately 160 between 1892 and 1893; only twice did the number of annual lynchings drop below 100 during the 1890s.[14] News of such violence and daily experiences of prejudice vividly reminded African Americans that as long as Jim Crow existed in Kansas, full inclusion would be far out of reach. Although legislators did not legally mandate segregation in public spaces (except at some public grade schools in larger cities and in the state militia), de facto segregation and racial hierarchy permeated the state as it had in other parts of the nation. Yet, Kansas still maintained a tradition of espousing ideals of equality and opportunity.[15]

It was this contradiction of embracing both liberty and inequality that Gordon Parks's "Kansas Land" poem expressed in 1985. It was also this contradiction that black Kansans recognized one hundred years earlier and pressed to reconcile through integration strategies. Unlike Native American parents whose interactions with white reformers might result in changes to their individual children's lives, African American parents and other adult leaders worked together to call for systematic changes in laws and public sentiment in order to better their positions in society. They made educational equality an urgent necessity knowing that full citizenship would lead to their being able to exercise their vote, buy land, serve on juries, gain better employment, and benefit from an array of civil rights. Refusing a nominal or second-class type of citizenship, blacks wanted to change the institutionalized prejudice that had prevented them from enjoying all of the rights and privileges of full citizenship. Conversely, Native American children advocated for themselves or occasionally a parent intervened for specific children. What distinguished African Americans from Native Americans during this period was that blacks employed strategies of negotiation to overhaul the educational systems that kept their students segregated and undereducated. "The colored people are getting awake upon this matter [of racial prejudice]. The time is past when they can be deceived. They are beginning to think for themselves," a minister threatened in 1886.[16] Viewing the law as a mechanism for attempting to maintain peace and protect individual rights, African Americans repeatedly turned to local and national legal channels to provoke change in their lives.[17]

Origins of the Segregation Debate in Kansas

Contradictions between sentiments about freedom for all citizens and realities of prejudice date far back into the history of the Kansas Territory. Specifically, debates about African American access to education and integration started as early as 1855. Although there was only a small black population living in the territory before the Civil War (343, of whom 151 were free and 192 were slaves), providing education for black residents was at least a matter of concern for the legislature. The Laws of the Territory of Kansas ordered that schools "shall be free and without charge for tuition, to all children between the ages of five and twenty-one years."[18] Although the law stated that "all children" could attend public schools, the law did not indicate *where* they might attend, thus causing both white and black reformers and politicians to debate the issue of segregation for the next hundred years.

Some white reformers joined black leaders in their call for equal access to education. The Kansas State Teachers Association, for example, supported full access to education and resolved in July 1866: "That we as teachers use our best endeavors to overcome unreasonable prejudice existing in certain localities against the admission of colored children upon equal terms with white children as guaranteed by the spirit of law of our state." Two years later, the superintendent of public schools, Peter McVicar, argued for equal access to education for all children. Perhaps recalling his earlier battles on the Kansas border against proslavery Missourians during the Bleeding Kansas era, McVicar state, "The only course worthy of a free people, is to give each child — be he white or black, rich or poor — a fair and equal chance in life, and let him work out his own destiny."[19]

Equality, however, was not the end goal for all reformers. For example, in 1906 the state superintendent of public schools wrote to his counterpart in North Carolina to inquire about laws that would secure a legal path to segregated schools. Black teachers must teach black students, he reasoned, and that would lead to the salvation of the African American race. "Shall the standard be lowered to meet the negro pupil, who has less than a half-century of progress behind him, or shall the standard be maintained to meet the requirements of the white pupil, who has centuries of progress behind him?" he asked in his official annual report.[20]

Nearly everyone engaged in the debate agreed that African Americans should have some sort of access to education, but positions on integration and segregation varied across political party, race, and gender lines. In 1859, for example, John Greer and John Burris, both Republicans, came to opposite conclusions about the mixing of races in public schools. Greer argued that African American children should be excluded from public schools because race mixing could lead to higher demands for rights and privileges. He was "opposed to giving the Negro and Mulatto either the political privilege . . . or the social privileges . . . which we claim for ourselves." Burris countered Greer by acknowledging the possibility that blacks would continue to immigrate to Kansas, and upon arrival, they should be trained as productive citizens of the state and the country. "We must proceed upon the assumption that blacks are to live in common with whites," Burris stated. He added that "they should be made as intelligent and as moral as education can make them."[21] A variety of factors motivated proponents on either side of the debate, including economics (whether or not to pay for a second set of schools), idealism (whether or not to embrace Reconstruction-era hopes), and politics (whether or not to court the attention of black voters by publicly taking issue with segregation).[22]

By the end of the constitutional debates in 1861, the legislature had not reached consensus about whether public schools would be integrated and therefore determined that district superintendents should have the power to decide for their local schools. In a resolution foreshadowing *Plessy v. Ferguson* in 1896, the legislature allowed for separate schools as long as districts provided "equal educational advantages" for both groups of white and black students. This established an ostensibly "separate but equal" clause that would determine the fate of primary schools. Before finalizing the Kansas Constitution, however, legislators declared that *secondary schools* were to be integrated. These constitutional provisions essentially allowed white leaders to segregate most of their schools at will, but at the same time it appeared to foster principles of freedom by standing firm on the issue of integration at the secondary level.[23]

The legislature's simultaneous embrace of both segregation and integration frustrated African Americans who believed that education was critical for racial uplift. The law prohibited segregation at the secondary level, but at the same time, it allowed for local communities to determine whether or not black students would attend school with white students at the primary levels. A provision by the 1868 state legislature attempted to provide educational guidelines for establishing primary schools throughout the state: first-class cities, or large towns with populations over 15,000, were to establish separate schools for African American children. However, in small towns that had fewer students, teachers, and resources, blacks were supposed to have permission to attend whatever school existed in the town, usually a one-room schoolhouse. In the town of Olathe in the 1870s, for example, black children attended classes with white children; Wichita and Lawrence in the 1880s and 1890s and Atchison in the 1890s also had mixed schools. In a few cases, such as in Galena in 1917, the Kansas Supreme Court ruled against segregation, citing expense as a reason not to build separate schools. The end result was that the legislature effectively allowed for legal segregation in towns that were considered first-class municipalities, and, although it did not order segregation of second-class towns, it did not prohibit segregation either.[24]

Fort Scott provides a dramatic but unexceptional example of a town's efforts to maintain segregation even within the first- and second-class city guidelines. In 1887, when the Kansas Supreme Court ruled that Buford Crawford, an African American student, could attend Wilson Street School, an all-white primary school located near his home, instead of walking one and a half miles to the all-black Plaza School, the majority of white citizens objected to integration. Realizing that they could not defy a state supreme court ruling, leaders in Fort Scott used the size classification law to maintain a hold on racial segregation. In 1867, the town had originally organized its government under the second-class category, but in the face of the threat of integration, leaders had the city reclassified as a first-class city so that they could legally maintain segregated schools.[25]

African American newspapers deplored the outcome of the Fort Scott case, and even as late as 1900 warned, "A race war is on at Fort Scott."[26] In 1917, when another town used the same reclassification strategy to secure segregation in their schools, an African American newspaper, the *Topeka Plaindealer*, accused the town of patterning itself after "murders, lynchers, and riff-raff."[27] Despite this protest, Fort Scott had successfully reclassified itself, an indication that nearly any town could segregate grade schools when the white community demanded it. *Plessy v. Ferguson* made legal on a national level the separate-but-equal policies that locals had already instituted as the norm.[28]

Education laws led to a substantial amount of uncertainty about the extent of segregation that could exist in the public schools. Consequently, first-class cities operated segregated schools for African American students, and second-class towns—where most blacks lived—managed to avoid integrating schools using multiple strategies, such as holding alternating sessions for white and for African American children. The town of Seneca, for example, required an entirely separate room and teacher for the two black students who lived in the district.[29] In North Leavenworth, African Americans had their own school, which was like a "hut" situated in a "low, dirty-looking hollow close to a stinking old muddy creek, with a railroad running almost directly over the building."[30] In Topeka, blacks attended class in the attic of a small frame building, while white students used the lower rooms. Several high schools were not formally segregated but required blacks to take special examinations to qualify for admission. If white parents complained about their children attending classes with African American students, schools could simply expel the black students without recourse. African American students who attended public high schools with white students often found that their course work differed from that of white students.[31] When black parents protested or brought cases to court, they realized that communities wanting to keep white and black children segregated from each other found ways to do so.

The state legislature neither took a firm stance against segregation nor provided solid protection for equal access. Between 1865 and 1911, there were as many separate but equal bills as actions to allow for African American inclusion in white schools.[32] Such vagueness in the law left blacks frustrated and disappointed, but legal ambiguity also signaled potential fractures in the foundation of segregation policies and therefore provided an opportunity for blacks to intensify their battles by challenging laws and by taking desegregation cases through higher courts. Some African Americans opposed integration for fear of losing influence over their own communities or eliminating jobs for black teachers, but the belief that integration was essential to racial equality generally won out. Leaders such as John Waller, an African American attorney elected to the Lawrence school board shortly after he moved there in 1879, promoted policies to reverse institutionalized racism. Alfred Fairfax, the first African American representative elected to serve in the Kansas legislature in 1889, tried to repeal the segregation provision of the 1879 Kansas school statute by introducing a bill that would provide equal access to public schools for all children. Even though the proposal did not pass, it forged a path for future legal maneuvers.[33]

Blacks had small successes as well as some setbacks when they sought to integrate schools. Maintaining their belief in the law as a catalyst for creating equality, African Americans tested policy at specific schools, at school board meetings, and in the courts. With a focus on gaining equality by changing the structure of society, African Americans engaged in what Laura Edwards calls the "expansive historical contests over the content of public order, instead of the acquisition of individual rights."[34] They rejected a culture of dominance and articulated a desire for inclusion, so when African Americans asserted their right to education, they did so in terms of large-scale integration rather than through individual negotiations, as Native Americans had.

African Americans and their white allies brought the lawsuits against segregated school districts that led to the United States Supreme Court case *Brown v. Board of Education*, which overturned segregation in public institutions. Success did not come easily, however. In the eighty years leading up to *Brown*, blacks pursued a multitude of cases to integrate schools, swimming pools, and other public places. During the first four decades of the 1900s, 207 lawsuits were filed to challenge school segregation, and they found mixed success. In Kansas alone, between 1881 and 1949, eleven de-segregation cases rose to the Kansas Supreme Court.[35] Two cases, the 1924 *Thurman* case and the 1949 *Webb* case, were argued by Elisha Scott, a lawyer and alumnus of the Tennesseetown Kindergarten. By sustaining these challenges to segregation, Scott and his contemporaries demonstrated their long-standing commitment to defend the rights that they believed the Constitution guaranteed them and their steady faith in what David Tyack calls the "equalizing power of schooling or a clearer understanding of the democratic promise of public education."[36]

Strategies for Inclusion

African Americans believed that they had the capacity for—and the right to—full equality, and they employed many strategies to prove to the larger public that they deserved all of the rights and privileges of American citizenship. Newspapers, in particular, provided a forum for blacks to make claims on citizenship and to highlight the achievements of model citizens. Editors published accounts of successful blacks in the belief that readers would emulate individual pioneers. They also hoped that such stories would help to improve white observers' assessments of their African American neighbors. Journalists seemed especially eager to highlight the academic achievements of black students, such as Willie Jackson from Des Moines, Iowa, who graduated first in a class comprised mainly of white students.[37]

Through newspapers, black parents demanded improvement in education, including more schoolhouses, competent teachers, and a fair share of state funding. Newspapers called for parents' involvement in children's education, such as the time when the *Afro-American Advocate* argued, "You can do nothing grander for your children than to store their minds with useful information. Give them that which can not be taken away from them. As a race we must educate."[38] Racial uplift would depend on the ability of African Americans to band together: "As a race let us support race enterprises. Educat[e] the young, get prosperity, be economical and in this way the Race Problem may be successfully solved."[39] Blacks believed that true freedom would follow after attaining education, liberty, and economic improvement.[40]

Reverend William Tecumseh Vernon, president of Western University, certainly believed in the power of intellectual and moral education to encourage racial uplift, and he called upon other African Americans to be catalysts for social change. Vernon used newspapers as an important vehicle for expressing his views and calling others to action. Recalling social Darwinist ideas about racial hierarchy, Vernon wrote that Jews, like African Americans, were once "hated, despised, pariahs." In the twentieth century though, Jews were considered "influential, successful, powerful." Vernon believed that education had helped Jewish Americans acquire the "wealth, rank, and position in life coveted by their neighbors."[41] Therefore, education could raise the status of citizenship for blacks in the same way. The editor of the *Afro-American Advocate* agreed with Vernon and encouraged black parents to enroll their children in school. He wanted them to look to Native American students as role models because they had already awakened to the importance of education, realizing "that to be anything the Indian must be educated."[42]

The racial comparisons that African Americans made were often cliched, and sometimes they reinforced the same kinds of racial hierarchies and negative stereotypes that had been used to justify prejudice against blacks. Despite these ironies, newspapers used racialized language to elevate African Americans' status by demoting other potential citizens. Newspapers echoed imperialist thrusts of the federal government regarding Native Americans, eastern and southern European immigrants, and its colonial subjects. Perhaps in an effort to ally themselves with the rhetoric that white reformers espoused, the *Afro-American Advocate* declared in 1892 that "it is cheaper to civilize the Indians than to fight them."[43] Frederick Douglass had made distinctive comparisons much earlier in 1869, claiming that "The negro is more like the white man than the Indian, in his tastes and tendencies, disposition to accept civilization . . . You do not see him wearing a blanket, but coats cut in the latest European fashion."[44] Regarding the mass of immigrants who were flooding the nation's borders in the late nineteenth century, the *Advocate* proposed to reduce the quantity and increase the quality of immigration by placing educational restrictions—along with an assessment of their law-abiding character and respectability—on immigrants to help determine their fitness. The *Advocate* added that citizenship training should be promoted among foreign populations residing in the United States.[45]

Like the former slaves who viewed education as critical to their efforts to make real their new freedoms, in the first half of the twentieth century a new generation of aggressive African Americans challenged inadequate educational standards and demanded political equality. Despite the rising tide of racism that permeated their communities, blacks believed that the forces of prejudice were penetrable. With the growth of the Niagara

Movement and the NAACP, black activists found institutional support for their efforts to be fully recognized as Americans. Organizations such as the Eureka Colored Club, the Convention of Colored Men, the Negro Undertakers' Association, and the Urban League denounced racial prejudice, demanded government assurances for equality, and consistently returned to improved education as a primary catalyst for racial uplift.[46]

Clubs called for mass meetings of African Americans in order to unite politically in preparation for upcoming elections. African American leaders also organized conventions to determine how the educated blacks in the country could assist the uneducated ones. The Coterie, formed in 1889, and the Interstate Literary Association, started three years later, promoted culture and education through reading Shakespeare and Tennyson and sponsoring lectures, art exhibitions, and musicals. At a black club convention in 1883 in Lawrence, delegates called for a larger meeting to fight discrimination on a national level. The *Topeka Commonwealth* reported:

> As long as colored men are discriminated against all over this country in their accommodations at the public schools, hotels, theaters, and other places common to other citizens because of race, it is the sacred duty of intelligent men of the race to meet together in conventions to devise whatever laws they deem best to awaken a public and national sentiment that will make it impossible to continue such discriminations which are as unreasonable in their motives as they are . . . pernicious in their operation and results.[47]

When Booker T. Washington visited Topeka to lead a meeting of the National Negro Business League, a newspaper article highlighted his political convictions in favor of black citizenship. "The Negro should not give up a single right guaranteed to him by the Constitution," Washington said, and he added, "After the Negro has done all these things [acquired property, education, character], he is not seeking to dominate over others in matters of government, nor is he seeking to mingle with others in strictly social matters, where he is not wanted or asked, but he is asking that in every community and State where he resides that equal justice shall be meted out to him in the courts and elsewhere and that at all times his family and property shall be protected by those who administer the laws."[48]

Women's clubs fought for African American equality with as much commitment as men's organizations. They led religious and social organizations, sponsored families in need of welfare, developed literary associations, and arranged church sponsorship. They also engaged in political activity, such as evaluating party platforms, and in Topeka, organized the Colored Women's Suffrage Association in 1887. A founding member of an NAACP chapter in Kansas and elementary school teacher, Julia Roundtree, joined Reverend C. G. Fishback, pastor of Shiloh Baptist Church, in calling for "uniting the blacks into a body to fight Jim Crow laws, and . . . building up the race individually and collectively."[49] The Women's League formed in Kansas City to provide sewing classes and opportunities for women to sell their items. In addition, they offered reading and writing classes to women and joined national women's organizations in advocating for temperance and literacy and campaigning against lynching. They also supported needlework clubs, charitable organizations, homes for the elderly and orphans, woman suffrage, economic development, and political action. In 1916, at their Kansas convention, African American women teachers joined chapters from other states in sending letters to Congress to encourage lawmakers to make lynching a federal offense. The *Topeka Plaindealer* called such groups a "band of earnest, intelligent colored women who have given and are giving much of their lives to lift the race to a higher plane."[50]

The Kansas Federation of Colored Women's Clubs (KFCWC) gathered together local African American women's clubs to ensure that they did not restrict their efforts to their own state. KFCWC connected black women to a national network of federations from other states and the largest black women's clubs umbrella organization, the National Association of Colored Women. KFCWC's agenda included campaigning against lynching, and in 1921, the president of KFCWC, Beatrice Childs, joined a small delegation of women who visited President Warren G. Harding to support antilynching legislation. The club also developed art and music projects, raised money for scholarships, publicly critiqued racial stereotypes, contributed to flood relief, and hosted needlework improvement projects. Most importantly, KFCWC served to unite black women in a movement that increased race pride and solidarity among all African Americans. With both gender and racial uplift in mind, its outreach included organizing young girls into a junior federation to prepare them for their own future citizenship roles. Susie Bouldin and Marie Fines organized art and music contests, including both traditional black spirituals and classical songs. KFCWC also organized community service projects. In 1924, the organization gave away $6,000 in donations and also supported the Florence Crittenton Home for Colored Girls in Topeka (the only Crittenton home in the country that accepted black residents).[51] Suffrage did not necessarily set the main agenda for women's political involvement, but clubwomen saw their organizations as portals through which they could politicize their roles as mothers, wives, teachers, and professionals. Clubs also provided a point of contact for peer interaction and support in towns where oppressive racial prejudice was the norm.

Although African Americans felt largely responsible for improving the educational conditions for their children, they did not reject support from white organizations. For example, they collaborated with white members of the Freedmen's Aid Association who believed that education of the hearts, minds, and hands would not only improve African Americans' social conditions but also remove prejudice from society as a whole. The Kansas State Teachers Association called for the integration of all schools, resolving that by educating white and black students together, communities would be able to overcome their racial prejudices. Others argued that integrated schools provided more economic savings than a dual school system.[52] In 1874, State Senator Jacob Winter argued that segregated schools were morally wrong because they simply reflected "Negrophobia" and a deliberate effort by the white population to "keep the colored population from rising in the scale of intelligence and eject the colored children from the common school edifices, and thrust them into dilapidated shanties."[53]

Demands for Integration: The Case of Fort Scott

Because of their resolve to use education as the key to racial uplift, black parents waged battles for integration through the courts but also through local school boards. By working through the very legal systems and decision-making boards that had formalized segregation, African Americans not only made claims about citizenship for their children, they also demonstrated their understanding of their own citizenship roles. Their efforts in Fort Scott, in particular, demonstrated not only the tenacity with which blacks approached educational issues but also the structures that they had to fight against to make their strides.

During the 1870s and through the turn of the century, the town of Fort Scott went through a series of changes that engaged the entire community in debates about segregation of its elementary schools. Even though the Fort Scott school board involved black parents in its meetings, quality education for African American children was not guaranteed. During these meetings, black parents and their white allies consistently campaigned for better education—and at times, for integration—but their methods and arguments varied through the years. In 1872, African American parents petitioned the Fort Scott school board for "proper education facilities," arguing that as tax-paying citizens of Fort Scott, they should be able to see their money being used to support better schools for their children. Their demands were restrained but firm:

> We the undersigned tax-paying citizens of Fort Scott, feeling aggrieved at the want of proper school accommodations for the colored children of this City here in affirms that in proportion to the amount of property owned by ourselves, that we pay the same taxes as other citizens, for Educational purposes, while we do not enjoy equal school privileges; and we the undersigned citizens and tax-payers, do most respectfully ask the Board of Education that they allow this state of things to continue no longer.

Parents asked for neither an increase in taxes nor new buildings for African American schools but instead requested that the school board fulfill its duty to taxpayers and "secure to all our children proper education facilities in the schools now built."[54]

The same year, the board of education considered gradual integration of African American students into the public school system as another method of improving their educational situation. After the third grade, black students would be admitted into white grammar schools and then allowed to advance through twelfth grade with white children. Students would have to prove their qualification of admission into the ostensibly white schools with a certificate of examination signed by the superintendent. There is no evidence that this proposal passed, but the school board continued to take suggestions regarding the condition of black education, and in 1874, it appointed a special committee on black schools that reported on the suitability of the buildings.[55]

Those concerned about education used new tactics as the fight for improved educational conditions intensified throughout the 1870s. In 1874, for example, African American parents accompanied their children to the Central School Building to try to obtain admittance to the white school but were denied. The school official who blocked their entrance told the group that teachers and schoolrooms had been provided for them "the same as usual" at a separate African American school and suggested that any further discussion should take place at the next school board meeting.[56]

Black parents also used petitions as a tactic to prompt attention to their schools. In 1878, for example, they asked for a new school building and a new teacher for a black grade school. While the board passed a motion recognizing the need to furnish another room for black students at the school and required future repair as well as the employment of a new teacher "at a salary not exceeding $25 per month," the board did not approve building a new school until 1884. At that point, the board felt compelled to respond to the outrage of parents at the dangerous conditions of their children's school. The bulging walls, settling of the building, and effects of blasting at a nearby brick plant finally forced the school board to respond with a new building.[57]

But the parents continued to protest because the proposed site was not centrally located and, therefore, would prove challenging for children to reach, especially in cold weather. Parents initially threatened not to patronize the school, but evidence suggests that the proposed First Plaza School was built as planned and that African American students ultimately attended it. In 1919, a new generation of African American parents held meetings to secure yet another new building for young African American students because the First Plaza school building, now thirty-five years old, seemed unsafe. This time, those who called for a new school prevailed right away, and in 1920 the First Plaza School was condemned. For two years, while the First Plaza, Washington, and Logan schools shut down, students attended a temporary facility until the Second Plaza opened to consolidate all of the black grade schools (first grade through ninth) in Fort Scott.[58]

Even in the 1880s African American parents evidently had some effect on education because the school board issued several bonds for both white and black schools and maintained a student-teacher ratio at black schools approximately the same as at white schools. The school board also convened a Colored Committee to provide advice about African American educational issues. In at least one case, the board deferred a decision about black schools until "the wishes of the colored citizens are more fully known."[59]

Although the Fort Scott school board incorporated the concerns of African Americans into development plans, black community leaders still demanded fuller inclusion. Overall, elementary schools remained segregated—and consequently the black schools remained inferior—through the turn of the century, so black parents protested to the school board and sought out white board members to ally with them. In 1888, when S. B. McLemore, a white board member, investigated the situation of students at First Plaza School, he argued that "discrimination made against any citizen is unjust, and has a tendency toward class legislation which is revolutionary and dangerous to the public safety, and will culminate in a war of races, if practiced to a great extent." McLemore called discrimination "barbaric" and contended that segregation "teaches children to disregard law on any subject that may come before them where selfish ends are at stake, and if they are religious, it teaches them to be hypocrites."[60]

Despite the seemingly democratic conversations that the Fort Scott school board held regarding African American schools, white school board members and politicians maintained control over the condition and population of every school in Fort Scott. The persistence of black parents to engage repeatedly with the school board, however, suggests that they saw themselves as citizens with legitimate rights that required enforcement.

The Kerr Park Shooting

Through the turn of the twentieth century, African Americans employed strategies to both show their capacity for citizenship and improve educational conditions for their children, and yet Kansas persisted as a plateau of uncertainty, where whites could be inviting to African Americans in some moments and hostile toward them in others. In the midst of these battles over segregation from the nineteenth century up to the *Brown* decision in 1954, a dramatic incident in Kansas City forced white and African American communities to establish the first state-mandated segregated high school in the state of Kansas.[61]

On an April afternoon in 1904, during a baseball game at Kerr Park, a dispute between Roy Martin, a white youth, and Louis Gregory, an African American youth, ended with Martin's death. Although conflicting reports arose about whether Gregory had shot Martin in self-defense, by accident, or on purpose, Gregory was immediately arrested and taken to jail. News of Martin's death traveled quickly throughout Kansas City and alerted both the white and black communities. When townspeople approached the jail the evening of Gregory's arrest, authorities were convinced that a race riot would explode. As angry members of the white community moved closer to the jail and threatened to lynch Gregory, a crowd of African Americans, including fifteen uniformed Spanish American War veterans, met the mob and protectively surrounded the jail to save Gregory's life. The Reverends George McNeil and Thomas Knapper led the African American group and voiced its sentiments. As the white mob approached, McNeil cocked his rifle and firmly stated, "Any man who crosses that curbstone will open his eyes in hell tomorrow."[62] He reminded the entire crowd that enough blood had been shed that day and with that, the crowd dissipated. The police arrested four other blacks for participating in an armed mob. Although none of the men were in possession of firearms at the time of their arrest, there was a report that an African American preacher, E. A. Greene, passed around whiskey, inciting the crowd to throw insults and pick up arms.[63]

Louis Gregory was tried in the Ninth City Court, where his court-appointed attorney entered a plea of not guilty. After three witnesses pointed to Gregory as the shooter, and the sheriff identified the gun recovered from Gregory as the murder weapon, the defense attorney asked for an acquittal by reason of self-defense. The jury was not persuaded by Gregory's lawyer, and they convicted Gregory of murder in the first degree. He received a sentence of life in prison.[64]

The significance of the Kerr Park incident is neither in the murder conviction of Louis Gregory (the black youth) nor in the death of Roy Martin (the white youth). Rather, its importance lies in the fact that this single event ultimately unraveled the tightly woven web of tension between the whites and African Americans that had otherwise kept race relations from losing control. Both Martin and Gregory were school-aged boys, and although Gregory did not attend the integrated Kansas City, Kansas High School (KCK High School), the shooting of a white student who did attend the school—especially one from a prominent family—sparked one of the most important debates about race relations and educational reform that the state had seen since the Bleeding Kansas era. Because of the ages of the youth, those who had long advocated segregation in schools used the Kerr Park incident to launch a campaign to close KCK High School to African Americans and order the opening of a separate high school for them.[65]

The segregation plan started the morning following the shooting, when African American students arrived at school to find white boys blocking the entrances, white girls sitting in the windowsills, and their parents gathered around the school building. Nearly six hundred white students and parents refused to allow any African American students to enter the school building. When the class bell rang at half past eight o'clock, instead of entering the building, "the white pupils formed a solid wall of human flesh, through which no negro [sic] might pass without a clash." During what the press called a "race demonstration," an African American student, Jim Stewart, approached the crowd of white American students to point out that the black young man who caused trouble at Kerr Park the day before was not even a KCK High School student, and therefore, he and his classmates should not be blamed for the death of Roy Martin. The white students listened but did not acquiesce. Physically barred from entering the high school, and without the support of the local police, the eighty African

American students who tried to enter their school that day turned away from the building and went home.[66]

After the African American students left, white students entered their classrooms, but they apparently spent much of their morning reading newspaper accounts of Roy Martin's death. A large number of them pinned the headline of the *Kansas City Journal*, "In Cold Blood," on the lapels of their coats. Shortly before noon, the principal closed the school to all students for the rest of the day. In order to prevent further escalation of the conflict between the two groups of community members, the school board decided to keep the school closed until the following Monday.[67]

The all-white board of education called an emergency meeting to address the racial tensions with KCK High School at its core. Arguments to segregate high school students by race immediately emerged. Both white and African American Kansas City residents were uncertain about the prospect of two separate high schools, however, because the Kansas Constitution prohibited segregation of secondary schools. Grade schools could be legally segregated, but the school board's responsibilities only allowed them to "organize and maintain separate schools *except* in the high school, where no discrimination shall be made on account of color."[68] As the *Kansas City Star* reminded its readers, "the board of education is powerless to provide separate schools."[69]

During the emergency school board meeting and in subsequent meetings, some white and African American leaders condemned the idea of removing black students from KCK High School, calling such an act unconstitutional and a "gross violation of the school laws of the state of Kansas."[70] Others argued that African American students who attended KCK High School simply should not be held responsible for Martin's death. Even Roy Martin's mother, upon hearing news that black students had been excluded from school by white students earlier that day, sent a note to the principal asking for their reinstatement. She pleaded, "I know that there are a great many innocent and deserving parties who would suffer if that were done and my desire is not to injure anyone."[71]

Disregarding these pleas and the law that prohibited separate high schools, the school board moved ahead with a temporary plan to separate white and African American students. Most concerned with the matter met in a spirit of reconciliation, and although some deplored the expulsion of African American students from KCK High School, most agreed that that if they attended a separate high school, the racial tensions that had erupted after the Kerr Park shooting would subside. They requested the state legislature to repeal the existing law prohibiting separate high schools in Kansas City, so that a sense of order could be restored.[72]

The Kansas State superintendent of public instruction went further by arguing that segregation in all public schools would ease the race problems that existed in Kansas. Segregation, he concluded, "is not based on prejudice, but on common sense and pedagogical principles." His version of "common sense" rested on the belief that if children were taught by teachers of their own race, their common consciousness, historic elements, and intuitions would help students speed up the process of race elevation. He further argued that race development had to come from within the race, not through extraneous agencies. He clearly believed in inherent racial hierarchy and used that belief to justify segregation: "The same pedagogical principles that apply to the instruction of the white child cannot possibly apply to the instruction of the average colored child; hence the importance of separating the races." He concluded that separate schools would, therefore, be the salvation of the race, promoting independence among black students.[73] John Waller countered such segregationist arguments by vehemently stating that "separate" could never be "equal." Waller argued that since separate facilities and institutions were the products of racial prejudice, they were, and would continue to be, inherently different and inferior. In addition to integration in schools, Waller called for increased representation of blacks in prohibition campaigns and among elected officials within the Republican Party. Such arguments went nowhere, and momentum in favor of establishing a separate school moved the discussion forward.[74]

The school board faced a logistical problem in going ahead with a segregation plan because the Kansas legislature was not due to meet until January 1905, more than eight months from the time of the Kerr Park shooting. As a result, the school board and leaders from both the black and white communities determined that the most legal and efficient, short-term solution to ease heightened racial tensions in the city was to allow both black and white students to attend classes at KCK High School—but at *different* times of the day and with *different* principals presiding. White students attended school with white teachers and Principal W. C. McCroskey in the morning, and African American students took their courses from African American teachers and Principal J. E. Patterson in the afternoon. The superintendent of schools, M. E. Pearson, met with the senior officers of the police department to ask for their support in maintaining peace when the school reopened with this new schedule. They planned to arrest anyone who protested or prevented black students from entering the school building. With the new school schedule and the decision to consult the legislature when it reconvened in January, order ensued for the rest of 1904.[75]

When the legislature did meet in 1905, it debated the segregation issue. White high school students, who were in favor of segregation, had circulated petitions throughout the city and claimed to have secured over ten thousand signatures in favor of a segregation bill. They delivered the petitions to the state capital, Topeka. At the same time, African Americans worked together to block the bill. They circulated their own petition with nearly four thousand signatures against segregation. Members of the black community stood in the statehouse while the legislature was in session to protest the bill.[76] William Vernon was one of the many black leaders who stood against the bill, even though he apparently received threats of losing appropriations for his own high school, Western University, by arguing against the bill. Later, when the bill had finally passed, African Americans continued their opposition, asking the governor for a veto and later trying to have the law declared unconstitutional.[77]

On 22 February 1905, the Kansas House of Representatives passed bill 890, the "Segregation Bill." By amending Section 6290 of the General Statutes of 1901, the act gave the Kansas Board of Education the power to "elect their own officers, make all necessary rules for government of the schools of such cities under its charge and under the control of the board, subject to the provisions of this act and the law of this state." For the first time in the history of the state of Kansas, school boards could "organize and maintain separate schools for the education of white and colored children, including the high schools of Kansas City, Kansas."[78] The Segregation Bill effectively defied the Kansas Constitution by ordering the establishment of separate African American high schools, specifically manual training schools, as part of the public school system of Kansas City.[79]

Upon signing the bill into law, Governor Edward Hoch, who declared that he believed "from boyhood that the black people should have all the rights and privileges under the law enjoyed by the whites," remarked that although the law seemed to be "a step backward, a concession to the southern ideas in such matters with which I have no sympathy whatever," he also believed that it would be "better for both races in Kansas City, Kas., that the separation proposed in this bill should be made." Hoch added that he did not consider the decision one that conceded to racism: "Without yielding an iota of my conviction in reference to the race problem, with all my sympathies going out toward these struggling people, and with no sympathy or patience with those who would put a straw in the way of their progress,

I have simply come to the conclusion that under present unfortunate local conditions the paramount and best interests of whites and blacks alike in Kansas City, Kas., will be best subserved by permitting this bill to become a law, and in this opinion I seem to be sustained by an overwhelming majority of the many able and conservative men with whom I have counseled from other parts of the state."[80]

As a show of support for the new resolution, white leaders pledged their willingness to pay extra taxes to the state to maintain two high schools. Finally, it was decided that Kansas City, Kansas would issue forty thousand dollars in bonds to fund a new school building for black students. The passing of the Segregation Bill made white Kansans rejoice; but blacks immediately worked to try to have the law overturned to ensure that they had the same access to educational opportunities as whites.[81] They objected to separate schools because the "present arrangement" encouraged inequality and although children did not "care whether they attend with the whites or not," African American children should have the same quality of education as white students. Emphasizing parents' ability to employ the legal system, a white parent stated, "If our children are refused admission to the school we intend to back them in a contest in court, but we will not back them in any disorderly actions."[82]

One of the first steps that African Americans took to contest the law took place in autumn 1905 when KCK High School reopened for the next school session. Twenty African American students approached Principal McCroskey to ask to be enrolled in the morning session with the white students. McCroskey refused, telling them that they should report at one o'clock to Principal Patterson. The students left and presumably returned in the afternoon with one hundred other black students. The *Kansas City Journal* reported that the purpose of the students' request for admission was so that they could prove that they had been refused. In the nearby town of Bonner Springs, where twelve African American students had been forced to attend classes in a separate room following the passage of the Segregation Bill, their parents replicated the Kansas City effort to have their children admitted to courses with white students. "The members of the board of education stood at the doorway and when a Negro parent approached with his child, he was compelled to take his children home," reported the *Journal*.[83]

Black parents and advocates challenged the Segregation Bill and took their case to the Kansas Supreme Court, arguing that it was unconstitutional. In January 1906, the court upheld the law allowing the separation

of African American and white students in Kansas City. The decision officially signaled the fall of the last integrated educational institution—the
high school. The local newspapers, the *Kansas City Star* and the *Kansas City
Journal*, reported that the decision not only entrenched segregation at the
high school level in Kansas City, it also paved the way to segregate the rest
of the schools in the state.[84] While debates about segregation continued at
the local and court level, in September 1905, a new high school building for
black students opened. The Manual Training High School, the first public
high school in Kansas established for the sole purpose of segregated secondary education, became a symbolic validation of segregation. The school was
no doubt a disappointment for many black Kansans, but eventually it also
became a galvanizing institution for African Americans to continue their
push for racial uplift and equal rights, including integration. Highly educated black teachers flocked to the school from across the nation and took
on the responsibility for its goals and its mission. African American leaders
quickly changed the name from Manual Training High School to Sumner
High School and transformed the school into a platform from which to reject systems of dominance and wage further battles for equality.

Part III

NEW LEADERS IN THE TWENTIETH CENTURY

Chapter Five

TEACHERS

FROM INDUSTRIAL EDUCATION
TO AFRICAN AMERICAN RACE PRIDE

Missouri's shores and muddy waves,

In fairest landscape's view,

On bleeding Kansas' famous soil

Stands Dear Old Western U.

—Reverend Calvin Douglass, "Kansas Western University"

Sumner [High School] is a child not of our own volition, but rather an offspring
of the race of a bygone period. It is a veritable blessing in disguise.

—Teacher at Sumner High School, 1935

In 1905, when Reverend William Tecumseh Vernon addressed the Kansas
Day Club, he was the first African American to do so. The title of his speech,
"A Plea for Suspension of Judgment," implied that Vernon intended to ask
the audience of white Kansans to ease their criticism of his African American brethren, and he started by stating, "The cause of my people is my
cause, their struggles my struggles." The rest of his speech, however, did
not detail the plight of blacks in hopes of gaining pity or understanding.
Instead, Vernon used this platform, along with many of his other speeches
and publications throughout his career, to call for nothing short of racial inclusion and equality. He demanded new terms for citizenship.[1]

In the 1880s and 1890s, when Elizabeth Comstock, Laura Haviland, and
Charles Sheldon established their schools for African American children,
their efforts reflected the intentions of other white reformers in the late
nineteenth century—to educate African Americans for positions in society
that would remain on the margins. But in the early twentieth century, when

Reverend William T. Vernon. Vernon was part of the generation of African American teachers that changed the purpose of black education to include race pride and uplift as well as preparation for professional careers. Vernon served as registrar of the U.S. Treasury, headed Western University, and served as a missionary in South Africa during his long career. (Courtesy of Kenneth Spencer Research Library, University of Kansas Libraries)

black reformers like William Vernon rose to prominent administrative positions in black schools, they subverted the original curricular goals of white reformers and pushed forward an agenda to fully incorporate blacks into the mainstream of American society. Although many white reformers still viewed African American education as a way of preparing black students to accommodate the dominant society by accepting social, economic, and political positions below whites, black reformers were determined to fight for full social and political integration.

By the 1910s, a new generation of African American reformers had taken from white teachers the responsibility of educating black children. There had been a long tradition of African American informal and formal teaching of black students, but a significant shift occurred in the early twentieth century when groups of college-educated African American teachers—many of whom had been educated in segregated schools themselves—changed the scope and purpose of segregated education. They were not the post-emancipation freedpeople who sought refuge in Kansas as their parents might have done; they belonged to the next generation, who entered into teaching and administrative positions in order to politicize education and use schools as platforms for classical education, leadership training, and preparation for college and professional careers, including teaching or the ministry. When necessary, they did continue nominal industrial courses as a ploy to meet the expectations of state funders or to provide instruction to students who did not have the aptitude to enter a professional field. But overall, teachers positioned themselves as role models in black schools and used segregation to shield themselves from white onlookers who might otherwise object to the ways they encouraged race pride and class mobility among their students.

African American men, in particular, created positions for themselves as administrators of segregated schools in order to alter the goals of black education, while women filled the teaching rank and file and accelerated their activism through club activities and group organizations. Although white reformers had hoped that African American schools would produce a class of well-trained, well-mannered workers, black reformers recognized that they were in the process of creating something different: a new African American middle class made up of themselves and their students. Therefore, faculty taught more than skills and knowledge; they equipped their students with the pride and strategies needed to sustain the twentieth-century fight for legal and social equality. They enlarged their faith in educational institutions as the best platforms to subvert racial hierarchies and train future citizens, expanded their own roles as reformers, and changed the purpose of African American education.[2] During the early part of the century, while Native Americans tried to maintain an element of cultural separateness and did not want their Indian identities to be erased, black leaders at schools like Sumner High School, the Industrial Educational Institute, and Western University struggled to give their students the kind of direct involvement in mainstream society that white reformers had never intended to allow.

From Race Riots to College
Prep: The Case of Sumner High School

In 1905, in Kansas City, where the Kansas Supreme Court allowed for the first time an exclusively African American high school to be built, black teachers felt especially loaded with a sense of responsibility and duty to their race. The memories of the Kerr Park shooting and subsequent riots and protests still haunted the minds of black teachers who joined other African American community members in objecting to the school board's proposed name for the new school, Manual Training High School. They immediately requested changes to the school's name and its industrial training-based curriculum. With these requests, the black community created both physical and intellectual spaces for African American teachers to redefine academic expectations and their students' paths toward citizenship. One of the original teachers summarized his dissatisfaction with the school's initial name by claiming that African American community members "did not want it understood that their children were to be confined to trade courses."[3]

Meeting with white school board members, teachers Greene B. Buster and G. F. Porter, along with principal-elect J. E. Patterson, demanded a new name for the school in honor of the abolitionist Senator Charles Sumner. They had considered other names, including those of Abraham Lincoln, Frederick Douglass, or Booker T. Washington, but immediately eliminated Lincoln and Douglass because grade schools in the city already bore those names. They decided against Washington because many perceived him as endorsing only industrial education, and the new faculty did not want their own curricular plans misunderstood. At this point, white politicians, businesspeople, and philanthropists still endorsed Washingtonian-style industrial education for blacks, or what was commonly known as the Hampton-Tuskegee Idea, but most black leaders did not. Charles Sumner proved to be an appropriate namesake because he had argued one of the earliest cases for integration against the Boston School Committee in the 1849 Supreme Court case *Roberts v. City of Boston*. In 1856, his condemnation of champions of slavery in a two-day oration, "The Crime against Kansas," provoked a brutal attack that rendered him unconscious and temporarily disabled yet an ever-committed champion of racial equality.[4]

Some African American community members saw Sumner High School as a step back in the fight for integration, yet others saw its establishment as a step forward in terms of expanding the educational potential for African

Sumner High School Faculty, 1919. The majority of Sumner High School teachers
had master's degrees and came to Kansas from other parts of the country. G. B. Buster
(front row, second to last on the right) helped to change the name of the first African
American high school in Kansas from Manual Training School to Sumner High School,
in honor of the abolitionist senator. (Courtesy of Kenneth Spencer Research Library,
University of Kansas Libraries)

American youth. Although one black educator considered Sumner High
School "an offspring of the race antipathy of a bygone period," the segregated school proved to offer better educational experiences than most integrated high schools in the area.[5] Unlike many black schools, which placed
industrial training at the center of their programs, teachers at Sumner High
School had more advanced goals in mind for their students. Namely, the
academically trained faculty designed a college-preparatory curriculum
that would eventually include junior-college-level courses.

The college-preparatory curriculum of Sumner High School attracted
students from local communities as well as distant neighborhoods in South
Park, Merriam, and Olathe. In the early years when the faculty was small,
Sumner High School did offer some home economics and industrial training courses, including typewriting, cooking, and sewing; yet students spent
the majority of their time in classical education courses, such as English,
algebra, geometry, botany, physics, and history. Boys took three courses in
shop, and girls took three years of sewing and cooking, but faculty considered such courses electives, and eventually they expanded the choice of
classes to include public speaking and other courses with more intellectual content, such as readings on Caesar and Cicero. By 1920, Sumner High
School had created four curricular tracks: College Preparatory, General

Sumner High School Science Class, 1920. Founded after a race riot in Kansas City, Kansas, Sumner High School offered a college-preparatory curriculum and African American studies classes. (Courtesy of Kenneth Spencer Research Library, University of Kansas Libraries)

Arts, Commercial Arts, and General. Additionally, the school offered a normal training course to seniors who wanted to prepare for careers in teaching. The offerings proved attractive, as evidenced by the growth of student enrollment from 80 students when Sumner High School first opened its doors to 795 by 1935. One-third of the graduates went on to college, which was enough to allow the people of Kansas City to regard the institution as a college-preparatory school—black teachers equated that fact with racial uplift.[6]

College-preparatory classes proved to be so important that the faculty promoted them among all students, including those who did not plan to continue their education after high school. The faculty reasoned that many of those students might eventually go to college and therefore advanced classes would help to prepare them for that later decision. They also believed that such courses offered "the best training that fits one for life."[7] In addition to coursework, Sumner High School faculty recognized the importance of extracurricular activities in promoting students' personal development and positive social attitude. Students engaged in student council, debate clubs, Girl Reserves, and drama groups; and during activity period, they sought academic guidance from their homeroom teachers or held club meetings.[8]

With the highest percentage of faculty with master's degrees of any school in Kansas City, Sumner High School attracted teachers with graduate training from institutions like Fisk University, Dartmouth College, and Wilberforce University. The school attracted an elite faculty because of its curriculum and the high standards that its founding faculty set; but it is likely that part of the reason the school retained its highly qualified black faculty was they simply had fewer alternative professional options than white teachers.[9]

Sumner's teachers represented a generation of educated African Americans who were born free and had access to primary, secondary, and higher education. Learned, engaged in politics, professionally ambitious, and imbued with a missionary zeal for racial uplift, black teachers and ministers provided important sources of leadership in African American communities.[10] Greene B. Buster's teaching career exemplified his generation. One of the first teachers at Sumner High School, Buster spent forty-three years of his forty-nine-year career there. He taught social sciences from 1905 to 1931 and served as vice principal from 1931 to 1948. A dedicated teacher who never missed work in the fifteen years between 1906 and 1921, Buster encouraged his students to attend college and develop leadership skills.[11]

The grandson of slaves, Buster was born and raised on a 123-acre farm in Ohio. After attending segregated grade schools, he was the only African American student in his class in a predominantly white high school and graduated as valedictorian of his class in 1902. Buster graduated from Wilberforce University, again as valedictorian, and then attended the University of Kansas, where he earned a second bachelor of science degree in 1925 and a master of science degree in 1931. He pursued other postgraduate study at Miami University (Ohio), the University of Iowa, and the University of Colorado.

Buster believed that schools should provide students and the larger community "a high degree of leadership through the intellectual ability and the moral integrity of its faculty members." Such leadership included faculty, who could be members of the expanding black middle class, and who would teach their students the highest intellectual, moral, spiritual, and practical values in preparation for entry into that class. Convinced of a direct correlation between education and citizenship status, Buster thought that schools should train young people to get along with others and equip them with values and self-discipline—mental, moral, and physical.[12]

Like Elizabeth Comstock, Laura Haviland, and Charles Sheldon, G. B. Buster argued that schools should rely on Christian principles, especially a belief in "God as ruler and provider of the universe," so that students would develop "certain inner controls which will make it easier for them to do right for right's sake, and not from compulsion from the outside."[13] On many more occasions, however, Buster differed from the white reformers. For example, Buster believed that African American students should not discard their past but rather should learn about how every generation stands upon the shoulders of preceding generations. In order to attempt to repay the past debt owed to their ancestors, students should be required to add to the sum total of the heritage that they had inherited. Putting his own ideal into practice, Buster wrote a novel called *Brighter Sun*, which explores experiences of slavery, highlighting his own grandfather's perspective. Through the novel, Buster wanted his readers to learn more than biographical information about his grandfather; he wanted them to see a cross-section of slavery "from the inside, a portrayal . . . of the heart-struggles, the unsatisfied yearnings, of those poor souls in chains who dreamed and suffered."[14]

Outside of the classroom, Buster encouraged parents to involve themselves in their children's activities and learning. He moderated the debate club and organized a contemporary history club for students and teachers to discuss African- and African American–centered topics, such as European occupation of African countries, the Pan-African Congress, W. E. B. Du Bois, and the Ku Klux Klan. The school brought speakers to promote Frederick Douglass and Ida B. Wells as important models to emulate.[15] Buster also organized the Du Bois Club, comprised of African American teachers whom Buster and his wife, Katie Buster, a Sumner High School teacher, welcomed to their home.[16]

In the classroom, Buster taught African American history and highlighted black achievements such as the service of twenty African Americans in Congress from 1868 to 1895, slaves' ability to speak more than one language fluently, and Benjamin Banneker's mathematical and scientific discoveries. He had the paintings of white leaders that hung in the school's hallways replaced with images and busts of black leaders—a different approach than the one at Hampton Institute, where pictures of President Andrew Johnson and General Robert E. Lee remained on display in the school chapel. Presumably Buster taught without the aid of a textbook that contained African American history, because in 1916 he had his students assemble an instruction guide (with images that were literally cut and pasted from other books) called *The Negro in American History, Written by the Students of the American History Class of Sumner High School, 1916*. Buster listed himself as the editor in chief of the book, and in the introduction he stated, "It is only natural for one to be vitally interested in the life-history of his own race." He added that the text was an important contribution to African American history that others should read because "we know much of the history of the Americans, the Englishman, the Frenchman, the German, the Italian, the Russian, the Roman, the Greek, the Egyptian, but when it comes to our own race-history, our race as a whole is woefully ignorant. It is for the purpose of throwing some light on this dark subject, of dispelling ignorance and [misinformation], of correcting misconceived ideas concerning our race, of instilling race-pride, self-confidence, and thoughtful consideration that the members of the American History Class of Sumner High School have set themselves to the task of compiling the following history of the Negro race in its relation to American History."[17]

G. B. Buster's determination to increase his students' race pride and self-confidence might have hindered his ability to teach his students to think critically about their African American history projects. In one essay, for example, a student wrote with hyperbole, "The Negro physically is one of the strongest races to be found. During slavery he was found to be doing the heaviest and hardest work. White men were tried on these jobs but were discharged on the account of their physical conditions." The student also opined, presumably without a critique from Buster: "Along the moral line the Negro is said to be the most religious and honest of races."[18]

While the task of compiling the *entire* history of African Americans might seem ambitious, for a teacher who spent a lifetime teaching and analyzing American history books and finding consistent omissions of black actors, Buster's *The Negro in American History* is not an extreme example of his commitment to his race. Rather, it is part of a larger series of documents that Buster produced to insert African Americans into the historical narrative of the United States and to make a contemporary call for more racial integration. In a 1909 essay, for example, Buster wrote of his hope for a social revolution to overturn racial inequality. "This is the problem for America," he wrote. "Will she solve it? I answer in the affirmative." Buster pointed to the potential that a young country had to correct the wrongs of previous generations: "She is not burdened with traditions, hence she is not conservative. Freedom in America's heart will assert itself. The principle of fair play will conquer, and man will come into his own, whether it be the steel king or the humble workman in the mine." National freedom required such a social revolution; and a revolution could not take place without the aid of African Americans in education, religion, and politics. Buster must have been ecstatic when black nationalist movement leader Marcus Garvey spoke to a crowd of one thousand in Sumner High School's auditorium in 1923.[19]

The theme of social revolution permeated Buster's career and allowed him to work in three of the areas that he had identified as essential catalysts for change: education, religion, and politics. In addition to teaching at Sumner High School for over four decades, he became a community leader holding office in the Eighth Street Christian Church and teaching adult Sunday school classes for that same amount of time. He also sat on the board of the Urban Renewal Commission of Kansas City, Kansas, between 1955 and 1960, where he encouraged the commission to hire more African Americans on its secretarial staff. Additionally, in 1919, he supported the founding of the *Kansas City Call*, a vital African American newspaper in Kansas City, Missouri, that still publishes today. Buster served as secretary to the state representative from the Eighth District, Myles C. Stevens.[20] Through these important community positions, his teaching, extracurricular activities, and public speeches, Buster consistently encouraged African Americans to invest in their own individual uplift, but also called for social agitation, such as standing up against segregation and demanding equal access to public places. He thought that black-white collaboration was an effective civil rights strategy and applauded black and white youths who went together to public locations, such as cafes, restaurants, hotels, theaters, and ice-cream parlors, "where they know the color-line is rigidly drawn, and insist on service for both."[21]

Industrial and Educational
Institute Transcends Its Name

The circumstances of the founding of Sumner High School were unique—rooted in heated conversations about racial mixing after the Kerr Park shooting in 1904—but the school's shift from an industrial training school to a college-preparatory institution and the role that G. B. Buster took in revising the curriculum were part of a larger trend in African American education. The Industrial and Educational Institute followed a similar pattern, and in 1923 even managed to remove the word "industrial" from its name.

The Industrial and Educational Institute, located in Topeka, started as an offshoot of nineteenth-century reform. Like Sumner High School, the institute expanded its course offerings beyond the initial scope of industrial education. Dependent on state funding to meet its budget demands and expand its programs, the school had to use subtle strategies to shift its initial purpose. But by the 1910s it was able to make more visible changes, including expanding traditional courses in history, science, and English, as well as professional training in health services and religious leadership. These efforts were meant to produce a comprehensive curriculum that would help African American students develop a "whole pattern of learning how to live."[22]

Founded by a white reformer, Edward Stephens, who had started in a one-room house in the eastern part of the town in 1895, the Industrial and Educational Institute initially offered an industrial curriculum centered on agricultural industries, millinery, and fancy work. In 1899, the Kansas legislature appropriated $1,500 per year for maintenance of industrial training at the school, an appropriation that continued until 1907, when the amount doubled. With such public funding, the school indeed promoted industrial education as the "beckoning hand of promise," a path on which students would learn the dignity of labor. A student of Booker T. Washington, William Carter, became the school's first principal, and Andrew Carnegie, a longtime Tuskegee Institute supporter, contributed $15,000 between 1908 and 1911 for new buildings. Industrial education would fit students for the "duties of life" and help them to prepare for better work and command higher wages, the school promised.[23]

Although the Industrial and Educational Institute received state funding in the first decade of the twentieth century, a new generation of college-educated African American teachers arrived there and deemphasized industrial training in favor of a broader curriculum that included theology, music, drama, and athletics. Except for a reemphasis on industrial training during the 1930s Great Depression years, the school otherwise emphasized academic learning as a path to professional work well into the 1940s. By 1927, there were twenty-eight faculty members, most of whom were African American. The school's cohort of teachers belonged to the same generation as those who taught at Sumner High School and were equally well educated, having graduated from the University of Kansas, the University of Chicago, Howard, Fisk, and Wilberforce Universities.[24]

In 1920, teachers at the Industrial and Educational Institute learned that white Kansas schools had encouraged their teachers to attend summer school by offering a bonus payment to cover all or part of their expenses. The institute's teachers demanded the same privileges, arguing that they were important citizens in the community and therefore should have a place to discuss problems and devise methods to resolve them. They bolstered their argument by noting that during the previous summer they had gathered black leaders and ministers together and found that the results were "splendid." They urged the state to make an investment in such a summer school, where African Americans could discuss and develop "industrial, social, intellectual, physical and spiritual power."[25]

In addition to making demands for their own status as citizens, preparing the next generation of African American teachers was also particularly important to the institute's teachers in the first two decades of the twentieth century. In the 1910s, the Industrial and Educational Institute proudly reported, *"Persons graduating from the full normal course are granted diplomas recommending them as competent to teach in the public schools."* In 1924, teacher-training credits were not only awarded to students in the program, they were recognized at other institutions across the country.[26] And, like Sumner High School, the Industrial and Educational Institute incorporated African American studies into its curriculum, noting that teachers had made a special effort to secure books and articles written by black authors. Although state funding had been earmarked for industrial education, the teachers used the public money to expand the school's library and proudly displayed an African exhibit. The following year, the school exhibited prominent African American achievements meant to provide inspiration to the student body.[27]

In the early 1920s, African American teachers wanted to demonstrate their race pride to the larger public; therefore, the school proposed to construct a new entrance gate. Made of iron and bronze, the gate supported a bust of Abraham Lincoln on one pillar and a bust of Booker T. Washington on the other. On the crossbar, looking down on those men, were two doughboys "standing at parade rest" to honor the memory of African American soldiers who fought in World War I. On the front of the crossbar the name of the school flashed with the electrically lighted words "Lincoln-Washington Victory Gate." Although Booker T. Washington was identified with a kind of education that the school was moving away from, school officials wanted his image there to remind onlookers of his leadership and his contributions to the advancement of African Americans.[28]

The school also made changes to the curriculum that signaled the enhancement of its educational standards. For example, in 1923, the school changed the names of the industrial departments to more professional and collegiate names, such as Division of Mechanical Arts and Division of Auto Mechanics. It was also in the early 1920s that the faculty boosted the rigor of courses so much that, for the first time, students could transfer their credits to other schools across the country. And, just as Sumner High School had added a junior-college-level course, the Industrial and Educational Institute added a college department, which included upper-level classes in English, chemistry, biology, educational history, political science, Spanish, mathematics, psychology, sociology, and military science.[29]

Responding to both the desire of an African American community in need of better health care and the hope of black female students who wanted a broader range of professional opportunities, the school opened a hospital for African Americans, and in addition to providing care for the community, teachers, and students, the hospital also trained students in a new three-year nursing program. The nursing students—only seven in number by 1928—managed to tend to the illnesses of all of the school's students, its teachers, and their families, and they reportedly helped to forestall several epidemics during that year. Collaborating with the medical staff from the hospital, the students also sponsored Negro Health Week, during which nursing students gave lectures and showed moving and still pictures demonstrating care of the human body. As part of the school's effort to respond to the health needs of community members, the nursing students, hospital staff, and the Negro State Medical Association (to which the school played host) held a clinic in which they removed tonsils and adenoids and tended to other ills. African American physicians performed operations at the hospital, and the free clinical department looked after the needs of poor patients.[30]

The most significant change that the Industrial and Educational Institute made in the 1920s was removing the word "industrial" from its name. Just as supporters of Sumner High School had not wanted others to perceive their high school as limited to industrial training, blacks in Topeka did not want the public to misunderstand the purpose of their school. After years of listening to the comments of white visitors, who continually mistook the Industrial and Educational Institution for a penal institution, the Boys' Industrial School (another school located north of Topeka), or a reformatory, the faculty and board members finally decided to change the name of the school in 1923. They concluded that the word "industrial" caused most of the confusion about the school's purpose and therefore took out all reference to industrial education and renamed the school Kansas Vocational School.[31]

During the 1920s, under the new name, the school made concerted efforts to engage its students in activities that would produce religious leaders. The chaplain supervised Sunday school, but he put students in charge of organizing Sunday-school duties and running Thursday-night prayer meetings. He also encouraged them to participate in YWCA and YMCA meetings—both at the school and in the larger Topeka and Shawnee County communities. At the same time, the school devised a marriage between academic and vocational training so that when they professed their motto, "How to Live and How to Make a Living," they did not limit their students' options for earning a living. Vocational subjects trained students to develop special skills for making a living, while more academic subjects were to "help the students toward a more effective comprehension of vocational work and interpretation of life situations and problems." This educational philosophy, along with a greater emphasis on increasing students' awareness and pride in their African American roots, characterized the Industrial and Educational Institute/Kansas Vocational School of the twentieth century.[32]

Legacies of John Brown:
The Case of Western University

Approximately ten miles east of Sumner High School and fifty miles east of the Industrial and Educational Institute, Western University in Quindaro shifted away from its industrial educational roots as well. Opened in 1857 by a white Presbyterian minister, Eben Blatchley, the school was not actually a university but an African Methodist Episcopal (AME) Church–sponsored secondary school founded with hopes of gaining a reputation as an academically strong institution. Western University's name was not unusual because by 1895, there were fifty-four black schools with "college" or "university" attached to their names, and only twenty-two of them offered college-level courses.

William Vernon, an AME minister, led the campaign to move Western University from its industrial training foundation to a school that would eventually offer junior-college-level courses in 1916 and provide religious instruction for future religious leaders. Vernon, born in 1871 to parents who had been slaves, grew up in Missouri, where he attended Lincoln Institute, an African American school in Jefferson City started by members of the

62nd and 65th Colored Infantry after the Civil War in 1866. By 1890, when Vernon earned his college degree (with honors), his school had received aid from the state to institute teacher training and college-level courses, so he eventually received a master of arts degree from Lincoln Institute. Like G. B. Buster, Vernon attended Wilberforce University in Ohio, where he earned a doctor of divinity degree. After joining the ministry of the AME Church (just as his father had) and teaching at various public schools, Vernon received an assignment to serve as the president of Western University in 1896.

William Vernon acknowledged that industrial education for African Americans had some practical purposes. "I am happy to know that the plan of industrial education for the Negro is rapidly gaining ground," Vernon wrote, "for through it thousands are to be put into the way of making an honest, honorable living, of being the embodiment of success." He linked industrial education to the acquisition of land and houses, without which blacks would be excluded from "governmental prosperity."[33] Before Vernon's tenure, Western University had earned a reputation as the "Tuskegee of the West," alluding to the numerous industrial opportunities that the school offered its students. Vernon knew that this reputation benefited the school because as long as the state legislature viewed Western University as an industrial school, it would continue to appropriate thousands of dollars of funding support. State funding totaling $10,000 had started in 1898 with Governor W. E. Stanley's explicit support of industrial education; the following year, the legislature appropriated $22,000 for a three-story industrial building, known as Stanley Hall. In 1905, the legislature appropriated $35,000 for the school; Western University used $15,000 of the funds for a new trades building to house manual training, domestic science, and millinery departments, as well as Vernon's new office completed in 1906.[34]

During the time that the Kansas legislature supported Western University, the AME Church did as well—it provided $15,000 for a girls' dormitory, for example. It was state funding, however, that allowed financial stability for the school so that it could expand its campus buildings and course offerings. After World War I, Western University continued to receive state and federal aid to offer vocational training to its students. It also received financial support, equipment, and personnel to offer military training to the boys who attended the school.[35] In 1922, when trustees of Western University asked the United States War Department to detail a regular army officer to provide military instruction for the male students, the school established a military department with the charge of building character, teamwork, and leadership. Students who enrolled in three to five hours of studies per week in the military department could enter into the armed services as commissioned officers. It was the cadet corps of Western University that brought the first Reserved Officer Training Corps to the area—a prestigious honor by itself, but a move that also allowed the school to receive even more federal funding.[36]

At the same time that the school used state support to expand, Vernon led a quiet campaign to shift curricular offerings away from the industrial track to one that would offer junior-college-level courses and a larger School of Religion, all of which encouraged his students to value intelligence, industry, frugality, patriotism, Christian principles, and support of the government. In the 1920s, Western University finally lived up to its collegiate name and offered postsecondary bachelor degrees. Although Western University took pride in its college-level course offerings, as a strategic consideration it still offered courses in the industrial trades through the 1930s "to the extent that we may qualify 100 per cent for federal reimbursement."[37]

Lecturing extensively around the country, William Vernon gained national prominence for his views on African American education. At the peak of his popularity, when he gave a speech about his missionary work in Africa, the lobby of the YMCA overflowed with listeners.[38] He claimed that while black schools played a part in training African Americans to be future workers, schools like Western University did not simply serve as training grounds for "serfs." Vernon's vision of the role of black workers differed from white reformers' views. African American schools should "train independent, competent workmen, who are masters of themselves and masters of their environment." In white reformers' nineteenth-century model for black education, industrial education led students into jobs that would serve or support white employers, but Vernon's version of industrial education prepared students for self-mastery. Their work not only benefited their employers, but also helped them gain their own material wealth as they became active citizens enjoying political participation. At the same time that Vernon publicly embraced industrial education in order to maintain funding and support from white onlookers, he skillfully took steps to transcend the traditional boundaries that industrial education had set. Most notably, Vernon proposed that education provide African Americans the opportunity to engage in jobs where they could meet white Americans on common ground and work together for social justice.[39]

William Vernon believed that African Americans were in need of up-

Western University, Class of 1914. Originally founded as a high school for African Americans in 1857 by a white reformer, Western University, under the leadership of William T. Vernon, changed its curriculum from industrial training to more academic courses that prepared black students for professional careers, especially in health, music, and religion. (Courtesy of Kenneth Spencer Research Library, University of Kansas Libraries)

lift because they had not yet achieved a level of citizenship on par with whites. Their position, however, was not for a lack of effort, Vernon argued. He noted their participation in wars, and in particular how they fought for emancipation, because they believed "that in some far-off day their children's children would know the freedom which that day came to you and yours." African Americans had given service to the country through their labor—"We delved in earth; we tunneled mountains"—and through their constant devotion to the country—"We broke no faith; we betrayed no trust." After the Civil War, blacks had contributed to the country by being loyal to Lincoln's Republican Party and by taking on racial uplift campaigns aimed to benefit the entire country. Vernon pointed to financial achievements, including the establishing of farms, banks, and railways and the paying of taxes, as evidence of African Americans' movement toward self-reliance. Despite these achievements, Vernon identified the persistence of social inequality as a problem that both blacks and whites still had to work to resolve. Referring to a comment made by H. T. Johnson, the editor of Philadelphia's *Christian Recorder*, Vernon explained that the "Negro Problem" that had been defined by white reformers in earlier decades was a misnomer. Although Vernon believed that some vestiges of slavery remained within black communities and African Americans themselves had to overcome that history, the problem of inequality between the races was as much a problem for whites as it was for blacks: "This problem is the problem of our whole country since the citizenship of all sections determines our national character." Therefore, because of both their Christian and national duties, whites were obligated to engage in the project of African American social uplift through education. If they did not support black education they would be responsible for the downfall of the entire nation, because "he who denies education to any class of citizens . . . gives us a dangerous element, places a millstone around the neck of all, and jeopardizes the welfare of our common country." Educating blacks would make America safer, he reasoned in concert with white reformers.[40]

Education provided the catalyst for full integration. Vernon argued that African Americans were not "constitutionally lacking in the elements of success"; industrial, intellectual, and moral education would bring African Americans to a higher status. "It will take years to overcome our weaknesses and faults," Vernon believed, "but it can be done." He called on black parents for support, but this project depended on whites as well. With assistance from whites in this effort, Vernon pledged, "we will not disappoint you."[41]

William Vernon quickly earned a reputation as the "Booker T. Washington of the West," and his strategy of recruiting whites as allies in the project of black racial uplift was certainly similar to Washington's. Vernon's rhetoric, however, was often less conciliatory than Washington's and frequently confrontational, launching firm reminders to whites about what they had already promised to do. He noted his faith in all Americans, but he also admonished whites to regard their Christian duty to keep "no men down and all men up." Blacks, too, had a Christian duty, as he noted, "a high Providence calling us onward."[42]

Vernon placed most of the pressure on African Americans themselves to bring about social change. Claiming that "the Negro parent who educates his boy and teaches him to covet principles of life may feel assured that for that boy there is no failure in life," he added that "in the professions or trades [African Americans have] the power within [themselves] to make conditions around [them] better, and to turn to good account all [their] faculties." With the aid of teachers like himself, who had once attended the kinds of segregated schools that they now led, African American students could develop into future citizens worthy of respect and privileges. Because of this philosophy, he encouraged faculty to join a grassroots political organization, the National Negro Constitutional Conservation League of America, which recruited blacks throughout the nation to demand full political rights for all African Americans.[43]

While leading Western University, Vernon espoused the value of industrial training in ways that would entice the state legislature into continuing its financial support of the school, yet he also promoted a strain of race pride among his students that would increase their expectations about their roles as potential citizens. For example, when he expanded the music department, the Western University Singers, modeled after the Fisk Jubilee Singers, traveled to various parts of the region, giving concerts in churches and schools, singing African American spirituals during their summer tours, demonstrating pride in their own heritage, educating their listening audiences, and raising money for their school. Crowds gathered at performances and students flocked from Colorado, Oklahoma, and other states to Western University's music department "to preserve and glorify the songs of our mothers and fathers which are acknowledged to be the only true American music."[44]

With the support of eager parents and AME preachers, Vernon also used his public positions to subvert popular notions about racial hierarchy, arguing for reforms in education that would lead to citizenship roles "directed not so much to the survival of the fittest as to the fitting of as many as possible to survive." Believing that along with expanded educational opportunities would follow an expansion of political rights, in 1903, he called for a new order when "the whitest man and the blackest man of America shake hands and say 'Verily we all are brethren.'"[45]

While Vernon's educational background and philosophy reflected a generation of black reformers that expanded the purpose of African American education at segregated schools to include race pride, potential for higher education, and movement toward full integration, his career after leaving Western University also reflected a pattern of twentieth-century African American leaders who immersed themselves in local, state, and national leadership roles in order to expand their sphere of influence. An active member of the Republican Party, Vernon was appointed registrar of the United States Treasury by President Theodore Roosevelt, reappointed by President William Howard Taft, and served from 1906 to 1912. At the time, he held the highest governmental position occupied by an African American. Vernon later served as supervisor of the United States government schools, and in 1912, he returned to Western University and to his AME church ministry. After serving as president of Campbell College in Jackson, Mississippi, and AME bishop during the 1910s and 1920s in various midwestern and southern districts, he traveled to South Africa, where he had been assigned the role of bishop of the 17th AME Church District in 1920. Between 1933 and 1938, he spent his final years before retirement in a position appointed by Governor Alfred Landon, as superintendent of the State Industrial Department at Western University—an ironic position, given his long-term efforts to move the curriculum beyond the limits of industrial education.[46] Despite his own achievements, Vernon still felt the oppression of inequality. His father's stories of slavery haunted him, and his frustration with racial prejudice led him to wonder "if the world is going forward" because at the age of fifty-five, he exclaimed, "*I have seen human slavery.*"[47]

William Vernon headed Western University for ten years, but his legacy lasted well beyond his death in 1944. While the Industrial and Educational Institute had its Lincoln-Washington Victory Gate, Western University displayed an even bolder symbol of race pride—a life-size statue of the antislavery crusader John Brown. The statue, installed in 1911, proclaimed, "Erected to the memory of John Brown by a grateful people." Donations, "freely given by the patriotic and race-loving Negroes of the Fifth Episcopal District," funded the statue of the man who had organized Underground Railroad stops on the very grounds and through the very buildings of Western University.[48] A visible representation of the school's connection with Brown gave Western University "an air of inspiration to the campus." School officials considered Brown a martyred yet somewhat immortal man, who had fiercely held a rifle in one hand while feeling the pulse of one of his dying sons in the other.[49] On the occasion of the dedication of the statue, the *Kansas City Journal* reported, "Old John Brown's spirit went marching on with the real Kansas spirit yesterday afternoon at Western University for Negroes at Quindaro, Kansas. Three thousand Negroes and three hundred white personages from Kansas and the United States forgot the hot weather and crowded into a tent on campus to witness the unveiling of the first statue ever erected to the man of Harper's Ferry."[50] The list of guests for the dedication was long and prominent. It included the former Kansas governor who had initially welcomed the flood of black migrants into Kansas three decades earlier, John P. St. John, several Exodusters, a founding member of the Niagara Movement, and teachers from Sumner

John Brown Statue. In 1911, Western University erected a statue honoring the controversial vigilante abolitionist John Brown, who waged a bloody campaign in Kansas in the 1850s and freed many slaves through the Underground Railroad, which passed through Quindaro, where the school was founded. (Photo by author)

High School. Champions for woman suffrage, temperance, and the newly organized NAACP spoke during the dedication.[51]

Like Sumner High School and the Industrial and Educational Institute, Western University took significant steps in the twentieth century to change the nature of African American education. The statue of John Brown provided one of the most explicit displays of race pride by a Kansas school and aptly symbolized the school's determination to leave behind its humble beginnings as an industrial school for freedpeople and instead promote its reputation as a school that was "leading the black youth to the higher things of life on the spot where forty years ago was heard the clank of slavery's chain."[52]

In the late nineteenth century, white reformers had established citizenship training so that blacks would have all of the responsibility of a middle-class lifestyle, but none of the economic privileges; but in the twentieth century, African American reformers sought social and economic privileges for their students. Although white reformers had encouraged black students to learn restraint, modesty, and decorum, black reformers expanded their opportunities for gaining greater knowledge and social mobility, learning about the past, and taking pride in African American cultural heritage. Moreover, black schools served as sites for social change, where African American parents, students, and reformers worked for their own uplift and built the foundation for future civil rights work.

Chapter Six

IDENTITY

NATIVE AMERICAN BICULTURALISM

We may know a people, but we cannot truly know them
until we can get within their minds, to some degree at least,
and see life from their peculiar point of view.
—Ella Cara Deloria, *Speaking of Indians*, 1944

The Indian problem is one of adjustment.
—Henry Roe Cloud, radio address, 1933

The local newspapers in and around Lawrence predicted that five to ten thousand Native Americans would gather at Haskell Institute in October 1926 for the boarding school's homecoming celebration and dedication of its new football stadium. Months before anyone arrived to pitch canvas tents and tepees on the forty-acre plot of land that the school had set aside for the gathering, journalists, students, and Haskell Institute officials anticipated something more significant than a homecoming celebration. They believed that the events surrounding the dedication would represent the largest assembly of Indians in peacetime and the most diverse meeting of Native Americans in the twentieth century. Newspapers issued headlines throughout the summer and early autumn declaring, "Primitive Tribe Coming," "More than 8,000 Redskins from All Over U.S. Will Be Present at Dedication of New Haskell Institute Stadium," and "Indians to Show Progress Made in Modern Arts: Greatest 'Homecoming' in History of Redmen Slated at Dedication of Big New Haskell Stadium."[1]

Earlier in the spring Haskell Institute's own publication, the *Indian Leader*, noted that alumni had commenced preparations for the autumn celebration, including forty former students who had a "midway pow-wow" in the Santo Domingo pueblo, north of Albuquerque, New Mexico. Those same students intended to caravan to Lawrence. For months preceding the stadium dedication, administrators used school publications to recruit students to help with the preparations and to encourage excitement among readers by listing names of former students who had already promised to attend. When mentioning the groups that planned to travel together, the *Indian Leader* claimed, "All Indian trails lead to Lawrence, October 27 to 30, 1926."[2]

When the weekend finally arrived, all "Indian trails" did seem to lead to Lawrence as seventy tribal representatives gathered for the four-day event. Forty-two years after Haskell Institute was founded, the 1926 weekend marked the school's first homecoming celebration. White reformers, reporters, and onlookers wanted the homecoming to represent the triumph of education for assimilation or "the real progress of the native American."[3] Indian visitors, alumni, and students used the festivities to describe their own notions about the bicultural nature of Native American citizenship in modern America. Whether or not they had been students of Haskell Institute, Indian participants demonstrated their own version of citizenship with their ability to finance the new football stadium and project pan-Indian unity throughout the weekend. In the 1920s, whites still held onto old savage-civilized paradigms and had a difficult time recognizing that Native Americans' version of modern citizenship was not based on complete assimilation, but rather anchored in an ability to mix cultural pride with modern opportunities. By this time, Native American leaders, many of whom had been educated at segregated schools in the late nineteenth century, discarded the notion that to be American precluded an embrace of Indian culture. Instead, their version of citizenship included developing bicultural abilities to navigate both white and Native American communities. Henry Roe Cloud and Ella Deloria, two Indian activists and educators who modeled this type of identity, demonstrated that white reformers had failed to destroy Native American culture and instead had created the very educational institutions that Indians would use to promote their modern version of American citizenship.

Homecoming Weekend

The 1920s saw an increase in financial support of federal Indian schools even though public enthusiasm had started to wane. As late as 1925, the government still provided a substantial $7,264,145 for the 77,577 students who attended boarding, day, mission, and public schools, but concern about student welfare circulated widely. The Committee of One Hundred, appointed by Secretary of the Interior Hubert Work, reported in 1924 that students in government boarding schools essentially "work their way through school."[4] A few years later, the Meriam Report detailed an investigation by the Institute for Government Research (later named the Brookings Institution), exposing the horrors of a half century of kidnapping by Indian agents, children engaged in forced labor, students subjected to physical abuse and a lack of adequate health care, in addition to the physical and curricular deterioration of boarding schools. In the 1930s, federal monies for boarding schools declined.[5]

The 1920s also marked a critical decade for Native American legal, cultural, educational, and professional citizenship. Most significantly, after a series of land laws, including the 1887 Dawes Act, the 1924 Citizenship Act established once and for all that any Native American could acquire legal citizenship regardless of land ownership or tribal status. Despite these laws, however, debates still continued about the true nature of Indian citizenship, and schools persisted with citizenship training, stressing virtues of obedience, promptness, self-discipline, and hard work.

During the 1926 homecoming, Haskell Institute officials directly engaged in the ongoing debate about the nature of Indian citizenship. Reformers were quick to contrast Haskell students with visitors to prove to observers how successful the school had been in training its students for life and work in the twentieth century. To this end, the school framed students as well educated and prepared for a desirable future, unlike the presumably unschooled Native American visitors who represented a static and unwanted past. Even though hundreds of the Indians who ventured to Haskell Institute during the stadium dedication weekend had, in fact, attended boarding schools and many were financial donors to the building of the new stadium, administrators focused on the contrasts rather than similarities and consequently the press reported them. "Civilization then made its debut before savagery," reported the *Kansas City Times*, describing seventy-five female students marching in black bloomers and white blouses to demonstrate their knowledge of gymnastics. The press portrayed such students as distinct from the visitors, whom they often photographed in traditional dress or wrapped in blankets.[6] The *Indian Leader* noted that whites could easily distinguish Haskellites from visitors because the students wore uniforms "so significant of dignity and honor," and the nearly three hundred alumni in attendance represented "the real progress of the race" by wearing "the latest conservative modes." In contrast, visitors reportedly wore attire described as "their characteristic colorful holiday dress."[7] The presence of such visitors confirmed for whites a narrative in which older Indians represented a vanishing race, while younger students represented the potential for survival and progress.

Even some alumni believed that contrasting students and visitors would help Haskellites be more readily accepted by whites as legitimate citizens. When asking for funds to support the building of the stadium, Frank Jones (Sac and Fox), class of 1898, asked his fellow alumni not to "forget the lessons of service and loyalty," asserting that they had been "equipped by Haskell training, to go out into the world to fight our way into good citizenship and to compete in business, agriculture, the professions and in every walk of life." Jones reminded his classmates that education had placed them in a category distinct from the visitors who would attend the festivities. "They need your help," Jones wrote. "The full-blood members are like children. They need your counsel, your inspiration and if you are sincere, honest, and clean in your own personal life, they will have confidence in you and will follow your example," he added. By attending the powwow and dedication, visitors could observe a younger, modern generation, but not necessarily merge with it.[8]

The dedication of the football stadium and the celebration festivities took on different meanings for the various groups involved. Whether they were tied to Haskell Institute, visiting for the weekend, or observing as an outsider, all involved used the celebration to make their own assessments about the roles that twentieth-century Native Americans played as citizens of the United States. For officials, students, and alumni, the weekend provided a highly publicized opportunity to draw attention to the ways in which Haskellites represented the most modern version of being American. In contrast to the thousands of Native American visitors, who were frequently referred to as the "most primitive in the United States," and who were accused of still adhering "to many old tribal customs of dress, dance and language," students were to represent Haskell's success in creating American identities as demonstrated by their domination on the football field, the ease with which they could put on and take off traditional costumes, and their use of vocational skills learned in class to earn gainful employment.[9]

The visitors did not see themselves as representatives of primitive cultures, although they were happy to celebrate the new football stadium by showing off tribal customs. Instead, they saw the event as a chance to display pan-Indian pride and American patriotism. White observers—represented by Lawrence, Topeka, and Kansas City newspapers—highlighted the contrasts between students and visitors but ultimately portrayed both sets of Native Americans as exotic and frequently harkened with some nostalgia to images of Indians in battle with whites.

During the weekend, Haskell Institute officials organized a number of activities for Indian visitors, including dance performances and contests and a barbecue. Carefully orchestrated and distinctly separate from the students' theatrical performance and parade, the visitors' activities were designed to reinforce a divide between the past and the future. Reformers first created a contrast by welcoming the homecoming visitors to what they called "Indian Village." Canvas tents and tepees dotted Indian Village on the south side of campus, where staff had rerouted electrical wiring and running water from the main part of campus in preparation for the first two hundred arrivals.[10] Reformers built Indian Village to represent their vision of a typical Native American camp, so the school program described it as a place where Indian women busied themselves with "keeping fires burning, jerking meat, making squaw bread and looking after little papooses." Even though many inhabitants of Indian Village actually had graduated from Haskell Institute and would not have burned fires or made their own food for their families, whites nostalgically described Indian Village as a place for "real Indians."[11] At most, the press noted with a tinge of disappointment the visitors who arrived in motorcars, but otherwise, many reporters focused on exceptionally traditional visitors, including a group of Blackfeet who wore ceremonial costume and sometimes relied on an interpreter to communicate in English. Alice Bear Paw, the granddaughter of Chief Two Guns White Calf (Blackfoot), was only four years old at the time, but her attendance was widely noted because her grandfather had been the model for the Indian head of the buffalo nickel.[12]

On Friday evening, the student band held concerts and performed drills, but most attention turned to a presentation of traditional Native American dances and competitions. Chiefs of visiting tribes judged the second contest, and audience applause levels determined the winner of the last dance. Dancers wore costumes, headdresses, and paint, while drummers accompanied their performances of the snake, eagle, rainbow, and sun dances. The press called the dances "primal" and "aboriginal" and claimed that some of the costumes were "cloak blankets such as were worn by their ancestors for a thousand years," some replete with "bead-work of a hundred years ago."[13] The press ignored the fact that many of the dancing costumes had been rented just as the costumes for the student performances had been.

The press also failed to mention how similar rituals, such as the sun dance and the ghost dance, had not been performed consistently throughout the years, but recently had been revitalized by Native American veterans after World War I. Whereas Indians might have seen veterans' participation in such dances as contemporary and patriotic, the press only saw the celebration dances as remnants of the past.[14]

A barbecue, during which men slaughtered buffalo and women cooked the meat along with the meat of thirteen cattle, provided a large community feast and another opportunity for the press to note the traditional nature of the visitors. The *Kansas City Times* emphasized old-fashioned methods of food preparation by describing a cooking scene as a group of "squaws [who] sat on their legs, skinned the beeves, dissected them, distributed the quarters and sliced the quarters into ragged steaks, many of which were hung on poles to dry in the wind and sun."[15] The buffalo had been "hand selected" from the Wichita Mountain Game Reserve near Cache, Oklahoma, in Kiowa and Comanche Indian Country "by a committee of old Indians who had their pick of a large herd." The Lawrence Chamber of Commerce provided the additional beef for the feast. In its advertising section, the *Haskell Stadium Dedication Program* included a photograph of a live buffalo with the caption, "This former resident of Oklahoma furnishes part of the meat for the Barbecue Saturday morning."[16]

Although earlier that year there had been a report that Charles Wright, a former Haskell Institute student and manager of the homecoming picnic, had promised to have a Canadian bear killed at the picnic, no evidence suggests that bear meat became part of the main menu. Louis Bighorse (Osage) chaired the barbecue committee, and his job included choosing "other Indians from the various tribes to assist him in putting on a real old time, old fashioned Buffalo Barbecue." Bighorse's tent was the first pitched in Indian Village since he had arrived ten days before the start of the celebration. Although the publication acknowledged that Bighorse's children were in attendance at Haskell Institute, Bighorse himself was not included when mentioning members of the modern generation.[17]

The entire feast was free to visitors, and the printed menu proudly listed barbecued buffalo and squaw bread as the main meal, jokingly adding that dessert would consist of even more meat and bread. The spectacle of the barbecue created much excitement among participants and onlookers. Only a few critics, such as E. D. Mossman, the superintendent of the Standing Rock Agency in Fort Yates, North Dakota, worried that gathering a large group of Native Americans would allow "reactionary" elements among tribes to resist the "progressive" work that had already been accomplished by schools.[18] Mossman's concerns were unfounded; even though the "the meat was prepared in the old Indian style" and even though reformers and the press argued that the barbecue represented a familiar version of a traditional feast, most of the visitors had never eaten buffalo meat before the homecoming. Barbecue participants could hardly have reclaimed a tradition that seemed unfamiliar to their generation.[19]

While visitors actively engaged in dancing competitions and eating barbecue, students had their own series of events for the weekend, including a parade, the school's annual production of *Hiawatha*, and the football game between Haskell Institute and Bucknell College. A parade of twenty floats traveled from the school through downtown Lawrence exhibiting the unique educational training that students received in Haskell Institute's various departments. To dramatize the contrasts, students dressed as pilgrims, Catholic priests, and Native Americans in headdresses and other traditional wear stood on a float titled "Indians of the Past." A float labeled "Indians of the Present" followed closely carrying students in nursing, soldier, and sailor uniforms. Students dressed as office workers sat at typewriters and held ballot boxes, and others displayed signs labeled "Electrician," "Steamfitter," "Engineer, or "Blacksmith." Those on the Business Department's floats held signs reading "Trained Accountant" and "Hundreds of Successful Graduates." Troop C, the student military cavalry troop, and Company D, its machine gun company, marched in the parade, as did the band, which the press—perhaps overzealously—called the "largest band in the world."[20]

The parade proceeded down Massachusetts Street, where streetcars had suspended their operation and automobiles remained parked. School officials sadly noted that the city had not cleared cars from the street in advance, and "much of the beauty of the parade was unappreciated." Still, a year later, the *Haskell Annual* called it the "greatest parade ever attempted in Lawrence," and the press was fascinated with the parade.[21] The *Lawrence Journal-World* claimed difficulty choosing which float was the best, but it suggested that the Normal Department showed most accurately the "service to the Indian people that Haskell gives" because it displayed "Indians of early times, without education to-day, and the Haskell student of to-day, with classrooms, books, and instructors to aid him." There was little subtlety about the priority that officials placed on assimilation and modernity

Performing *Hiawatha*. Native American students at Haskell Institute put on an annual production based on Henry Wadsworth Longfellow's 1855 poem *The Song of Hiawatha*. Plays and pageants earned money for their school, and dressing up in Indian costumes aided the development of their bicultural identities. (Courtesy of Kansas State Historical Society)

as it publicly positioned students wearing suits and dresses under a sign that read "Modern" next to those costumed in traditional Native American attire under a sign that read "Primitive."[22]

In addition to dressing up in different costumes for the parade, students donned headdresses and war paint to perform *Hiawatha*. The school had been producing the play every other spring for years as a fund-raiser, but in 1926, officials deliberately scheduled the production to coincide with the powwow and to entertain both white and Native American audiences. Productions of *Hiawatha* had been widely successful throughout the region in the first decade of the century. In 1909, the performance had gained so much popularity that Superintendent Hervey Peairs estimated having turned away one thousand spectators because the theater could not accommodate them.[23] Across the nation, Henry Wadsworth Longfellow's 1855 poem *The Song of Hiawatha* had quickly gained fame as a stage production. Native Americans performed pageants, stage spectacles, songs, dances, and dramas based on it throughout the country, and "by the early twentieth century, the poem had been translated into virtually all the world's languages, including Latin, Hebrew, Ojibway, and Yiddish," thus becoming almost universally known. Indian students performed *Scenes from Hiawatha* at Carnegie Hall in New York and throughout New England for approximately thirty years beginning in 1881, and Haskell students continued that tradition for many years.[24]

From the point of view of reformers, the very act of dressing in traditional costume for the parade and production of *Hiawatha* proved that students had achieved a citizenship status as Americans. With rented costumes, students could *perform* roles as Indians, presumably a mark of the school's success in having eradicated the habitual use of traditional dress and other native characteristics.[25] Performing as an Indian, however, was not necessarily evidence of assimilation. In fact, scholars have pointed to the act of dressing up as a strategy for Indians to confront the very stereotypes held by whites and as a way of asserting their own modern identities.[26] Students who participated in the parade or in *Hiawatha* might not have been able to articulate their own understanding of the assertive nature of performance, but native teachers and leaders in the 1920s certainly recognized and encouraged the use of traditional languages, dances, rituals, and costumes as a way of blocking complete assimilation and claiming bicultural identities. For example, from about 1900 through the 1930s, Indian leaders Henry Roe Cloud and Ella Deloria donned traditional costumes and used their native languages when speaking to white audiences as a way of getting the attention of onlookers whom they could then carefully educate about native cultures.[27]

Reformers, reporters, and onlookers failed to recognize students' ability to perform as a strategy for defining citizenship for themselves. They also failed to see that the visitors whom they had so readily viewed as primitive and antimodern were engaging in the same kinds of performance as the students. Newspapers consistently described visitors' festivities as exotic and strange, even likening them to animals. The *Kansas City Times* claimed that there was madness infusing the dancing and drum beating. The paper added, "Knees bend grotesquely; moccasined feet descend toe downward; arms rise and fall. Beribboned weapons are twirled and swung menacingly. But the dance is stopped before the ecstasy comes. Enough is enough." John Bloom argues that such descriptions of the dances made visitors seem dangerous, exotic, and sexually charged—"far more a reflection of cultural tensions within the dominant society than of anything inherently sexual or exotic in the dances themselves." Visitors were supposed to be consigned to exotic and unassimilated roles, while students represented a desirable future. However, if the act of performance, of putting on a disguise, "calls the notion of fixed identity into question," as Philip Deloria (Ella Deloria's grandnephew) argues, visitors could be considered comparable to students.[28] Visitors, after all, had spent the weekend engaged in activities that were not necessarily part of their everyday experiences: living in tepees, eating buffalo meat, and dancing. Moreover, they were the ones who had provided the essential funding for the new stadium and memorial arch, testaments to modern citizenship.

Funding the New Stadium and Arch

When Haskell Institute officials decided that the school needed a new football stadium to replace its small field and wooden bleachers, alumni decided to raise the endowment for the stadium strictly through Native American contributions. Put simply, money from white donors would be refused. Through small subscriptions, and an occasional larger donation of $4,000 to $15,000, the graduates collected enough money for the materials and part of the construction costs of the $250,000 stadium.[29] Students, along with alumni and other friends of Haskell Institute, provided much of the manual labor needed to build the new 20,000-seat stadium. The new stadium would accommodate large crowds and promised to bring athletic teams "of national reputation here to meet the Indians."[30]

Small donations provided seed money for the stadium. Even enrolled students made financial contributions in small but creative ways. For example, upon learning about the fund-raiser, eight students volunteered to walk to their homes in Oklahoma from Kansas in 1924 so they could donate their transportation money to the building fund. Frank McDonald, the athletic director who promoted the campaign to raise stadium funds, admitted that it was the "recently oil- and mineral-rich Osage and Quapaw Indians of Northeast Oklahoma" who "unquestionably built the stadium."[31] The Quapaw tribe made a contribution in 1925 totaling $56,195, and they sent over two hundred delegates to the powwow, as did the Osage tribe. Esther Bighorse Jefferson (Sac and Fox), a Haskell alumna, donated a portion of her wealth from payments for oil on her land. She joined two Quapaw women, Agnes Quapaw-Hoffman and Alice Beaver Hallam from Miami, Oklahoma, whose fortunes came from lead and zinc, in paying for the memorial arch. Harry Crawfish (Quapaw), a resident of Baxter Springs, never attended Haskell Institute, but he had visited often, and during the campaign to raise money for the school, he was the greatest single contributor. Major donors found notes of appreciation and their photographs in Haskell Institute programs and yearbooks, although a few years later, Superintendent Henry Roe Cloud would expose some illegal methods used by the Athletic Association to procure such funds. In the meantime, neither the press nor officials acknowledged the irony that these wealthy donors, who had made their money from modern advances in oil and mineral mining, were the same visitors who had been described by the press as primitive. At most, the *Kansas City Kansan* expressed confusion at the juxtaposition of "Indians in blankets" driving "high-powered automobiles" or seeing "older Indians dance the steps that were old when Columbus discovered America, [and] other Indians dance the Charleston."[32]

Frank McDonald proved instrumental in securing needed funds for the stadium, and he later admitted that taking Haskell Institute student and star football player John Levi (Arapaho) to talk to members of the Osage nation was one of his most effective strategies in convincing Indian donors to give their money to the stadium fund. For many years Levi had been admired by students and teachers alike; in 1923, an anonymous poet described his football achievements:

> But no proud chieftain ever has left
> A mark so well revealed,
> As the print of big John Levi's cleats
> In the turf of the football field.[33]

Levi was a legendary figure reminiscent of the Olympian Jim Thorpe; the *Kansas City Star* described him as a "superb football player, one who could pass the ball accurately almost the length of the field," weighing in at 280 pounds and boasting a twenty-two shoe size. On fund-raising trips, Levi received numerous invitations to powwows and people's homes to talk about the stadium project. McDonald called Levi's athletic ability the "best 'calling card' a salesman ever had."[34]

By donating most of the money for the stadium and memorial arch, the visitors demonstrated that they were not so primitive and backward as they had been described. Their donations helped to build tangible representations of native unity, biculturalism, and patriotism. The stadium itself proved to be impressive: the third largest stadium in the state and the first lighted stadium in the Midwest. As for the arch, Haskell Institute officials claimed that it was one of the first memorials to honor World War I veterans; but it would have been more accurate to say that the building of the memorial arch represented part of a larger trend, namely an outpouring of patriotism throughout the nation during the interwar years. There were,

Haskell Institute Memorial Arch. A World War I memorial dedicated in 1926, the arch both celebrates Native Americans' pride and unity and commemorates their patriotic contributions and sacrifices to the war effort. (Courtesy of Kansas State Historical Society)

in fact, several other memorials erected before Haskell Institute's. Most notably, approximately forty miles east of the school, in Kansas City, Missouri, the Liberty Memorial had its building site dedicated in 1921 and was completed in 1926. In Kansas alone, more than fifty World War I memorials, including statues, obelisks, high schools, American Legion halls, college student unions, and arches, were built in honor of World War I veterans.[35] Officials insisted on declaring the stadium the "first and only Indian Stadium in America," and when Secretary of the Interior Hubert Work acknowledged the tremendous effort that it took to build it, he credited Haskell Institute and other Indian schools that had encouraged such progress.[36]

Visitors took great pride in the two physical structures that represented their contributions to the recent war effort. Initially, enlisted Native Americans were to be segregated from whites into their own companies, but the War Department quickly reversed that decision. As soldiers integrated into military companies, Indians would fall under the command of white leaders, or as Lieutenant Z. B. Vance stated, "constantly be kept under the eye of a white man."[37] But at the same time, integrated companies allowed Indian men to claim the role of citizens, regardless of their specific legal status. Of the ten thousand Indians who served in World War I, 85 percent volunteered regardless of their official status as United States citizens. In 1918, a year after the United States had entered the war and called its first draft, the Office of Indian Affairs decided that all male Indians were eligible for the draft, but not necessarily eligible for American citizenship.[38] Despite this ambiguity about their status, Indian soldiers believed their service proved their patriotism and readiness for American identities. As one soldier commented, "I am glad, because it shows Washington knows we are men."[39] A few years after the war, in 1921, at the consecration of the original tomb of the unknown soldier, Chief Plenty Coups (Crow), who had encouraged Indians to join the military during World War I, made a spontaneous speech: "I feel it an honor to the red man that he takes part in this great event, because it shows that thousands of Indians who fought in the great war are appreciated by the white man."[40] Although Native Americans have participated in war efforts since the colonial period, their service had been largely ignored until World War I when recognition of their service included the creation of Native American sections of the American Legion, the establishment of two companies of all-Indian troops, and the erection of memorials such as the one at Haskell Institute.[41]

The climax of the weekend's events was the football match, during which the Haskell Fighting Indians beat the Bucknell College Bisons from Pennsylvania in a 36–0 blowout. Athletics, specifically football, had grown in importance at Indian schools in the 1920s. Male students had been writing to Indian boarding schools about the prospects of playing on athletic teams since the early part of the century. As sports programs grew in the 1910s and 1920s, so did opportunities for students to develop masculine citizenship through competition.[42] Indian leaders also endorsed athletics programs as training grounds for future citizenship. For example, Henry Roe Cloud explained that when athletes competed they expended energy comparable to bringing a crop to harvest. In Roe Cloud's estimation that was enough cerebral activity "to have passed the competency test for citizenship for one hundred Indians!" In the 1920s, he also referred to football using the pacifist William James's phrase: "the moral equivalent of war."[43]

The metaphor of battle was not lost on students, who echoed rhetoric that equated football with preparation for citizenship. In 1924, Henry Lewis Smith wrote, "The real glory of the game is not measured in gate-receipts but consists in the joy of battle, the overcoming of obstacles, the fair and final winning of a hard-fought goal. These constitute the *Lessons* of the GAME." A culturally sanctioned expression of violence and masculinity, football also represented athletes' determination, prowess, and character in preparation for engaging with the rapid and complex changes of the modern world. "Modern football is too rapid and complex for the ignorant and untrained, however strong and zealous they may be," Smith wrote.[44] Analogous to twentieth-century society, football served as a reminder to fans that Indian athletes could manage the intricacies and organization of both athletics and society. Athletes signaled to white onlookers that self-discipline and training on the field could transfer to the presumably masculine world of business—the gridiron, after all, was literally a level playing field and a place to claim a common manhood. Football, then, allowed viewers to indulge their nostalgia for a past time when Indians and whites battled each other and simultaneously encourage players to make a claim for citizenship in a rapidly changing world.[45]

Shifting between Two Worlds

In 1926, white Americans tended to point to the powwow and stadium dedication to accentuate contrasts between older Native Americans and Haskell Institute students. A new generation of Indian leaders, however, insisted on projecting an alternative vision of modern American citizenship that did not require a divorce from the past; instead, reformers of Native American descent who assumed leadership in the 1920s developed American identities that were bicultural, demonstrated pride in their heritage, and forged expanded cultural and legal citizenship roles for Indians. They did not feel forced to choose between Native American culture and white culture as mutually exclusive entities. Rather, they developed strategies enabling them to shift between worlds and to navigate terrains of language and customs in both white and Native American societies as if they were ambassadors in each. They used their biculturalism to challenge recycled stereotypes of Indians, improve Native American relationships with white society, and increase their influence over the design of Indian education. Like their African American peers, Native American reformers inverted the goals of their own educations in order to teach their students to embrace their cultural heritage. Unlike African American reformers, however, their strategies did not necessarily focus on broad racial uplift and full integration. If African Americans have continually seen themselves as integral to

American society, Native American reformers spent their careers vacillating between cultures, interpreting one for the other, and arguing that keeping Indian cultures distinct from the rest of society was important to their modern American identities.[46]

If the complexity of Native American citizenship during the homecoming demonstrated the precarious nature of Indians who were both incorporated into the dominant society yet still unequal with whites, then the lives of Ella Deloria and Henry Roe Cloud certainly did as well. In the 1910s through the 1930s, both Deloria and Roe Cloud persistently called for Indians to be treated like American citizens without having to give up their heritage. To be a modern American citizen, they argued, was to draw from both white and Indian cultures. Representing a new generation of reformer distinctly different from the assimilationists of the past, they thought that modern Indians ought to take advantage of educational opportunities but should not have to eradicate their knowledge about their own cultures in order to become educated Americans. Indians could engage in performance, but not merely as a way of entertaining whites; they could do so to persuade whites to be more accepting and respectful of their cultures. Indians could adopt whites' language and job practices, and even work for the very government that had been responsible for large-scale assaults on their cultures, but they could also be at the forefront of cultural preservation, documenting native languages and folklore and teaching them to the next generation. To be American meant shifting between both worlds; it did not mean giving up native identity in favor of full assimilation into the dominant society, and neither did it mean fully integrating or giving up self-determination as a strategy for preserving Native American identities.

Throughout their careers, Deloria and Roe Cloud grappled with definitions of bicultural citizenship that would allow Indians to enjoy the benefits of inclusion while still maintaining their distinct cultures. Deloria became a teacher, activist, performer, pageant author, linguist, and writer. She ardently worked to become the most prolific writer on Sioux languages (Dakota, Lakota, and Nakota) and culture. Roe Cloud became the youngest founding member of the influential pan-Indian group, Society for American Indians (SAI), in 1911; started a Native American high school, Roe Indian Institute (later renamed American Indian Institute), in 1915; held superintendent positions at federal boarding schools and administrative positions with the BIA; and proved to be a catalyst for the Indian New Deal in the 1930s. Believing that the question of official citizenship was most fundamental, he also kept his campaign for Indians' full legal citizenship at the forefront of his concerns and frequently used his position in SAI to lobby Congress.[47]

Both Deloria and Roe Cloud concentrated their reform efforts on removing the prescriptions of nineteenth-century Native American education, advancing cultural and legal Native American citizenship, and reaching out to whites to improve their perceptions of Indians. Although both were long-time teachers, they also considered themselves activists and advocates for Indian reform. Their work influenced a shift in boarding school curriculum to include Native American studies and other efforts to increase Native American pride and cultural preservation.[48]

Neither Roe Cloud nor Deloria was originally from Kansas, but both were drawn to Kansas to make pivotal changes in their careers. Roe Cloud— first named Wo-Na-Xi-Lay-Hunka or Wonah'i layhunka (War Chief)— was born in 1884 in Nebraska on the Winnebago Reservation and spent his college years at Yale University. Deloria—also named Anpetu Waste (Beautiful Day)—was born in 1888 at White Swan on the Yankton Dakota (Sioux) Reservation in southeast South Dakota and spent her college years at Columbia University.[49] Roe Cloud had a particular affinity for Kansas because he wanted American Indian Institute to be located in the center of the country in order to radiate its influence from the middle back out to the four corners. Wichita was the "cross-roads of Indians traveling north and south, east and west," and therefore the ideal location for an institute of higher learning.[50] Deloria's reasons for moving to Kansas were less stirring: a job as a dance and physical education teacher at Haskell Institute simply provided more financial security than contractual payments for her various jobs. During her tenure at Haskell Institute, Deloria also maintained a position as a YWCA officer, which allowed her to travel throughout the country giving lectures on Sioux culture for white audiences with the intention of intellectually shaping their perceptions of Indians. Roe Cloud, too, traveled throughout the country as a member of investigative commissions, including the 1914 Phelps-Stokes Fund survey on Indian school conditions, the 1923 Committee of One Hundred to advise the Secretary of the Interior on Indian affairs, and the Meriam Report. Serving as the head of the American Indian Institute and Haskell Institute for the years 1915 through 1935 anchored him in Kansas for nearly two decades of his career, but it was his national travel that increased his knowledge of multiple Indian tribes and contributed to his public image as a national expert on Indian affairs.[51]

Ella Deloria's Agenda

Ella Deloria continually recognized how bicultural strategies had been integral to her life and encouraged other Indians to learn how to straddle both Native American and white worlds. As Philip Deloria argues, his great aunt Ella, like many Native American adults in the early twentieth century, "was quite conscious of her bicultural identity. The positive female images she reflected back at the Camp Fire Girls undoubtedly drew not only from her knowledge of Dakota kinship, but from the middle-class American gender standards advocated by the Episcopal church mission in which she had grown up and attended school."[52] Deloria's parents embraced both assimilation—her father was an Episcopal priest, for example—and native traditions, including speaking traditional dialects, Dakota and Lakota, in the home and among community members.[53] Margaret Mead characterized Deloria, her contemporary and collaborator in anthropology, as someone able to "bridge the gap between aboriginal Indian and modern American life."[54]

As a linguistics researcher among the Sioux, Ella Deloria quickly found that her insider status allowed her access to more information than white anthropologists. Yet it was her affiliation with Franz Boas and his prestige as an anthropologist at Columbia University that lent her the necessary credibility to publish her research. Deloria's professional experiences had also shown her that it was precisely her biculturalism that allowed her to control the filters that determined what information she would share with her white audiences. For example, during her field work, she gained extensive knowledge of Sioux religious practices and customs and carefully documented stories, but when she lectured to white, Christian audiences she presented information in a way that could not be misconstrued as what she called "devil worship." At the same time, Deloria—herself a devout Christian—gave detailed accounts of tribal dances and traditions with what Beatrice Medicine describes as "total respect for their significance to those participants."[55] By carefully determining how or if to share information with her audiences, Deloria learned to strike a balance between effectively influencing white audiences and maintaining her respectable standing as a member of the Sioux community. Margaret Mead once observed that working with Franz Boas allowed Deloria to effectively combine roles as informant, field worker, and collaborator. Mead also pointed to Deloria's "very rare feeling for Dakota life and style" as her unique contribution as a scholar, and Boas even admitted that her knowledge was "unique."[56]

Modeling a bicultural identity and preserving Sioux languages and traditions were two strategies that Deloria employed to improve the status of Native Americans, but her preferred approaches also included elements of creativity and performance. In particular, writing historical pageants provided Deloria with her most satisfying creative outlet, or what many thought of as her real avocation. She had studied the genre of pageantry as a Columbia graduate student and understood the importance of spectacular visuals, literary and historical metaphors, and ornate costumes for artistic effect. But Deloria considered her pageants, along with her other performances (often in elaborate costumes) of Indian songs and dances, more than entertainment. In her mind, they were the most effective means of building a bridge between Native American and white societies.[57] Through her performances, she worked toward her more important goal of making Native Americans (or Dakota people, in particular) "understandable, as human beings, to the white people who have to deal with them."[58]

Of Ella Deloria's use of performance, Philip Deloria has observed that she sought "access to American cultural institutions in order to reshape popular conceptions of Indianness."[59] Ella Deloria met white audiences at the point of their negative stereotypes or preconceptions, but then expanded their perceptions into positive images. She had started giving lectures about Sioux culture when she was a college student (as did Roe Cloud while he attended Yale),[60] and she continued this kind of informal (although incredibly effective, in her mind) instruction throughout her adult life. Through her performances, Deloria became what scholars have called a "cultural mediator" or "cultural broker," someone who created a bridge between white American and Native American cultures, often challenging assumptions and stereotypes and raising awareness among academic and popular audiences about the histories of Indian peoples.[61]

In 1927, a year after Haskell Institute's stadium dedication and powwow, the school hosted a second homecoming, but with much less flair and far fewer participants than the previous year. This time, there was no Indian Village to house thousands of visitors, no traditional powwow, no student parade through the town of Lawrence, and no public relations effort from the school to contrast guests with students. The second homecoming weekend did offer a valiant football match and attracted 4,000 to 5,000 audience members for an epic pageant written by Deloria, titled, "Indian Progress: Commemorating a Half Century of Endeavor among the Indians of North America."[62]

Through "Indian Progress," Deloria echoed some of the themes of the

Ella Deloria in Costume. Dressing in traditional clothing allowed Deloria, teacher
and activist, to challenge white audiences' stereotypes and then lead them to a new
appreciation of Native American history, culture, and people. (Courtesy of Ella
Deloria Archive, Dakota Indian Foundation)

activities coordinated for the previous homecoming and demonstrated her understanding of the importance of students' ability to navigate in both white and Indian worlds. The pageant depicted scenes from "The Old Life," illustrated Deloria's belief in the gifts of Christian education to Indian students, and ended with scenes that portrayed students as fully prepared for American citizenship—including an American flag. Deloria did not criticize early colonizers and missionaries (a technique that Roe Cloud also employed), but rather saw them as part of a continuum of growth, an ideology that characterized the Progressive Era.[63] The final scenes, which included a depiction of Native Americans in military service to their country and mention of the Citizenship Act, reinforced Deloria's point and drew immense cheers from Native American audience members.

Just as the 1926 parade commemorated Haskell Institute as instrumental in the modernization of Indian students, Deloria's penultimate act provided a celebratory overview of the school's departments and ended with a scene harkening back to the highlight of 1926, "The Gift of the Haskell Stadium," complete with the key fund-raiser for the stadium and heroic athlete, John Levi, in the role of a football coach. In the section commemorating the football stadium, Deloria considered the massive structure a tribute to Haskell Institute for sending Native American students onto a "higher enterprise":

So well is she succeeding at her task
That our own people saw her earnestness,
And in acknowledgment they gave to her
This spacious stadium, where now we stand.[64]

Deloria even celebrated Native American mobility in the pageant—first by travois, then horse and buggy, and ultimately what she described as "an impatient Chevrolet sedan which honked imperiously"—which certainly would have been witnessed at the previous year's homecoming.[65] Deloria noted that by the end, the pageant, with its presentation of patriotic and heroic themes, dancers from the Potawatomi Agency, and elaborate costumes furnished by the Lyon Curio Store in Nebraska, made a "flattering impression on the audience," and she was pleased to receive affirming notes from the "University professors," presumably from the nearby University of Kansas.[66]

Producing "Indian Progress" represents a strategy that Deloria frequently used throughout her career: appealing to both Native American and white audiences by combining praise for white reformers' assimilation strategies with traditional elements of Native American culture. In 1920, her "Oicimani Hanska Kin (The Fifty Years' Trail)" commemorated fifty years of organized Christian service by the Episcopal Church, her minister father's church, among the Dakota Indians. And in 1940, Deloria wrote another pageant, "The Life-Story of a People," which followed the same formula of reflecting on traditional ways of Indians in the first act and concluding with evidence of Native Americans' adaptability and loyalty to home, country, and God. In Deloria's mind, the pageants provided large venues for her to shape the white onlookers' perceptions of Native Americans.[67]

Deloria also viewed occasions to write and produce pageants as opportunities to improve her own professional status. She was happy to receive a leave from teaching classes during the semester that she wrote the pageant, and she believed that if she were afforded other sabbaticals, she could support herself financially through creative endeavors and ultimately reach larger audiences than her regular job as a physical education teacher allowed. She optimistically wrote to Boas, "If I could get out where I could gradually let it be known that I can do that, I could earn money that way."[68] Deloria would never achieve this goal. She was able to involve her students in deliberate acts of performance and thereby directly engage them in the process of cultural mediation that became a hallmark of her own career, and in 1927, she proudly made one thousand dollars with her pageant, or enough money to pay for the expenses related to the powwow and more money than the football game earned.

Deloria's ability to navigate back and forth between Native American and white communities helped her reclaim and preserve Native American culture in general and Sioux culture in particular. As a linguist in Franz Boas's employ for over twenty-five years, she used her Dakota ethnicity to facilitate fluid travel among Sioux reservations to document language, family and tribal structures, religion, roles of women, biographical information, myths, and stories. At the same time, her collaboration with the well-credentialed anthropologist helped her to occasionally earn national grants to support her research and to compile the largest body of information on any Plains Indian tribe collected to date. Validation, language abilities, and cultural adaptation from both communities allowed Deloria to develop a new, more complex version of citizenship than white reformers had originally encouraged when she was young. She built a long career in linguistics and ethnography and went on to publish *Dakota Texts*, *Dakota Grammar* with Franz Boas, and *Speaking of Indians* before the end of her life. She also wrote *Waterlily*, a book often referred to as the first Native American novel, which was published posthumously in 1988. In her own estimation, however, the 1927 pageant, with thousands of people in attendance, counted as one of her largest audiences of both Native Americans and whites, and she therefore considered pageantry and performance her most effective means of building bridges between Indian and white constituencies.

Henry Roe Cloud's Career

In 1933, seven years after Haskell Institute's first homecoming, Henry Roe Cloud returned there to accept a position as the school's first Native American superintendent. By that time, Haskell Institute had enrolled nine hundred students representing eighty tribes, and Ella Deloria had left Kansas for South Dakota (to take care of her extended family) and for New York (to dedicate more of her time to linguistic work with Franz Boas). The Haskell community had not forgotten Deloria, however, and even posted a congratulatory note in the *Indian Leader* after her book of Siouan folklore and language, *Dakota Texts*, was published.[69] Although it is unclear whether Roe Cloud witnessed Deloria's 1927 pageant, it is reasonable to assume that he was in attendance because Haskell Institute frequently drew prominent Native American leaders to its campus, and by the 1920s Roe Cloud undoubtedly ranked among the most influential leaders. For over a decade, he had been heading his private boarding school, American Indian Institute, the first school solely dedicated to secondary education for Indian boys. After his graduation from Yale University in 1910, Roe Cloud married Elizabeth Bender (Chippewa), an active SAI member, and became actively involved in Indian reform at a national level, including a trip to President William Howard Taft's White House as the head of a Winnebago delegation in 1912.

Like Ella Deloria, Henry Roe Cloud's professional work promoted bicultural citizenship as a model of American identity for Indians. In particular, the curricula that he established at American Indian Institute and at Haskell Institute provided platforms to preserve Native American cultures, thereby ignoring the lessons that he had learned from his own boarding school experience and directly reversing decades of assault on Indian culture. Most notably, as superintendent, Roe Cloud encouraged practices that had been forbidden in the first fifty years of Haskell Institute's existence, including sharing native languages, Indian dances, pageants, and legends. As a symbolic endorsement of pan-Indian pride, he also replaced the names of the school's recreation halls with traditional Indian names. Roe Cloud embraced a policy of Indian preference in hiring, and he orchestrated intertribal powwows as part of the annual school activities. On the occasion of Haskell Institute's fiftieth anniversary, he supervised a large, three-day powwow in November 1934 during which the school erected another Indian Village for the hundreds of guests expected to attend the celebration. As with the 1926 celebration, costumed dancers and alumni stood at the center of the celebration, and the longtime administrator Hervey Peairs also returned, this time in a theatrical role playing Haskell's first superintendent in a pageant.[70]

White reformers of the late nineteenth century could not have imagined the possibility of living in both the white and Indian worlds, but as Alan Trachtenberg points out, that is exactly what Native Americans of this generation did. In Henry Roe Cloud's case, he continued to expand industrial programs for Haskell Institute students to prepare them for practical work, but he also remained committed to increasing the number of college preparatory offerings, hoping to provide students with training in leadership and social concerns. His decision to publish essays in the school's newspaper (he had assumed the role of editor, unlike previous superintendents) on leadership and activism rather than on vocational education emphasized his priorities as the school's new head. Modern Indian leaders would learn about Native American cultures, read Indian biographies, write about their own heritage, and then use that knowledge to reach out to whites to gain their support.[71]

As much as Roe Cloud wanted Indians to be perceived as Americans responsible for their own lives and able to "understand civic responsibility," he also expected students to "know how to enrich tribal and family life." He argued that white teachers in the past had mistakenly believed that the only method of advancing Native American students "into white man's civilization" was to "coerce the young Indian student to abandon this reigning spirit of his forefathers." His own introduction to a coercive education had started at the age of seven when the police arrived at his home on the Winnebago Reservation to force him to attend the Genoa School in Nebraska, where his teachers changed his name to Henry Clarence Cloud.[72] Reflecting on the strict rules forbidding Indian languages, Roe Cloud noted, "How well do I remember marching with a dozen other Indian lads half a day round and round in a room in the government school because we were caught talking our native language."[73]

Decades later after attending the Winnebago Industrial School in Nebraska, Mount Hermon School, and eventually going on to Yale, Roe Cloud declared that his leadership style would abandon that "ignorant method" of

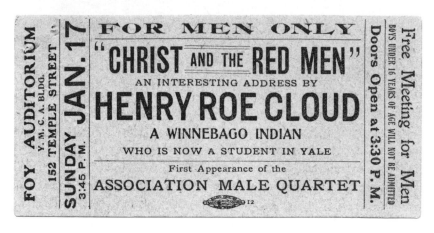

Henry Roe Cloud Lecture Ticket. The first Native American graduate of Yale University (1910), Roe Cloud dedicated his career to Indian uplift through education and legal reform. He often gave speeches to inform white audiences about Native Americans and to win support for granting them legal citizenship and preserving their cultural practices. (Courtesy of Roe Family Papers, Manuscripts and Archives, Yale University Library)

the past.[74] He would not perpetuate what he called "the retarding process in the Government schools." Roe Cloud did believe that vocational education served a purpose for some Indian students, but he hoped that more Native American students would pursue a college education as he had. All would not earn college degrees, he reasoned, but he still wanted students to embrace educational opportunities so that they could one day become leaders of their race and grapple with economic, political, educational, religious, and social problems. Therefore, their studies would include traditional academic subjects but also Indian cultures, traditions, and heritage. He called on students to "take up the righteous cause among their people, interpret civilization to their people, and restore race confidence, race virility."[75]

Henry Roe Cloud's hope was that the dominant society would finally see Native American culture as a central part of the larger American culture. He believed that Native Americans had been essential to United States history just as antiquity had been to the nations of Europe and that "no dominant race has the right to destroy the past of any people in any iconoclastic fashion."[76] Before whites could fully consider Indian culture integral to the larger history of the United States, however, Native Americans themselves would have to preserve and respect their own traditions and stories. When Roe Cloud introduced Native American studies to his students at American Indian Institute and Haskell Institute, he did so to promote self-respect. Using Indian mythology as an example, Roe Cloud urged students not only to learn different stories but also to understand their multiple purposes. "Many of the myths are purely for entertainment, some being romantic, some heroic, some satire, humor and adventure, and a great many of them teach moral allegiance," he instructed. Referring to a creation story and "a story of romance that belongs strictly to the Indian," he told his students that studying Indian mythology would make them proud of their culture. He encouraged them to compare their stories with mythology originating from other cultures. Once they had studied other mythologies, Roe Cloud reasoned, they would "be just as proud of the Indian mythology."[77]

Henry Roe Cloud continually promoted cultural preservation among his students, but his plan to incorporate native traditions into students' daily life did have some limitations, especially where religion was concerned. Roe Cloud was known to defend Native American religious beliefs and practices, and when the City of Wichita wanted to build a forty-acre cemetery on a tract of land immediately west of American Indian Institute, he intervened, asking planners to honor students' religious beliefs by preventing the building. Throughout his career, Roe Cloud would consider traditional Indian beliefs superstitious, controversial, supernatural, and even "fallacious," but he also argued to whites that such beliefs constituted the foundation of Native American culture, and therefore needed attention, respect, and appreciation. At the same time, as a Protestant minister, a graduate of Auburn Theological Seminary, and an adopted son of missionary parents, Roe Cloud never wavered from his belief in Christianity as the fundamental element to survival and success. After his ordination in 1913, he proudly announced to his adoptive mother, Mary Wickham Roe, that his first baptism was performed for a six-week-old Indian baby, scorned those who did not seriously observe the Sunday Sabbath, and argued that it was Christianity—not native religions—that allowed the "Red Man" to be "able to resist the vices of civilization."[78] While he certainly wanted Indians and whites to respectfully preserve traditions, he also believed that "to go back to the old days is unthinkable." Education would uplift Native Americans, "but the power which will regenerate us and lead us to a glorious future is the Christian religion," he professed.[79] Once students accepted Christianity, they could learn to serve others and claim full participation in American society.

Roe Cloud believed that American citizenship and dependency on the government were mutually exclusive, so when he established American Indian Institute, he included training in agriculture and the trades, and even drew comparisons to Booker T. Washington's curriculum in school pro-motional brochures.[80] However, Roe Cloud's school was different from gov-ernment boarding schools in that the primary purpose of American Indian Institute was to prepare students for higher education and national leader-ship. Government schools could not provide proper Christian training alone and needed the aid of the YMCA, YWCA, and other religious entities to help them, but American Indian Institute was designed to evangelize self-determined students, who could create a "distinctive native leadership for the Indian Race" and serve as a "powerful factor in the solution of the long-tangled Indian problem."[81]

In addition to producing leaders, Roe Cloud's vision of Indian education included helping Native Americans learn how to alter the perceptions of white Americans. In 1933, when he addressed the student body at his first Haskell Institute school assembly, he explained that education should im-prove their lives but should also prove to white onlookers that Indians were capable citizens. "The Indian race is on trial," Roe Cloud announced. He added that government offices were watching students, faculty, and staff and that the "general public is mightily interested to see this experiment of native leadership in the making." He expected the outcome of this trial to be a fleet of students who were "good American citizen[s] in the quickest and best manner."[82] Nearly a decade earlier, he had addressed a crowd of five thousand boys, declaring, "We are gathered here today as young Ameri-cans. 'Americans'! How proud we should be of that name."[83]

As a member of the committee that investigated the condition of Indian schools in 1928, Roe Cloud used the Meriam Report to propose expand-ing citizenship roles for students. Specifically, he wanted more attention be given to poverty rather than race when confronting the problems in Native American communities, an end to the policy of removing children from homes and placing them in boarding schools, more Native Americans to go on to higher education, and the support of federal scholarships and loans to send them to college. Believing that the modern version of the Indian Problem would be resolved through the mixing of races, disman-tling of reservations, and decentralization of government policies for Indi-ans, Roe Cloud was loathe to ask for government intervention in students' lives. But in order for Indians to feel their individual worth, become free from dependency on government help, assume individual responsibility, and meet whites on an equal social and economic footing, educational sup-port had to increase. Therefore, education loans were the only form of as-sistance from the federal government that Roe Cloud deemed acceptable for Indians. He was otherwise highly suspicious of the government's intentions toward Indians. Like William Vernon, the head of Western University, Roe Cloud was determined to find a way to accept government funding for his school without submitting to the limits of industrial education. Initially, he could not see how he could receive government money and still have control over his curriculum, so he refused government subsidies, fearing interference with his own plans. Instead, he received financial support from white Wichita families, Native Americans, the Kansas chapter of the Daughters of the American Revolution, and churches and missionaries affiliated with Reverend Walter and Mary Roe. In the 1920s, however, Roe Cloud changed his mind about government aid and began a decades-long campaign for higher education scholarships. He reasoned that children whose parents could not afford to send them to school should have access to scholarships and recommended that the government provide them. Congress did not heartily agree with Roe Cloud's proposals, although the BIA increased higher education opportunities by transforming some existing Indian schools into high schools in 1923.[84]

In 1930, Congress established a $15,000 educational loan fund for Native American college students in nursing, home economics, forestry, and other disciplines. Some American Indian Institute students went on to college with federal aid, and as superintendent of Haskell Institute in 1935, Roe Cloud proudly sent twenty-eight Native American students to nearby University of Kansas with the support of federal education loans.[85] Although Roe Cloud never suggested that all Indians attend college, he did want any capable students to have the opportunity. Low collegiate enrollments, especially in the first decade of the century, did not reveal a failure on the part of Indians, he argued, but with the educational system. Despite his attempts to improve access to higher education, Roe Cloud failed to maintain a substantial enrollment at American Indian Institute, let alone send a high percentage of the student body on to college. The school never gained enough momentum to reach its initial goal to produce one thousand new Indian leaders, so it closed in 1939.

With an emphasis on cultural preservation, Native American studies, and higher education, Roe Cloud spent the remainder of his career as an administrator employed by the federal government. He had once told his college classmates about his vision for his improved model of Indian education: "By the time we are old and grey, shaking hands on the Yale Campus in 1960, I hope to tell you that the American Indian Institute is the leading institution for Indian tribes in this country and radiates its influence to the twenty-odd millions of Indians in Central and South America."[86] Instead of reaching into Latin America, Roe Cloud concentrated on his work with the United States government. In the latter part of his career he became a potential candidate for the commissioner of Indian affairs, but a Native American administrator would not head the Bureau of Indian Affairs until the mid-1960s, approximately 140 years after the BIA started. From 1935 to 1940, he served the "representative-at-large" of Indian education for the BIA. From 1940 until his death in 1950, Roe Cloud accepted an appointment as superintendent of the Umatilla Agency in Oregon, although not without a struggle with white BIA administrators who challenged his requests for promotion.[87]

Although his dream of international influence was not realized, Roe Cloud felt that he had achieved his goals of expanding citizenship roles for Native Americans and producing Indian leaders for religious and secular uplift. His longtime fight to get the Citizenship Act passed, participation in the Lake Mohonk conference and SAI meetings, and maintenance of government posts certainly helped to catalyze within the BIA a shift in the 1930s toward preserving Indian culture and allowing most students to live at home while they attended Indian day schools or local public schools with white children.[88] In the 1930s, the BIA's director of education, Dr. W. Carson Ryan Jr., estimated that of the 90,000 to 100,000 school-aged Native American children, 83,000 attended school, and half of those attended school with whites in public schools. An estimated 20,000 still attended federal boarding schools, even as the federal government was starting to shift its emphasis away from these institutions.[89]

Both students and his own children echoed Roe Cloud's sentiments in their writing and their speeches. Harry White, valedictorian of American Indian Institute's class of 1924, declared that Indians were no different in ability than other races that occupied the country. Physical, mental, and spiritual education were necessary for uplift, but with that education, Native Americans could be among "the greatest civilization of the world."[90] White's classmate Coleman Byrd (Creek) made a similar argument that same year, declaring that all residents of the United States, whether immigrants or native born, should be educated to prepare for responsible citizenship. "The time has come to show that we are more than just Indians, but good American citizens," Byrd added. Comparing Native Americans to immigrants, Byrd also declared that Indians would make better citizens because they had the "foundation necessary for good citizenship."[91] Anne Woesha Roe Cloud North, daughter of Henry Roe Cloud and Elizabeth

Bender Cloud, an SAI member, astutely learned from her parents' influence that "I should work to 'save my race.'" She attributed her desire to the role-modeling of her parents, including "their leadership for Native Americans, their examples as Christians, their participation in the Wichita community as exemplary citizens, and their recognition even on the educational efforts." Roe Cloud's influence made an impact on his own daughter's life in ways he could not have anticipated. Less than two decades after North made this statement, she became one of the leaders of the occupation of Alcatraz Island, one of the watershed events that launched the Native American movement of the 1970s.[92]

The Outcomes of Bicultural Identities

From the time he graduated from college, Henry Roe Cloud managed to find employment that offered relative financial security of a kind that Ella Deloria never enjoyed. Deloria spent her career patching together a salary by combining jobs for Franz Boas, writing, lecturing, performing, and teaching. Beginning in 1916, the year her mother died and a year after her college graduation, "Aunt Ella," as so many would call her, assumed much of the emotional and financial responsibility for the brothers and sisters born out of her father's three marriages. Deloria rounded out her career as director of her former school, St. Elizabeth's, from 1955 through 1958, and assistant director of the W. H. Over Museum at the University of South Dakota in the early 1960s.[93] Although employed from 1938 to 1940 by the BIA to write on the topic "The Navajo Indian Problem," she did not otherwise have an opportunity to obtain the kind of secure, salaried government position that she had always wanted. As a scholar, Deloria was successful at earning grants to support her research. For example, in 1962 the National Science Foundation offered her $15,000 for her study of Sioux languages. She also earned some awards, among them the 1943 Indian Achievement Award of the Indian Council of Fire of Chicago. In the end, she spent most of her career struggling to make enough money to support her work, herself, and her family obligations. Even though her personal costs were great, Deloria's influence over Native American citizenship roles spread through her writing—notes, papers, and translations so voluminous that scholars continue to publish her research. Her greatest acclaim came posthumously with the publication of *Waterlily* and the establishment of the Ella C. Deloria Research Professorship in Indian Language and Culture at the University of South Dakota.[94]

Like the graduates who raised money to build the stadium in 1926, Ella Cara Deloria and Henry Roe Cloud had been educated in schools that taught them that Native American culture would prohibit their incorporation into the dominant culture. However, Deloria and Roe Cloud changed the intended outcomes of their own educations, and therefore illustrated the initial failure of Indian boarding schools. Through their lives and work, they were able to make Indian culture, language, ideas, and goals more accessible to white audiences, funders, and collaborators. At the same time, their ability to take pride in their Native American heritage and make it a part of their scholarly and professional endeavors allowed them to prove their teachers wrong by showing that Indians could be American citizens by embracing the values and customs of both the dominant culture and their own.

Conclusion

UNINTENDED CONSEQUENCES

THE NEXT GENERATION

He was no longer willing to accept second-class citizenship.
Oliver Brown wanted to be a whole man.
—Sam Jackson, Washburn law student, 1951

I had received the message during my upbringing that I
should assume the leadership role for my people.
—Anne Woesha Cloud North, c. 1980

On 6 April 1955, Charles Scott received a Western Union telegram at his Topeka law office from lawyer Thurgood Marshall, who was in New York. Marshall wrote, "Have just received information on the latest action Topeka School Board completely abolishing all segregation September this year. Please advise." The telegram noted Marshall's continued concern for the enforcement of the *Brown* case that he and Scott had successfully helped to argue a year earlier. It was the 1954 decision that made segregation in public places unconstitutional, but Charles Scott, along with his brother John Scott and colleague Charles Bledsoe, had first argued the *Brown* case in federal district court in Topeka in 1951 when Charles was a member of the law firm of his father, Elisha Scott, a former student of the Tennesseetown Kindergarten.[1]

In the 1890s, the young Elisha Scott lived in Tennesseetown when he caught the attention of school founder Charles Sheldon. When Sheldon took the young man under his wing, he had no idea that his student would later help usher in a critical watershed moment of the civil rights movement. Born in 1890, Scott was the youngest of thirteen children. His family had moved from Memphis, Tennessee, to Topeka with a group of fifty families who settled in the African American colony. As Scott grew up, Sheldon supported him by periodically buying him clothing and paying his tuition at the Industrial and Educational Institute. Although Sheldon had hoped that Scott would become a minister, Scott's academic interests took him to Washburn University Law School, where he was the only African American in his 1916 graduating class and only the third black student to graduate from the law school.[2]

As an attorney in Topeka, Elisha Scott gained a national reputation as an effective, although sometimes unconventional, civil rights lawyer. Whether his reputation was so widespread or he was simply a conspicuous anomaly, the post office knew to direct mail to him addressed as "Colored Lawyer, Topeka."[3] Scott and his wife, Esther V. Vandyne Scott, had three sons, John, Charles Sheldon (named for the elder Scott's benefactor), and Elisha Jr., who became lawyers like their father. The boys' mother died in 1928, leaving Scott and his sister Viola, or Aunt Duck, to rear them. The children and their father often welcomed famous guests in their home, including W. E. B. Du Bois, Walter White of the NAACP, and Jack Johnson, the ex-heavyweight champion boxer.[4] All three sons completed their college educations and entered their father's alma mater, Washburn Law School, in addition to serving tours in the military during World War II. While Elisha Jr. moved to Flint, Michigan, to take over his uncle's law practice, John and Charles joined their father's practice.

Before the *Brown* case, Charles Scott worked with his father on racial integration cases in elementary schools and, in particular, won a Kansas Supreme Court decision in *Webb v. School District No. 90, South Park Johnson County, Kansas* that ruled equal facilities must be provided for all children. He also partnered with his brother John to argue for African American plaintiffs seeking access to swimming pools, restaurants, theaters, and other public spaces that were otherwise segregated in Topeka. On 28 February 1951, Charles and John Scott, assisted by a team of NAACP lawyers, filed the United State District Court for Kansas the landmark *Brown v. Board of Education of Topeka*. The case was unsuccessful at the District Court level, but on 17 May 1954, the United States Supreme Court unanimously overturned the decision, declaring that separate public and educational facilities were inherently unequal, and therefore, violated the guarantee of "equal protection of the laws" by the Fourteenth Amendment to the United States Constitution. The important decision neither immediately desegregated schools nor quickly ushered in a change in racial attitudes, but it did lay the groundwork for future legislative, political, and social changes across the country.[5]

Fifteen years after *Brown*, Native Americans joined together to occupy Alcatraz Island, a protest that is often thought of as a defining event of the Indian rights movement. The Native American educator and activist Henry Roe Cloud had taught his students and his children that they were responsible for their own uplift.[6] This legacy may have been one of the reasons that in November 1969, his daughter, Anne Woesha Cloud North, helped to lead the nineteen-month occupation of the island off of the California coast near San Francisco. Between November 1969 and June 1971, a group of one hundred activists, many of whom were young, urban college students, claimed the island for "Indians of All Tribes." In addition to seeking the deed to the island, the occupiers demanded a Native American university, cultural center, and museum. Armed federal marshals, FBI agents, and special force police brought an end to the occupation before the federal government met these demands. Still, the siege united Indians from different tribes around issues of self-determination, autonomy, and respect for Native American culture. Occupiers of Alcatraz would later participate in the 1972 occupation of the BIA headquarters, Wounded Knee II in 1973, the 1975 Pine Ridge Reservation (South Dakota) shootout between American Indian Movement members and the FBI agents, and other protests that some have referred to as "Red Power."[7] The occupation proved to reignite a flame of Native American activism that Wilma Mankiller (Cherokee) said had not exactly died out but had diminished to a "very low, low flame." Mankiller argues that "Alcatraz sort of relit that and out of that fire came all these different people, spread in all the different directions to do incredible work."[8] She points to her own interest in the occupation of Alcatraz as a turning point in her activism in Indian rights—"The occupation of Alcatraz excited me like nothing ever had before"—including organizing antipoverty, education, and health care programs, as well as serving as the first woman chief of the Cherokee Nation of Oklahoma from 1985 to 1995.[9]

The *Brown* decision and the occupation of Alcatraz Island are two events that sparked a visible increase in African American and Native American civil rights efforts. In each case, participants descended from parents who had had their early educations in segregated schools. Although the white reformers who established the schools that the young Elisha Scott and Henry Roe Cloud once attended wanted their students to conform to limited citizenship roles, Scott and Roe Cloud managed to move beyond these expectations to redefine for themselves their American identities and to teach their children to actively improve citizenship roles even further.

Most of the segregated schools founded in the late nineteenth and early twentieth centuries in Kansas have disappeared from the physical and historical landscapes. Diminished funding led to the closings of most schools, including Halstead Institute and the Industrial and Educational Institute. In Fort Scott and other cities, African American elementary schools closed after the end of legal segregation, and black students eventually attended classes with white students. Of all the schools mentioned in this study, only two presently remain: Haskell Institute and Sumner High School.

Haskell Institute, the federal boarding school that opened in 1884, is now Haskell Indian Nations University. In 1970, Haskell expanded from an elementary and high school to a junior college, and in 1993, the school changed to its current name and started offering bachelor's degrees. Today there are nearly a thousand students, representing over 152 Native American tribes, who enroll in courses. Tuition is free to any member of a federally recognized tribe. Haskell is home to the American Indian Hall of Fame, and in 2001, the school broke ground on a $1.2 million Cultural Center and Museum. The new Cultural Center, funded by the American Indian College Fund and the American Indian Higher Education Consortium, provides research facilities and access to archived collections, and it displays artifacts representing Native American cultural heritage. Athletically, the school competes within the National Association of Intercollegiate Athletics and still hosts games in the football stadium built by Native American–only contributions in 1926.

The curriculum at Haskell Indian Nations University has shifted significantly since its early days in the 1880s. With a focus on college-level teaching and learning, Haskell's academic majors consist of Education, American Indian Studies, Business Management and Administration Services, and Environmental Science. Through a partnership with the University of Kansas Law School, Haskell also offers a tribal lawyer training program to its students.

Like Haskell Institute, which grew from a boarding school to a four-year college, Sumner High School, the first segregated high school in Kansas, exists in a different form today. It is now Sumner Academy of Arts and Sciences, a college-preparatory magnet school in the Kansas City, Kansas Public School District. Although segregation was banned in 1954, it was not until 1967 that Sumner athletic teams were incorporated into the public school district athletic leagues.[10] In 1978, court-ordered desegregation forced the closing of Sumner High School and finally returned racial integration at the high school level in Kansas City, Kansas. When Sumner High School closed, the district reassigned students to other schools until the school reopened as Sumner Academy. At the turn of the twentieth century, Sumner Academy's student population was racially and ethnically mixed, largely reflecting the population of Kansas City, Kansas: African Americans (43.19%), whites (40.31%), Latinos (11.63%), Asian Americans (3.43%), and Native Americans (1.44%). The curriculum is anchored in college-preparatory courses; 97 percent of the school's seniors matriculate in college.[11] In 2003, *Newsweek* ranked Sumner Academy in the top one hundred schools in the nation offering courses to prepare students for college.[12]

The transformation of the United States Indian Industrial Training School to Haskell Indian Nations University and the Manual Training High School to Sumner Academy of Arts and Sciences marks the failure of white reformers to impose their own definitions of citizenship on Indian and African American students and the success of subsequent generations to define their American identities for themselves. White reformers intended to assimilate Indians and keep blacks separate from the rest of society, but by the early 1900s, both groups rejected the prescriptions that whites had outlined for them. Native Americans turned to acts of distinct cultural preservation—including maintaining tribal identities, languages, and customs—that manifested in pan-Indian pride and the occupation of Alcatraz. African Americans fought for full inclusion and civil rights through systematic integration and numerous legal battles culminating in the *Brown* case. By transforming African American and Indian education and by asserting their own definitions of citizenship, blacks and Native Americans demonstrated what Gary Okihiro calls agitation from the margins to help "preserve and advance the principles and ideals of democracy" and therefore make "America a freer place for all."[13] In the face of educational campaigns aided by millions of dollars, thousands of religiously excited reformers, and increasingly hierarchical notions of racial difference, the struggles of blacks and Indians made good on the promise that the Free State did not—the freedom to define themselves as Americans.

Notes

Abbreviations

The following abbreviations are used throughout the notes.

BWTV
Bishop William T. Vernon Collection, Kansas Collection,
Kenneth Spencer Research Library, University of
Kansas Libraries, Lawrence, Kansas

CMS
Charles M. Sheldon Memorial Room, Central
Congregational Church, Topeka, Kansas

EDA
Ella Deloria Archive, Dakota Indian Foundation,
Chamberlain, South Dakota

FSSBM
Fort Scott School Board Minutes, Arnold Schofield
Private Collection, Fort Scott, Kansas

GBB
Greene B. Buster Collection, Kansas Collection,
Kenneth Spencer Research Library, University of
Kansas Libraries, Lawrence, Kansas

HCCM
Haskell Indian Nations University Cultural
Center and Museum, Lawrence, Kansas

HI
Records of Haskell Indian Junior College

IEI
Industrial and Educational Institute of Topeka, Kansas

IL
Indian Leader (published by the Haskell Institute, Lawrence, Kansas), Haskell
Indian Nations University Cultural Center and Museum, Lawrence, Kansas

IO
Indian Outlook (published by the American Indian Institute,
Wichita, Kansas), Roe Family Papers, Manuscript and
Archives Collection, Sterling Memorial Library, Yale
University, New Haven, Connecticut

KC
Kansas Collection, Kenneth Spencer Research Library,
University of Kansas Libraries, Lawrence, Kansas

KSHS
Kansas State Historical Society, Topeka, Kansas

LMCI
Proceedings of the Lake Mohonk Conference of the Friends of the Indian

LMCN
Proceedings of the First [and Second] Lake Mohonk
Conference on the Negro Question

MSBM
Minutes of School Board Meetings, Unified School District 234, Fort Scott, Kansas

NARA
National Archives and Record Administration–Central
Plains Region, Kansas City, Missouri

RFP
Roe Family Papers, Manuscript and Archives Collection,
Sterling Memorial Library, Yale University, New Haven, Connecticut

RG 75
Records of the Bureau of Indian Affairs

SHSC
Sumner High School Collection, Kansas Collection, Kenneth Spencer
Research Library, University of Kansas Libraries, Lawrence, Kansas

SHSR
Sumner High School Records, Kansas City, Kansas Public
School District Office Archives, Kansas City, Kansas

Introduction

1 G. B. Buster, "Today's Challenge to Negro Youth," 4–6, Honors Convocation Address, Lincoln University, 1944, file 34, School-Administration-Faculty/Staff —G. B. Buster, SHSC.

2 Henry Roe Cloud, "An Anthropologist's View of Reservation Life," Address for Superintendent's Conference at Pendleton, Oregon, 1941, RFP. In this book, I use the following terms to distinguish among the three racial groups discussed: "white," "African American" or "black," and "Native American" or "Indian." I use other racial terms only when quoting or pointing to a reference from a specific historical figure. I have intentionally avoided using hyphenated names to describe each group, and if an individual's tribal affiliation is known, I have included that information in parentheses after the mention of his or her name. Occasionally I use the term "nonwhite" to refer generally to people of color in the United States. This term has its own set of problems, but it also seems appropriate to make clear the distinctive separation of white Americans and nonwhite Americans during this period.

3 Clark Wisslor quoted in ibid.

4 Trachtenberg, *Shades of Hiawatha*, xvii.

5 Hodes, "The Mercurial Nature and Abiding Power of Race," 97.

6 Harmon, "When Is an Indian Not an Indian?" 95; Hoxie, *A Final Promise*, 38–39.

7 Bederman, *Manliness and Civilization*, 10.

8 *Afro-American Advocate*, 15 April 1892; Carper, "The Popular Ideology of Segregated Schooling," 257; Buster, "Today's Challenge to Negro Youth," 8.

9 *IL*, 5 and 12 June 1931; Philip J. Deloria, *Playing Indian*, 7, 122.

10 Trachtenberg, *Shades of Hiawatha*, 310, x, xxii.

11 Underwood, "Civilizing Kansas," 292.

12 Sheridan, "From Slavery in Missouri to Freedom in Kansas," 30–31.

13 Painter, *Exodusters*, 4, 195–96; Cordley quoted in Sheridan, "From Slavery in Missouri to Freedom in Kansas," 31; Kousser, "Before *Plessy*, before *Brown*," 221; Carper, "The Popular Ideology of Segregated Schooling," 255; IEI, *Second Biennial Report* (1922), 11, KC; Woods, "Integration, Exclusion, or Segregation," 185–86; Hagan, "How the West Was Lost," 179–84; Taylor, *In Search of the Racial Frontier*, 136–43; Foner, *Free Soil, Free Labor, Free Men*; Schwendemann, *Nicodemus*; Athearn, *In Search of Canaan*.

14 Jacobson, *Whiteness of a Different Color*, 3–4, 9.

15 Trachtenberg, *Shades of Hiawatha*, xiv, xvi.

16 Jacobson, *Whiteness of a Different Color*, 9; Scott, "Gender"; Pascoe, *Relations of Rescue*; Wall, "Gender and the 'Citizen Indian'"; Perales, "Empowering 'the Welder.'"

17 See especially Hine and Faragher, *The American West*; Hurtado, *Intimate Frontiers*.

18 For histories of boarding schools, see Adams, *Education for Extinction*; Archuleta, Child, and Lomawaima, *Away from Home*; Child, *Boarding School Seasons*; Ellis, *To Change Them Forever*; Lindsey, *Indians at Hampton Institute*; Loma-

waima, *They Called It Prairie Light*; Mihesuah, *Cultivating the Rosebuds*; Trafzer, Keller, and Sisquoc, *Boarding School Blues*; Trennert, *Alternative to Extinction*; Trennert, *The Phoenix Indian School*.

19 Noted southern studies include Anderson, *The Education of Blacks in the South*; Litwack, *Been in the Storm So Long*; Williams, *Self-Taught*; Fultz, "African American Teachers in the South"; Jones, "Women Who Were More than Men"; for northern studies, see especially Douglas, *Jim Crow Moves North*; and for studies on desegregation in Kansas, see Dudziak, "The Limits of Good Faith," Kousser, "Before *Plessy*, before *Brown*," Woods, "Integration, Exclusion, or Segregation?" Taylor's *In Search of the Racial Frontier* pays some attention to black education in the West.

20 Brooks, *Captives and Cousins*; Brooks, *Confounding the Color Line*; Miles, *Ties That Bind*; Miles and Holland, *Crossing Waters, Crossing Worlds*. Also see Krauthamer, "Blacks on the Borders"; Naylor, *African Cherokees in Indian Territory*; Saunt, *Black, White, and Indian*; Katz, *Black Indians*. Two studies examine the brief inclusion of Native American students at a school founded for the education of African Americans, Hampton Institute: Adams, "Education in Hues"; Lindsey, *Indians at Hampton Institute*. For a call for multicultural educational history, see Donato and Lazerson, "New Directions in American Educational History."

Chapter One

1 Comstock, "The Freedmen," in Hare, *The Life and Letters of Elizabeth L. Comstock*, 397.

2 Comstock, "Announcement of the Agricultural and Industrial Institute for the Refugees," 1881, Pamphlets Collection, KSHS. At one point, Governor John P. St. John tried to encourage the tide of immigrants to turn from Kansas to Nebraska and Iowa before they arrived in Topeka. See Haviland, *A Woman's Life-Work*, 388, 490; also see McPherson, *The Abolitionist Legacy*, 143–44.

3 Charter of Industrial Institute for Colored People (Agricultural and Industrial Institute for Refugees), Pamphlets Collection, KSHS. Another school that KFRA supported was the Samaritan Mission and Wayside Home, known to neighbors as "Hell's Half Acre." See Haviland, *A Woman's Life-Work*, 532.

4 E. L. C. [Comstock] to L. R., 27 November 1880, in Hare, *Life and Letters*, 404.

5 McPherson, *The Abolitionist Legacy*, 150.

6 Charter of Industrial Institute for Colored People.

7 Dudley Haskell died in 1883 before the school opened on 17 September 1884. See *Kansas City Star*, 7 March 1937.

8 Untitled newspaper clipping, 1904, *Kansas City Star/Times* Clippings, Kansas City Public Library, Kansas City, Missouri.

9 Hoxie, *A Final Promise*, 83–113; Peairs, "Indians Trained to Compete on Even Terms with Other Races," *School Life* 11 (April 1926), 147, KSHS.

10 Fear-Segal, *White Man's Club*, 36–37.

11 LMCI (1891), 11–12. Hertzberg referred to a reformer who believed that human intervention could alter the course of evolution as a "reform Darwinist" rather

than a "conservative Darwinist." See Hertzberg, "Nationality, Anthropology, and Pan-Indianism," 59; also see Hertzberg, *The Search for an American Indian Identity*, 22.

12 LMCI (1885), 27–28; LMCI (1886), 9.

13 Haywood, *Victorian West*, 123; Adams, "Fundamental Considerations," 4; Adams, *Education for Extinction*, 26–27; Novak, "The Real Takeover of the BIA," 645; Hoxie, *A Final Promise*, Appendix 2, 253–54; Hoxie, "The Curious Story of Reformers," 206–7. Also see Keller, *American Protestantism and United States Indian Policy*. The roots of the Bureau of Indian Affairs date back to 1775, when Benjamin Franklin headed the Committee on Indian Affairs for the Continental Congress. For clarity, I will refer to the BIA even though Indian Office and Office of Indian Affairs are other names used for the office.

14 "Free to Learn."

15 McPherson, "White Liberals and Black Power in Negro Education," 1360; Williams, *Self-Taught*, 69; also see *Private Laws of the Territory of Kansas* in Smith, "Western University," 7. George Washington Carver attended a school established in Fort Scott after leaving Missouri in search of better schools across the state line. He left Fort Scott after a year because he observed the violent murder of a black man. See "A Brief History of Fort Scott African American Schools"; Carper, "The Popular Ideology of Segregated Schooling," 255; *First Annual Report of the Freedmen's Educational Society*, 5–8, Pamphlets Collection, KSHS.

16 Comstock quoted in *Topeka Weekly Times*, 11 March 1881. Also see *Topeka Daily Capital*, 9 March and 5 April 1881; *Topeka Weekly Times*, 25 March and 22 April 1881.

17 E. L. C. [Elizabeth L. Comstock] to L. R., 21 August 1880, in Hare, *Life and Letters*, 387; Susan B. Anthony to Governor John P. St. John, 21 April 1879, St. John, Correspondence Received, Governor's Records, KSHS. Also see Haviland, *A Woman's Life-Work*, 512, 520; "Articles of Corporation and By-Laws of the Kansas Freedmen's Relief Association"; Taylor, *In Search of the Racial Frontier*, 143.

18 Excerpt from unnamed American newspaper, 14 January 1882, in Hare, *Life and Letters*, 430–31; Haviland, *A Woman's Life-Work*, 520.

19 Comstock, "The Freedmen"; E. L. C. to C. H. [Caroline Hare], 18 January 1881, in Hare, *Life and Letters*, 394, 415–16.

20 E. L. C. to L. R., 21 August 1880, in Hare, *Life and Letters*, 386; "Exodusters," 252–53.

21 Comstock died in Union Springs, New York, on 3 August 1891. Danforth, *A Quaker Pioneer*, 129; Elizabeth Comstock to John P. St. John, 16 June 1881, Correspondence Received, Governor's Records, St. John, KSHS; E. L. C. to L. R., 21 August 1890, in Hare, *Life and Letters*, 386–87. Also see ibid., 430, 436.

22 Haviland, *A Woman's Life-Work*, 518–19.

23 Danforth, *A Quaker Pioneer*, 129; Haviland, *A Woman's Life-Work*, 530–46.

24 Haviland, *A Woman's Life-Work*, 547; Lillian Miller, "'Aunt Laura,'" 203.

25 Lillian Miller, "'Aunt Laura,'" 206.

26 Haviland reported that between March 1879 and March 1881, 50,000 freed-

people arrived in Kansas. She thought that a total of 80,000 migrated in the 1880s, but Painter's numbers and census figures are much lower. Painter estimates that 15,000 African Americans migrated during the exodus. The census recorded 43,107 African American/Colored residents in Kansas in 1880, and approximately 52,000 by 1900. See Haviland, *A Woman's Life-Work*, 482–87; E. L. C. to L. R., 27 November 1880, in Hare, *Life and Letters*, 399; Painter, *Exodusters*, 256; Bureau of the Census, *Tenth Census*, 1880, 390–92; Bureau of the Census, *Fourteenth Census*, 1920, 338 (for 1900 statistics).

27 "The Agricultural and Industrial Institute for Colored People," Negroes Clippings, KSHS, 44–51. The thrifty Haviland once spent $500 on $2,000-worth of goods for refugees in Washington. Haviland's effect on different factions in Kansas was represented by the pallbearers who attended her casket. When she died in 1871, Haviland's pallbearers included two white ministers, two Grand Army men, and two African American men.

28 Peairs was a Republican, and some people believed that in 1916, if Woodrow Wilson had lost to Charles Hughes, Peairs, who at the time was the supervisor of schools, would have been appointed commissioner of Indian affairs. See "Memoranda on Experience and Some of the Accomplishments of H. B. Peairs in the Indian Service," Subject Peairs, H. B. Indian Service Career, 1928–30; Jas. B. Royce to Supr. H. B. Peairs, 11 November 1916, Subject 1916 Presidential Election, Education Division, RG 75, NARA.

29 Peairs, "Indians Trained to Compete on Even Terms with Other Races," 144, KSHS; Peairs quoted in *IL*, 2 March 1900.

30 "Memoranda on Experience"; Sculle, "The New Carlisle of the West," 198.

31 "Haskell Celebration," *IL*, 29 October, 5, 12, and 19 November 1926, 12–15, HCCM; Hervey Peairs to Commissioner of Indians Affairs, 31 January 1902, Hervey B. Peairs Papers, RG 75, NARA; "Superintendent Peairs' Address at Mohonk" reprinted in *IL*, 2 March 1900; LMCI (1885), 61. Samuel Armstrong suggested that the Indian could be "killed with kindness." See Adams, "Education in Hues," 165; *Kansas City Star*, 11 December 1904. For more on Pratt, see Hertzberg, *The Search for an American Indian Identity*, 16–17.

32 LMCI (1891), 11.

33 Dawes quoted in LMCI (1886), 31, and LMCI (1887), 63; Hertzberg, *The Search for an American Indian Identity*, 21. For the importance of the Lake Mohonk meetings, see Prucha, *American Indian Policy in Crisis*, 132–68; Prucha, introduction to *Americanizing the American Indian*, 5–6; Hoxie, "The Curious Story of Reformers and the American Indians"; Burgess, "The Lake Mohonk Conferences on the Indian." In 1904, the conference included "other dependent peoples," including Hawaiians, Puerto Ricans, and Filipinos. See Burgess, *The Lake Mohonk Conference of Friends of the Indian*, 7.

34 LMCN (1891), 62.

35 Hoxie, *A Final Promise*, 12; Danforth, *A Quaker Pioneer*, 129; Haviland, *A Woman's Life-Work*, 530–46; Prucha, *Indian Policy in the United States*, 242; Jacobson, *Whiteness of a Different Color*, 146–48.

36 LMCN (1890), 9.

37 Ibid., 8.

38 Pratt, *Battlefield and the Classroom*, 7–8.

39 Child and Tappan quoted in Kerber, "The Abolitionist Perception of the Indian," 272, 295.

40 Harmon, "When Is an Indian Not an Indian?" 95; Hoxie, *A Final Promise*, 38–39.

41 Jacob Winter, "Speech of Honorable Jacob Winter Delivered before the Senate of Kansas on Civil Rights, January 26, 1874," 12–13, Kansas State Legislative Documents, KSHS.

42 LMCI (1884), 21; LMCI (1885), 33, 55.

43 Prucha, *American Indian Policy in Crisis*, 227–64; Takaki, *A Different Mirror*, 234.

44 Richard Peterson to Dear Sirs, 12 March 1930, Superintendent of Indian Education (Lawrence, Kansas), Subject Correspondence, Education Division, RG 75, NARA; Hoxie, *A Final Promise*, 64; Tyack and Cuban, *Tinkering toward Utopia*, 2.

45 Thomas J. Morgan, "Studies in Pedagogy," in Prucha, *Indian Policy in the United States*, 242.

46 LMCN (1890), 7–8.

47 Jas. Harlan to Morgan L. Martin, 28 June 1866, in Hare, *Life and Letters*, 241; Kerber, "The Abolitionist Perception of the Indian," 285. The Peace Policy resulted in policies anchored in assimilation. See O'Brien, *American Indian Tribal Governments*, 71.

48 Ahern, "Assimilationist Racism," 24–25, 29.

49 Carper, "The Popular Ideology of Segregated Schooling," 263–65.

50 Armstrong quoted in Jones, "Women Who Were More than Men," 49.

51 LMCN (1890), 58–64.

52 *First Annual Report of the Freedmen's Educational Society* quoted in Cox, *Blacks in Topeka*, 68.

53 Peairs, "The Difference in the Starting Point of the Indian Child as Compared with that of the Average Civilized Child," 70.

54 Pitzer and Howard quoted in *New York Times*, 4 June 1891; Trennert, "From Carlisle to Phoenix," 271; Hoxie, *A Final Promise*, 106, 237.

55 Gates quoted in LMCI (1899), 12; Abbott quoted in LMCI (1901), 38; M'Cosh quoted in LMCI (1890), 14; Drexel quoted in Katherine Burton, *The Golden Door*, 311; Hayes quoted in LMCN (1890), 9. Also see Prucha, *Indians in American Society*, 10; Litwack, *Trouble in Mind*, 52–113.

56 Hine and Faragher, *The American West*, 376. Also see Antoinette Burton, "The White Woman's Burden," 137.

57 Jacobs, "Gender and Colonialism in the American West," ⟨http://www.historians.ie/women/jacob.pdf⟩.

58 Stoler, "Tense and Tender Ties," 830; Stoler, *Carnal Knowledge and Imperial Power*, 10; Hurtado, *Intimate Frontiers*, xxix. Hurtado refers to "intimate frontiers" as "frontiers of the mind, frontiers of the heart, frontiers of difference."

59 Hoxie, *A Final Promise*, 235.

60 McPherson, *The Abolitionist Legacy*, 197.

61 Elson, *Guardians of Tradition*, 67–73; Hoxie, *A Final Promise*, 106; Pfister, *The Yale Indian*, 10–11, 45–46; Woods, "Integration, Exclusion, or Segregation?" 196–97.

62 Exam reprinted in Adams, "From Bullets to Boarding Schools," 227. This examination was originally published in an issue of the Hampton Institute school newspaper, the *Southern Workman*, under the heading of "Work and Fun in the Geography Class."

63 Washington, *Up from Slavery*, 46, 49. Also see Lindsey, *Indians at Hampton Institute*, 95–97.

64 Lucile Doersch to Dear Gentlemen, 19 March 1930, Subject Correspondence, Superintendent of Indian Education (Lawrence, Kansas), Education Division, RG 75, NARA.

65 Mrs. Stanley M. Piland to Sirs, March 1930, Public Schools, 1930, Subject Correspondence, Superintendent of Indian Education (Lawrence, Kansas), Education Division, RG 75, NARA.

66 Parker, "Race Assimilation," 299.

67 Leupp quoted in Child, *Boarding School Seasons*, 74.

68 LMCN (1890), 8.

69 Antoinette Burton, "The White Woman's Burden," 139; Hoxie, *A Final Promise*, 242, 235.

70 Thomas Morgan, "Patriotism," in *Annual Report of the Commissioner of Indian Affairs to the Secretary of Interior* (1890), clxvii.

71 Peairs, "Indians Trained to Compete on Even Terms with Other Races," 147, KSHS.

72 *IL*, 11 September 1931.

73 Harmon, "When Is an Indian Not an Indian?" 106.

74 LMCN (1891), 58–64.

Chapter Two

1 Sheldon, *In His Steps*, 20.

2 Ibid. Also see Kluger, *Simple Justice*, 384; Miller, *Following in His Steps*, 24–28, 47, 50–51. There were actually two kindergartens founded — one for white children at the church and one in Tennesseetown for black children to attend. The black kindergarten moved to permanent quarters in the Tennesseetown Congregational Church building.

3 Sheldon, "The Bible's Place in Schools," *Dr. Sheldon's Scrap Book* (New York: Christian Herald Association, 1942), 161–62, CMS; T. E. Bowman, "The Value of Kindergarten Training in a Business Education," Kindergarten Scrapbook, CMS; *Topeka Daily Herald*, 1 November 1901; Kluger, *Simple Justice*, 383–84.

4 Minister quoted in the *Mennonite*, July 1895.

5 Handy, "The Protestant Quest for a Christian America," 10; Handy, *A Christian America*, 63.

6 Tyack and Hansot, *Learning Together*, 73.

7 Child quoted in Kerber, "The Abolitionist Perception of the Indian," 272, 283–

85; Gates quoted in LMCI (1893), 12, and LMCI (1886), 13. For a discussion of the evangelical spirit of the Indian reform movement, see Prucha's essay, "Indian Policy Reform and American Protestantism, 1880–1900," in Prucha, *Indian Policy in the United States*, 229–41.

8 Sheldon quoted in Miller, "Charles M. Sheldon and the Uplift of Tennesseetown," 128–29.

9 LMCN (1890), 127.

10 *Annual Report of the Commissioner of Indian Affairs* (1890), 185.

11 IEI, *Announcement for 1911–1912*, 28–31, KC; emphasis in original.

12 "Haskell Highlights, 1884–1978," Bureau of Indian Affairs Haskell Institute Publications file, Subject Correspondence, HI, RG 75, NARA; *Mennonite*, May 1889.

13 Krehbiel, *Prairie Pioneer*, 110; Valentine, [Commissioner of Indian Affairs], "General Regulations for Religious Worship and Instruction of Pupils in Government Indian Schools," Department of the Interior [stamped received 12 March 1910], Religious Instruction file, Subject Correspondence, HI, RG 75, NARA.

14 "September" and "Sunday Program," School Calendars file, Subject Correspondence, HI, RG 75, NARA; "The American Indian Institute at Wichita, Kansas," RFP. Although Haskell tolerated Catholicism among its students, there were no Catholic speakers listed on the schedule. See "Suggestions for Assembly: Topics for Speakers" and H. B. P. [Hervey B. Peairs] to Reverend F. L. King, 13 December 1918, Religious Instruction file, Subject Correspondence, HI, RG 75, NARA.

15 IEI, *Second Biennial Report* (1922), 3, KC.

16 IEI, *Announcement for 1911–1912*, 28, KC.

17 Kansas Vocational School, *Annual Catalogue, Kansas Industrial and Educational Institute, 1923–1924* (Topeka, Kans., 1923), KC. The name of the school had changed to Kansas Vocational School by this point, but its catalogue still listed its former name.

18 *Topeka Daily Capital*, 18 March and 6 February 1894; Tourgée quoted in LMCN (1890), 108.

19 Sheldon quoted in Edward Stephens, "The Kindergarten and the Colored People," Kindergarten Scrapbook, CMS, and in E. F. Parson, "What Shall We Do with 'Young America'?" *Kansas Farmer*, Churches—Congregational Central file, Sheldon Kindergarten folder, Topeka Room Collection, Topeka and Shawnee County Public Library.

20 *Topeka Plaindealer*, 7 November 1913, quoted in Cox, *Blacks in Topeka*, 152.

21 Cox, *Blacks in Topeka*, 150; Miller, *Following in His Steps*, 60.

22 Peairs quoted in Adams, *Education for Extinction*, 164.

23 Adams, *Education for Extinction*, 164–206.

24 Pascoe, *Relations of Rescue*, 112–45.

25 Shelly quoted in the *Mennonite*, February 1889, December 1888; Barnard quoted in Tyack and Hansot, *Learning Together*, 124; LMCI, 1894, 24. In the 1930s, Native American women belonging to a group called First Daughters of America would embrace this decidedly feminine role, claiming that women were well poised to train their family members to spend money wisely, as well as improve their homes and gardens. See the *Indian Leader*, 22 April 1932. Also see Marie L.

Baldwin, "Modern Home-Making and the Indian Woman," paper read before the First Annual Conference of the American Indian Association, Ohio State University, Columbus, 12–15 October 1911, RFP.

26 Carl Schurz quoted in Prucha, *American Indian Policy in Crisis*, 271.

27 [H. B. Peairs] to Clara S. Reed, 24 November 1916, YMCA file, Education Division, RG 75, NARA.

28 Peairs, "The Difference in the Starting Point of the Indian Child as Compared with that of the Average Civilized Child," 70; [Hervey B. Peairs] to Clara S. Reed, 24 November 1916, Subject YMCA, Education Division, RG 75, NARA. Also see Trennert, "Educating Indian Girls at Nonreservation Boarding Schools, 1878–1920," 272; Gilmore, *Gender and Jim Crow*, 31; Pfister, *The Yale Indian*, 96.

29 Gilmore, *Gender and Jim Crow*, 36; also see Rury, "Vocationalism for Home and Work," 22–24; Wall, "Gender and the 'Citizen Indian,'" 221; Trennert, "Educating Indian Girls at Nonreservation Boarding Schools," 286–90.

30 *Mennonite*, June 1886; Smith, "Western University," 70; Kansas Vocational School, *Fifth Biennial Report* (1928), 8, KC.

31 H. B. P. [Hervey B. Peairs] to Robert D. Hall, 1 May 1911, YMCA file, Subject Correspondence, HI, RG 75, NARA.

32 *Topeka Daily Capital*, 9 September 1885.

33 IEI, *Second Biennial Report* (1922), 6–7, KC.

34 *Annual Report of the Commissioner of Indian Affairs* (1890), 185; *Leavenworth Times*, 19 February 1888, 7; Horne and McBeth, *Essie's Story*, 33–35; IEI, *Announcement for 1914–1915*, 20, KC; HBP [Hervey B. Peairs] to Commissioner of Indians Affairs [E. B. Meritt], 5 April 1920, Flag Pledges file, Subject Correspondence, HI, RG 75, NARA.

35 IEI, *Announcement for 1911–1912*, 28–29, KC; emphasis in original. Child argues that the mail was sometimes screened before students could send messages home to their families. See Child, *Boarding School Seasons*, 30.

36 Of the twenty-three regulations stated in the 1911–1912 *Announcement*, including the regulation that prohibited students from possessing firearms, this was the only regulation printed in italics. It should be noted that there is a paucity of evidence regarding girls' sexual exploitation in their schools or their outing assignments. This omission likely has more to do with the schools' efforts to hide such violations than the actual security of the girls in these situations. In Manuel's play, *Strength of Indian Women*, she includes the risk of molestation, physical abuse, and pregnancy as part of the Native American boarding school experience. See Manuel and Oskiniko, *Two Plays about Residential School*, 104–13.

37 Horne and McBeth, *Essie's Story*, 38, 47.

38 In the Industrial and Educational Institute rulebook, uniforms had their own section, including costs: girls' uniforms were made to order at a cost of $2.50 for the work uniform and $6.50 for the dress uniform; boys' uniforms, which included a coat, pants, and a cap, cost $15. See IEI, *Announcement for 1911–1912*, 28–30, KC.

39 Ibid.

40 Ibid., 30.

41 LMCI (1884), 13; Trennert, "Educating Indian Girls at Nonreservation Boarding Schools," 280; Cox, *Blacks in Topeka*, 142. Even though Hampton was ostensibly a normal school, responsible for educating future teachers, it maintained a reputation as an institution that would prepare masses of black students for work. See Anderson, *The Education of Blacks in the South*, 33–78.

42 *Mennonite*, July 1888. See Goffman, *Asylums*, 3–124. For a lengthy discussion of the term "total institution," see the footnoted explanation in Adams, *Education for Extinction*, 357–58.

43 "Calendar and Announcements, 1918–19," School Calendars file, Subject Correspondence, HI, RG 75, NARA; IEI, *Third Biennial Report* (1924), 4, KC; Office of Superintendent of Indian Schools, *Course of Study for Indian Schools of the United States*, 146.

44 Anderson, *The Education of Blacks in the South*, 66, 72; Hanson, *Mary McLeod Bethune and Black Women's Political Activism*, 29; Prucha, *The Great Father*, 827; McPherson, *The Abolitionist Legacy*, 204, 213; Adams, *Education for Extinction*, 97–135.

45 LMCN (1890), 20.

46 Ibid., 15.

47 IEI, *Announcement for 1911–1912*, 21, 27, KC; emphasis in original.

48 Comstock quoted in Cooper, "History of the Agricultural and Industrial Institute (Nigger Hill), Crawford Township, Cherokee County, Kansas" (unpublished manuscript, 1962), 17–18, KSHS. Also see Pamphlet, Industrial and Agricultural Institute, Dunlap, Kansas, in the Agricultural and Industrial Institute file, Pamphlets Collection, KSHS; Haviland, *A Woman's Life-Work*, 512.

49 Litwack, *Trouble in Mind*, 69–70.

50 IEI, *Second Biennial Report* (1922), 3, KC.

51 IEI, *Announcement for 1911–1912*, 10, 17–28, KC.

52 IEI, *Third Biennial Report* (1924), 8, KC.

53 Trennert, "Educating Indian Girls at Nonreservation Boarding Schools," 278–79; Haskell Institute Clippings, 2, 4, 14, KSHS; *Topeka Daily Capital*, 16 March 1890; *Kansas City Star*, 22 July 1915; Horne and McBeth, *Essie's Story*, 35; Meserve, *A Tour of Observation among Indians and Indian Schools*, 35–36; Litwack, *Trouble in Mind*, 84; Miller, "Charles M. Sheldon and the Uplift of Tennesseetown," 131; Kansas Vocational School, *Fifth Biennial Report* (1928), 8–9, KC. In 1917, the BIA asked federal schools to increase their food production to tend to wartime needs. See the *Carlisle Arrow*, 20 April 1917.

54 Burke, "Indians Making Progress in Learning White Man's Ways," *School Life* (Washington: Department of the Interior, Bureau of Education, 1924), 241, KSHS.

55 Hailmann quoted in *Annual Report of the Commissioner of Indian Affairs* (1895), 344.

56 Office of Superintendent of Indian Schools, *Course of Study for the Indian Schools of the United States*, 5, 6, 143–47; Trennert, "Educating Indian Girls and Women at Nonreservation Boarding Schools," 278–79; Horne and McBeth, *Essie's Story*, 35; Prucha, *The Great Father*, 832; Meriam, *The Problem of Indian Administration*.

57 Mrs. [Mary] Stanley to Supt. H. B. Peairs, Report of Outing Trip, Outing Matron file, Subject Correspondence, HI, RG 75, NARA; emphasis in original.

58 Ahern, "Assimilationist Racism," 25.

59 Fairclough, *A Class of Their Own*, 21.

60 Wolters, *The New Negro on Campus*, 12; Litwack, *Trouble in Mind*, 90; Anderson, *The Education of Blacks in the South*, 67.

61 Krehbiel, *Prairie Pioneer*, 132.

62 Peairs quoted in Child, *Boarding School Seasons*, 74.

63 *Topeka Daily Capital*, 16 March 1890.

64 BIA commissioner Francis Leupp quoted in Child, *Boarding School Seasons*, 74.

65 Harvey quoted in *Proceedings of the Indian Educational Convention, for the Fourth Supervisors' District, Held at Arkansas City, Kansas*, December 1891 (Independence, Kans.: Tribune Steam Printing House, 1891), 8–9, KC; emphasis in original.

66 *Kansas City Star*, 11 December 1904; Child, *Boarding School Seasons*, 56–74. There were compulsory attendance laws that required African American children's attendance at school, but Kluger argues that there were high incidents of truancy among African Americans through the 1950s because attendance laws were not enforced to keep them in school. See Kluger, *Simple Justice*, 350–51.

67 Krehbiel quoted in *Proceedings of the Indian Educational Convention*, 12–13, KC.

68 Hervey Peairs to Hon. Walter Roscoe Stubbs, 24 February 1912, Stubbs file, Education Division, RG 75, NARA.

69 *Topeka Daily Capital*, 16 March 1890.

70 IEI, *Fourth Biennial Report* (1926), 12, KC; *A Book of Information about Kansas Vocational School* (Topeka, Kans.: The School, 1942), KC.

71 Leroy Halbert, "Across the Way: A History of the Work of Central Church, Topeka Kansas, in Tennesseetown" (1900), 26, Box 3, Charles Sheldon Papers, KSHS.

72 *Topeka Journal*, 17 November 1928; Greene, "Dr. Sheldon and Tennesseetown," 117; Hodge, "Problem of Self-Help," 73; Timothy Miller, *Following in His Steps*, 49–50, and "Charles M. Sheldon and the Uplift of Tennesseetown," 130.

73 Timothy Miller, *Following in His Steps*, 54–56, 136; *Topeka Daily Capital*, 27 March 1901; Hodge, "The Problem of Self-Help," 75; "The Sheldon Kindergarten" (pamphlet), vol. 1, no. 8, Central Congregational Church Collection, KSHS. June Chapman, the lead teacher at the Tennesseetown Kindergarten, made it part of her standard schedule to visit the homes of her students in the afternoon as part of her missionary work. In fact, the Central Congregational Church paid her wages for her mission work but not her role as a teacher.

74 Kathleen Koehn, "Christian Krehbiel: A Mennonite Leader," unpublished manuscript, History—W, Washburn University Collection, KSHS, 7; "The Indian Industrial School," *Halstead Independent*, 12 August 1937, KSHS, 32; Krehbiel, *Prairie Pioneer*, 110.

75 *Kansas City Star*, 16 October 1934; Adams, *Education for Extinction*, 153–63; Trennert, "From Carlisle to Phoenix," 276; Pratt, *Battlefield and Classroom*, 311–15; LMCI (1889), 19; *Kansas City Times*, 26 August 190[?].

76 Horne and Burnett, *Essie's Story*, 48.

77 Trennert, "From Carlisle to Phoenix," 274; Adams, *Education for Extinction*, 155.

78 C. H. Armstrong to H. B. Peairs, 5 July 1921; H. B. Peairs to C. H. Armstrong, 6 July 1921; H. B. Peairs to Mr. H. H. Killbuck, 19 May 1920; J. H. Killbuck to Mr. H. B. Peairs, 17 May 1920, Outing—Boys file, Subject Correspondence, HI, RG 75, NARA. Also see Trennert, "Educating Indian Girls at Nonreservation Boarding Schools," 283. Child notes a trend that boys' work was more varied than girls' and cites an example of a boy at Carlisle whose summer outing assignment was to wash glassware in a restaurant near the boardwalk in Atlantic City, New Jersey. See Child, *Boarding School Seasons*, 82. For wages, see C. F. Hawke to Mr. Wise, 17 July 1913, and "List of Wages," Outing Matron file; "Outing Rules Governing Patrons/Outing Rules Governing Pupils," Outing—Controls file; Mrs. [Mary] Stanley to Supt. [Hervey] Peairs, Outing Matron file, Subject Correspondence, HI, RG 75, NARA; Horne and Burnett, *Essie's Story*, 48.

79 [Third] Report of Outing Trip, Mrs. [Mary] Stanley to Supt. [Hervey B.] Peairs, 26 May 1919, Outing Matron file; "Outing Rules Governing Patrons/Outing Rules Governing Pupils, Haskell Institute," Outing—Controls file, Subject Correspondence, HI, RG 75, NARA.

80 [Second] Report of Outing Trip, Mrs. Mary Stanley to Supt. H. B. Peairs, Outing Matron file, Subject Correspondence, HI, RG 75, NARA. The rules did not have a corollary that forbade male students from visiting girls.

81 [Second] Report of Outing Trip, Mrs. Mary Stanley to Supt. H. B. Peairs; Report of Outing Trip, Mrs. [Mary] Stanley to Supt. H. B. Peairs in Outing Matron file, Subject Correspondence, HI, RG 75, NARA; Adams, *Education for Extinction*, 162–63.

82 Adams, *Education for Extinction*, 163; Trennert, "From Carlisle to Phoenix," 277, 288–91.

83 IEI, *Announcement for 1911–1912*, 30, KC; emphasis in original. See also IEI, *Announcement for 1913*, KC.

84 IEI, *Second Biennial Report* (1922), 12, KC.

85 "Sheldon Congress of Mothers, 1906–7," *Parents Meetings at Sheldon Kindergarten, Corner of King and Lincoln Streets, Topeka, Kansas*, Parenthood file, Pamphlets Collection, Central Congregational Church Collection, KSHS.

Chapter Three

1 C. E. Birch to H. B. Peairs, 24 October 1919, HI, RG 75, NARA.

2 Ibid. The students are quoted in this letter. Both Vučković and Child refer to this incident as one of the most dramatic and communal acts of resistance that Haskell students organized. See Vučković, *Voices from Haskell*, 229–30; Child, *Boarding School Seasons*, 93–94.

3 C. E. Birch to H. B. Peairs, 24 October 1919.

4 Child, *Boarding School Seasons*, 87–95; Adams, *Education for Extinction*, 207–69; Ahern, "An Experiment Aborted," 263–304.

5 Tyler, *A History of Indian Policy*, 97; Wall, "Gender and the 'Citizen Indian'";

Burgess, "The Lake Mohonk Conferences on the Indian," 8–12; Hagan, "How the West Was Lost"; Trachtenberg, *Shades of Hiawatha*, xxi; Hertzberg, *The Search for an American Indian Identity*, 3–5.

6 Henry Roe Cloud, "An Anthropologist's View of Reservation Life" (1941), RFP; Horne and McBeth, *Essie's Story*, 33, 41. Also see Vučković, *Voices from Haskell*, 3, 213–16; Adams, *Education for Extinction*, 209–38.

7 Adams, *Education for Extinction*, 223.

8 Stampp, *The Peculiar Institution*, 86–140; White, *Ar'n't I a Woman?*

9 Horne and McBeth, *Essie's Story*, 41; Milk, *Haskell Institute*, 74–77; Adams, *Education for Extinction*, 231.

10 Horne and McBeth, *Essie's Story*, xxxv, 32–33.

11 Adams, *Education for Extinction*, 232–35; Lomawaima, *They Called It Prairie Light*, 157–59, Child, *Boarding School Seasons*, 2, 66–67.

12 Johnson E. Tiger to H. H. Fiske, 15 March 1911; [H. H. Fiske] to Johnson E. Tiger, 21 March 1911, Students' Perspectives file, Subject Correspondence, HI, RG 75, NARA.

13 Students quoted in H. B. Peairs to the Commissioner of Indian Affairs, 15 July 1917, Subject Correspondence, HI, RG 75, NARA; *IL*, 13 October 1919; Child, *Boarding School Seasons*, 80.

14 The arson attempt is described in *IL*, 17 January 1908. Also see H. B. Peairs to Netta Allison, 31 July 1907, Subject Correspondence, HI, RG 75, NARA. For more on mysterious fires, see Adams, *Education for Extinction*, 229–31; *Kansas City Star*, 13 February 1915; *Topeka Daily Capital*, 13 February, 1915.

15 *IL*, 17 January 1908.

16 *IL*, 27 July 1906.

17 *Kansas City Journal*, 29 July 1907; Lovilla Mack to Supt. H. B. Peairs, 31 July 1907, Financial—Forfeiture file; H. B. Peairs to Netta Allison, 31 July 1907, Financial—Forfeiture file; various depositions in Fire—Dairy Barn file, 1905, Subject Correspondence, HI, RG 75, NARA.

18 Vučković, *Voices from Haskell*, 231–239; Adams, *Education for Extinction*, 224; Ida John to Dear friend, 26 August 1910, Students—Haskell file, Subject Correspondence, HI, RG 75, NARA; H. B. Peairs to Edson Watson, 11 May 1908, Numbered Correspondence with Indian Agencies and Schools; H. B. Peairs to Geo. L. Williams, 21 August 1906, Incoming Correspondence, Schools and Agencies, Records of the Potawatomi Agency, Mayetta, Kansas, RG 75, NARA.

19 Superintendent to Mr. J. L. Smoot [Superintendent of Industries, Haskell Institute], 24 March 1909, Students—Haskell file, Subject Correspondence, HI, RG 75, NARA. There are reports of three other male or female student runaways. See untitled document, Desertions, Arrests, White Slave Traffic file, Subject Correspondence, HI, RG 75, NARA.

20 H. B. Peairs to Mr. J. E. Downing, 22 April 1924, Students—Haskell file, Subject Correspondence, HI, RG 75, NARA.

21 H. B. Peairs to Edson Watson, 16 March 1910, Students—Haskell file, Subject Correspondence, HI, RG 75, NARA.

22 Mrs. Harriet W. Fairchild to Dear Sir, 19 May 1909, Students' Perspectives file,

Subject Correspondence, HI, RG 75, NARA; Child, *Boarding School Seasons*, 9–25; Adams, *Education for Extinction*, 255–57.

23 Adams, *Education for Extinction*, 261; Ralph Revere to My dear Sir, 29 January 1910, Students' Perspectives file; Tennie Lumby to Dear Sir [H. H. Fiske], 15 August 1910, Students—Haskell file, Subject Correspondence, HI, RG 75, NARA.

24 Trennert, "Educating Indian Girls at Nonreservation Boarding Schools," 289–90.

25 Lenore K. Bost to Superintendent H. H. Fiske, 12 May 1910, Students' Perspective file, Subject Correspondence, HI, RG 75, NARA.

26 MRP [Haskell official] to Ernest Goforthe, 8 March 1910, Students' Perspective file, Subject Correspondence, HI, RG 75, NARA.

27 Novak, "The Real Takeover of the BIA," 642, 647–48; Vučković, *Voices from Haskell*, 257; Bell, "Telling Stories Out of School," 340; Adams, *Education for Extinction*, 294; Ahern, "An Experiment Aborted," 271, 274; Hertzberg, *The Search for an American Identity*, 19; *IL*, 22 May 1908.

28 Mary Nash to Mr. [H. B.] Peairs, 7 October 1920, Students—Haskell file, Subject Correspondence, HI, RG 75, NARA; Johnson-Gover quoted in *IL*, 26 June 1908.

29 *New York Telegram and Evening Mail* quoted in "Haskell Highlights, 1884–1978," Bureau of Indian Affairs Haskell Institute Publications, HI, RG 75, NARA, 19; Horne and McBeth, *Essie's Story*, 44.

30 Ernest Goforthe to Dear Sir [MRP], 28 February 1910; Superintendent MRP to Ernest Goforthe, 8 March 1910, Students' Perspective file, Subject Correspondence, HI, RG 75, NARA. The dollar's worth of stamps must have been significant considering that the domestic letter rate in 1910 was two cents per ounce and the foreign rate was five cents per ounce.

31 *IL*, 22 May 1908; Wm. S. Jackson to H. B. Peairs, 23 and 29 April 1907; H. B. Peairs to William S. Jackson, 26 April 1907, Students' Perspective file, Subject Correspondence, HI, RG 75, NARA.

32 Philip J. Deloria, *Indians in Unexpected Places*, 127; Israelson, "The Haskell Indians," 25.

33 Amos Duggan to H. B. Peairs, 19 April and 5 April 1907; W. Friedman [?] to Amos T. Duggan, 8 April 1907, Students' Perspectives file, Subject Correspondence, HI, RG 75, NARA.

34 Sophia LaPointe to H. B. Peairs, 29 July 1907; H. B. Peairs to Sophia LaPointe, 31 July 1907, Students' Perspective file, Subject Correspondence, HI, RG 75, NARA.

35 Horne and McBeth, *Essie's Story*, 37.

36 HHF [H. H. Fiske] to Mrs. Susan Bohanan, 24 February 1911; H. B. Peairs to Miss Lovilla Mack, 21 August 1907, Students—Haskell file, Subject Correspondence, HI, RG 75, NARA. See Students—Haskell file for a collection of letters written by parents of Haskell students requesting their release from school. The collection also contains responses, usually written by Hervey Peairs. In a 1907 letter, Peairs wrote that the father of a boy still owed $5.28, and without repayment, Peairs sternly warned, "the boy will never be regularly released."

37 Hoxie, *A Final Promise*, 211–38.

38 Quotes from LeSieur and Peairs are taken from the following letters: T. B. LeSieur to H. B. Peairs, 26 May 1907, H. B. Peairs to T. B. LeSieur, 3 June 1907; T. B. LeSieur to H. B. Peairs, 24 June 1907; H. B. Peairs to T. B. LeSieur, 28 June 1907; T. B. LeSieur to H. B. Peairs, 15 July 1907, Students—Haskell file, Subject Correspondence, HI, RG 75, NARA.

39 *Mennonite*, February 1889, 65; Child, *Boarding School Seasons*, 54, 66–7. Child argues that Haskell did not accurately list all of the deaths that occurred. Milk lists the names on grave markers in the Haskell cemetery. See Milk, *Haskell Institute*, 128–67. Many scholars and community members continue to argue that several unmarked graves crowd the cemetery as well. Also see file marked "HINU Cemetery," Vertical Files, HCCM.

40 Quotes from Taber and Peairs are taken from the following letters: (Miss) Cora E. Taber to H. B. Peairs, 5 June 1907; H. B. Peairs to Cora E. Taber, 10 June, 18 June, and 15 July 1907; Cora E. Taber to H. B. Peairs, 19 June 1907, Students—Haskell file, Subject Correspondence, HI, RG 75, NARA. Also see documents in Maud Valley file, Student Case Files, HI, RG 75, NARA.

41 Haskell listed the Burson children as members of the Ute tribe, even though several letters written in 1910 dispute their status as Utes and claim that their deceased father, Nephi Burson, was from the Piute nation. Their mother is listed as a member of the Cherokee nation, although Haskell officials also thought that she was white. See, for example, Superintendent [Haskell Institute] to Mr. Chas. L. Davis [supervisor of Indian schools, Martinez School, Thermal, Calif.], 8 February 1910; Captain 5th Calvary, Acting U.S. Indian Agent to Superintendent, Haskell Institute, 24 February 1910, Blanche Burson file, Student Case Files, HI, RG 75, NARA.

42 Records for the Kansas State Penitentiary document a person named William Frye, who received a jail sentence in Douglas County on 9 December 1899. See Inmate Registers and Indexes for the Kansas State Penitentiary, microfilm roll AR7461, Library and Archives Division, KSHS.

43 Writ of Habeas Corpus, Case Number 1102, United States District Court of Kansas, 4 October 1909, Law Case Files, District Courts of the United States, Record Group 21, NARA. The suit was waged on behalf of Rachel, Blanch, and Uneta Burson. The spelling of the girls' names varies in the court and school documents.

44 Ibid.

45 Blanche [Burson] to Superintendent Peairs, 5 August 1909; Superintendent [Peairs] to Blanche Burson, 6 August 1909, Blanche Burson file, Student Case Files, HI, RG 75, NARA.

46 L. [Lily] McCoy to J. R. Wise, 22 September 1913; Superintendent [John R. Wise] to Chas. E. Dagenett, 14 March 1916, Blanche Burson file, Student Case Files, HI, RG 75, NARA.

47 Enrollment Record, Rachael Burson file, Student Case Files, HI, RG 75, NARA.

48 Mrs. [Olive] Burson to Superintendent [H. B. Peairs], 26 November 1909; Superintendent to Mrs. Olive Burson, 23 November 1909, Blanche Burson file, Student Case Files, HI, RG 75, NARA. Also see Application of Ollie Burson for En-

rollment of Weldon Burson, Weldon Burson file, Student Case Files, HI, RG 75, NARA.

49 Superintendent to Supervisor Jewell D. Martin, 23 October 1913, Weldon Burson file, Student Case Files, HI, RG 75, NARA.
50 Horne and McBeth, *Essie's Story*, 37, 41.
51 Lindsey, *Indians at Hampton Institute*, 36, 72.
52 *Kansas City Call*, 27 January 1928.

Chapter Four

1 Parks, *Voices in the Mirror*, 330–33.
2 Ibid., 1, 330. Parks wrote a number of semi-autobiographical and autobiographical books, including *A Choice of Weapons* and *Half-Past Autumn*. His most popular work of fiction, based on his experiences as a boy in Kansas, was *The Learning Tree*.
3 Bureau of the Census, *Thirteenth Census* (1910), vol. 4, 579–698; Douglas, *Jim Crow Moves North*, 88.
4 "Exodusters" (1886), 253, KSHS.
5 *Afro-American Advocate*, 15 August and 12 August 1892.
6 Kousser, "Before *Plessy*, before *Brown*," 221; Bureau of the Census, *Tenth Census* (1880), 390–93; for 1900–1920, see Bureau of the Census, *Fourteenth Census* (1920), 338. Also see Gibson and Jung, "Historical Census Statistics on Population Totals by Race, 1790 to 1990."
7 Peter W. Meldrim quoted in Litwack, *Trouble in Mind*, 90.
8 Litwack, *Trouble in Mind*, 106, 16–17.
9 Douglas, *Jim Crow Moves North*, 3–6.
10 Woods, "After the Exodus," 189–91; Woods, "Integration, Exclusion, or Segregation?" 182–83, 190–91; Cox, *Blacks in Topeka*, 111; Parks, *Voices in the Mirror*, 1.
11 Parks, *The Learning Tree*, 20.
12 Cox, *Blacks in Topeka*, 116; Woods, "Integration, Exclusion, or Segregation?" 192; *Topeka Commonwealth*, 31 August 1881.
13 *Afro-American Advocate*, 10 February 1893.
14 Bond, *The Education of the Negro*, 122; Woods, "After the Exodus," 181–95; Fairclough, *A Better Day Coming*, 23–24. Fairclough notes that 723 whites were lynched during this period. For more on conditions under Jim Crow, see Gilmore, *Gender and Jim Crow*; Litwack, *Trouble in Mind*; Woodward, *The Strange Career of Jim Crow*.
15 Woods, "After the Exodus," 187–95; Woods, "Integration, Exclusion, or Segregation?" 182–83. Also see Carper, "The Popular Ideology of Segregated Schooling."
16 Minister quoted in "Exodusters," 253.
17 Edwards, "Status without Rights," 365–93; Williams, *Self-Taught*, 70.
18 1855 Laws of the Territory of Kansas quoted in Blair, *History of Johnson County, Kansas*, 210.
19 Kansas State Teachers Association and McVicar quoted in Van Meeter, "Black Resistance to Segregation," 65.

20 State Superintendent of Public Instruction of Kansas, *Fifteenth Biennial Report, for the Years Ending June 30, 1905 and June 30, 1906,* ⟨http://brownvboard.org/research/handbook/sources/misc/1905edrept.htm⟩.

21 Burris and Greer quoted in Cox, *Blacks in Topeka,* 13.

22 Douglas, *Jim Crow Moves North,* 10.

23 1861 Kansas Session Laws quoted in Cox, *Blacks in Topeka,* 14.

24 *Leavenworth Advocate,* 3 May 1890 and 21 December 1889; *Topeka Plaindealer,* 27 December 1912; Kousser, "Before *Plessy,* before *Brown,*" 221–26; Dudziak, "The Limits of Good Faith," 346–48; Carper, "The Popular Ideology of Segregated Schooling," 263; Kluger, *Simple Justice,* 371–72; Woods, "Integration, Exclusion, or Segregation?" 187–88; Douglas, *Jim Crow Moves North,* 87; Taylor, *In Search of the Racial Frontier,* 215–19.

25 "Free to Learn."

26 *Topeka Colored Citizen,* 21 September 1900.

27 *Topeka Plaindealer,* 26 January 1917.

28 Cox, *Blacks in Topeka,* 167–68.

29 Carper, "The Popular Ideology of Segregated Schooling," 259.

30 *Leavenworth Advocate,* 4 May 1889.

31 Woods, "After the Exodus," 188.

32 See Table 1 in "Before *Plessy,* before *Brown,*" 222–23.

33 "In Pursuit of Freedom and Equality: Kansas and the African American Public School Experience, 1855–1955" (Topeka, Kans.: Brown Foundation for Educational Equity, Excellence and Research, 1996), KC.

34 Edwards, "Status without Rights," 393.

35 Eleven cases preceded *Brown* between 1881–1949: *Elijah Tinnon v. The Board of Education of Ottawa* (1881), *Knox v. Board of Education, Independence* (1891), *Reynolds v. Board of Education of Topeka* (1903), *Cartwright v. Board of Education of Coffeyville* (1906), *Rowles v. Board of Education of Wichita* (1907), *Williams v. Board of Education of Parsons* (1908), *Woolridge v. Board of Education of Galena* (1916), *Thurman-Watts v. Board of Education, Coffeville* (1924), *Wright v. Board of Education of Topeka* (1929), *Graham v. Board of Education of Topeka* (1941), and *Webb v. School District No. 90, South Park Johnson County, Kansas* (1949).

36 Tyack, *The One Best System,* 110.

37 *Afro-American Advocate,* 3 February 1893.

38 *Afro-American Advocate,* 29 July 1892.

39 *Afro-American Advocate,* 15 April 1892.

40 Carper, "The Popular Ideology of Segregated Schooling," 257.

41 Vernon, *The Upbuilding of a Race,* 32.

42 *Afro-American Advocate,* 29 September 1892 and 2 September 1891.

43 *Afro-American Advocate,* 10 June 1892.

44 Douglass quoted in Kerber, "The Abolitionist Perception of the Indian," 294, and in Trachtenberg, *Shades of Hiawatha,* 28.

45 *Afro-American Advocate,* 10 June, 1 July, and 5 August 1892.

46 Williams, *Self-Taught,* 77; Bardolph, "The Distinguished Negro in America,

1770–1936," 540–42; Woods, "After the Exodus," 181–95; *Afro-American Advocate* 17 June, 4 June, and 24 June 1892.

47 *Topeka Commonwealth* quoted in Cox, *Blacks in Topeka*, 119. Also see *Afro-American Advocate*, 1 September 1893 and 9 September 1891; Brady, "Kansas Federation of Colored Women's Clubs," 21; Cox, *Blacks in Topeka*, 161.

48 Washington quoted in untitled newspaper clipping (n.d.), 75–96, Negroes Clippings, KSHS.

49 *Topeka Plaindealer*, 14 March 1913.

50 *Topeka Plaindealer*, 15 June 1900. Also see Taylor, *In Search of the Racial Frontier*, 213–14; Brady, "Kansas Federation of Colored Women's Clubs," 21; Cox, *Blacks in Topeka*, 162; Higginbotham, *Righteous Discontent*.

51 Brady, "Kansas Federation of Colored Women's Clubs," 24–29; *Kansas City Call*, 26 August 1922; Giddings, *Where and When I Enter*, 95; White, *Too Heavy a Load*, 105.

52 *Kansas State Journal*, 16 February 1882 and August 1866.

53 *Topeka Commonwealth*, 30 January, 1874.

54 FSSBM, 1 July 1872.

55 FSSBM, 1 July 1872 and 21 March 1874.

56 Ibid.

57 MSBM, 1 July 1878 and 15 November 1878.

58 A special election in 1921 allowed for the issuance of $53,000 in bonds for the new African American school that included the first through ninth grades. See Margue Williams, "The Plaza (Hawkins) School," unpublished essay, in the possession of Kenneth Sharp. Between 1920 and 1922, when the First Plaza, Washington, and Logan schools were closed, all African American children attended classes in the Old Convention Hall until the Second Plaza School was completed in 1922. See "Free to Learn."

59 MSBM, 5 November 1884 and March 1884.

60 MSBM, 6 February 1888.

61 For the sake of clarity, it is useful to remind readers that Kansas City, Kansas, is a city separate from Kansas City, Missouri.

62 See quote in Johnson, "Why, How and When It All Began," *The Yesterdays of Summer*, Supplement to the *Kansas City Voice*, 8–14 June 1978. Also see Lawrence, "The Impact of Local, State and Federal Government Decisions on the Segregation," 79; Greenbaum, *The Afro-American Community in Kansas City, Kansas*, 65.

63 *Kansas City Journal*, 14 April 1904; McGuinn, "The Kansas City, Kansas, Public School System," 115.

64 See a summary of these events in Lawrence, "The Impact of Local, State and Federal Government Decisions on Segregation," 79–85; Peavler, "Drawing the Color Line in Kansas City," 191–193. Louis Gregory received parole after thirty years.

65 Johnson, "Why, How and When It All Began."

66 *Kansas City Journal*, 14 April 1904.

67 Ibid.

68 "Powers and Duties of the Board of Education," [1879] quoted in *Kansas City Journal* 14 April 1904; emphasis added.

69 *Kansas City Star*, 15 April 1904.

70 Scottie Davis, "The Story of Sumner High School," 1935, SHSR, 2.

71 *Kansas City Journal*, 15 April 1904; Roy Martin's mother, identified only as "Mrs. Martin," is quoted in *Kansas City Journal*, 14 April 1904.

72 Lawrence, "The Impact of Local, State and Federal Government Decisions on Segregation," 88; Davis, "The Story of Sumner High School," 2.

73 Superintendent quoted in Van Meeter, "Black Resistance to Segregation," 70–71.

74 Waller quoted in Woods, "After the Exodus," 178; also see ibid., 180–82.

75 *Kansas City Star*, 17 April 1904, 11 September 1905, and 6 January 1906; *Kansas City Journal*, 12 September 1905.

76 Peavler, "Drawing the Color Line in Kansas City," 194–96. Peavler points out that getting 10,000 signatures was improbable, and some may have been forged.

77 *Kansas City Journal*, 23 February 1905.

78 Davis, "The Story of Sumner High School," 2.

79 *Kansas City Journal*, 23 February 1905.

80 Ibid.

81 McGuinn, "The Kansas City, Kansas, Public School System," 120; Davis, "The Story of Sumner High School," 1; *Kansas City Journal*, 23 February 1905.

82 Jacob Tillman quoted in *Kansas City Star*, 11 September 1905.

83 *Kansas City Journal*, 12 September 1905. Although students were involved in this strategy of negotiation, I would still classify it as a part of a larger integration effort engineered by adults.

84 *Kansas City Star*, 6 January 1906; *Kansas City Journal*, 7 January 1906.

Chapter Five

1 Vernon, "A Plea for a Suspension of Judgment," n.d., Personal Records—Speeches, BWTV.

2 Litwack, *Trouble in Mind*, 81; Gilmore, *Gender and Jim Crow*, 32–33, 76; Coulter, *"Take Up the Black Man's Burden,"* 8, 2; Fultz, "African American Teachers in the South," 401–22; Anderson, *The Education of Blacks in the South*, 110–47; Jones, "Women Who Were More than Men," 47–59; Fairclough, *Teaching Equality*; Williams, *Self-Taught*.

3 Teacher quoted in "Some Facts about Sumner High School," SHSC.

4 Scottie Davis, "The Story of Sumner High School," 1935, SHSR, 4; Anderson, *Education of Blacks in the South*, 33, 67–72.

5 Teacher quoted in Davis, "The Story of Sumner High School," 3.

6 Coulter, *"Take Up the Black Man's Burden,"* 6; Woodson, *The Mis-Education of the Negro*, 14; Lawrence, "The Impact of Local, State and Federal Government Decisions," 124–25; "Enrollment Statistics," SHSR.

7 "Sumner High School Enrollment Guide: 1921–1922," SHSR.

8 Davis, "The Story of Sumner High School," 6; "Some Facts about Sumner High School," SHSC.

9 *The Sumneriana*, 1911, SHSC; *Kansas City Call*, 2–8 September 1994. The *Kansas City Call* is one of the few African American newspapers published in Missouri cited in this book. All other newspapers are Kansas publications unless otherwise noted.

10 Fairclough, *A Class of Their Own*, 9.

11 "Some Facts about Sumner High School"; *Sumner Courier*, 15 January 1921, SHSC.

12 G. B. Buster, "Adjusting to the Changing Times," file 14, box 1, SHSC.

13 Ibid.

14 Buster, *Brighter Sun*, vii.

15 *The Sumnerian, Class of 1925*; *Sumner Courier*, February 1920, SHSC.

16 *Sumner Courier*, May 1920, 16 January 1921 [1922], and 17 October 1921, SHSC.

17 See G. B. Buster, "The Negro in Washington's Time" (1935), GBB, which contains a list of thirty facts about African Americans under the heading "Did You Know." Buster [editor in chief], "The Negro in American History, Written by the Students of the American History Class of Sumner High School" (1916), 2, GBB. For reference to Hampton Institute, see Anderson, *The Education of Blacks in the South*, 63.

18 "The Negro in American History," 81–82.

19 G. B. Buster, "Revolution," GBB, 10; Coulter, *"Take Up the Black Man's Burden,"* 160.

20 "The G. B. Busters to Leave KCK Nov. 10 for California Residence," newspaper clipping, n.d. [1960?], GBB.

21 G. B. Buster, "Today's Challenge to Negro Youth," Honors Convocation Address, Lincoln University, 1944, file 34, School-Administration-Faculty/Staff—G. B. Buster, SHSC.

22 *A Book of Information about Kansas Vocational School, Topeka, Kansas (1942–1943)*, KC.

23 Ibid.; IEI, *Second Biennial Report* (1922), 3, KC. Also see Taylor, *In Search of the Racial Frontier*, 214–15.

24 *A Book of Information about Kansas Vocational School, Topeka, Kansas (1942–1943)*, KC.

25 IEI, *First Biennial Report* (1920), 6–7, KC.

26 IEI, *Announcement for 1911–1912*, 17, KC; emphasis in original. Also see IEI, *Third Biennial Report* (1924), 8, KC.

27 IEI, *Announcement for 1914–1915*, KC; *Announcement for 1915–1916*, KC. By 1924, Industrial and Educational Institute had 150 students and 20 teachers. Most of the students came from the state of Kansas, but the total enrollment represented twelve states. See IEI, *Third Biennial Report* (1924), 4, KC.

28 IEI, *Second Biennial Report* (1922), 13, KC. The construction of the gate was estimated to cost $1,000.

29 Kansas Vocational School, *Annual Catalogue, Kansas Industrial and Educational Institute, 1923–1924* (Topeka, Kans., 1923), KC.

30 IEI, *Third Biennial Report* (1924), 8, 13, KC; Kansas Vocational School, *Fifth Biennial Report* (1928), 8, KC; *Twenty-sixth Biennial Report of Western University and State Industrial Department, Kansas City, Kansas for the Two Years Ending June 30, 1932*, 12, KC.

31 IEI, *Second Biennial Report* (1922), 13–16, KC. The other names that faculty and board members suggested were Kansas Trade School, Agricultural and Mechanical College, Kansas Industrial and Educational Institute, Kansas Educational Institute, Kansas Vocational Institute, Kansas Technical Institute, and Kansas Technical College.

32 Kansas Vocational School, *Fifth Biennial Report* (1928), 8, KC; *A Book of Information about Kansas Vocational School*, KC.

33 Vernon, *The Upbuilding of a Race*, 32.

34 *Kansas City Star*, 24 December 1905. This is the major, mainstream newspaper for Kansas City, published in Missouri, although it reports news from both sides of the state line. Also see IEI, *Third Biennial Report* (1924), 4, KC.

35 *Twenty-sixth Biennial Report of Western University and State Industrial Department*, 4, KC. This document is dated 1932, but the report dates cover the years 1920 to 1922.

36 Smith, "Western University," 69–70; Orrin Murray, "The Rise and Fall of Western University" (unpublished manuscript, n.d.), 7, KC.

37 *Twenty-sixth Biennial Report of Western University and State Industrial Department*, 12, KC; also see Greenbaum, *The Afro-American Community in Kansas City, Kansas*, 75.

38 Coulter, *"Take Up the Black Man's Burden,"* 137.

39 Vernon, *The Upbuilding of a Race*, 110; also see *Kansas City Star*, 24 December 1904.

40 Vernon, "A Plea for a Suspension of Judgment," 4–5, 7–9, 12–13; Vernon, *The Upbuilding of a Race*, 110, 37.

41 Vernon, *The Upbuilding of a Race*, 32, 110.

42 Vernon, "A Plea for a Suspension of Judgment," 2, 14–16.

43 Vernon quoted in *Kansas City Star*, 24 December 1905; Vernon, *The Upbuilding of a Race*, 110; Coulter, *"Take Up the Black Man's Burden,"* 162.

44 *Twenty-first Biennial Report of Western University, Quindaro, Kansas, for the Two Years Ending June 30, 1922*, 9, KC. The date on the inside of this report states that it is for 1930–32. Also see Murray, "The Rise and Fall of Western University," 5.

45 Vernon, *The Upbuilding of a Race*, 112, 115–16, 129. Also see "Kansas Western University," 5, Quindaro Pamphlet, Pamphlets Collection, KSHS.

46 *Parsons Sun*, 28 July 1910, Negroes Clippings, KSHS; *Topeka Journal*, 20 April 1910.

47 [William T. Vernon], untitled, handwritten notes, n.d., BWTV; emphasis in original. Vernon earned $5,000 per year as registrar, but gave up that position to return to Western, where he earned $1,800 per year.

48 *Twenty-first Biennial Report of Western University*, 7, KC.

49 *Twenty-sixth Biennial Report of Western University and State Industrial Department*, 7, 10, KC.

50 *Kansas City Journal* quoted in Lawrence, "The Impact of Local, State and Federal Government Decisions," 105.

51 Greenbaum, *The Afro-American Community in Kansas City, Kansas*, 93.

52 Vernon, *The Upbuilding of a Race*, 106–7. This essay is a reprint of an address delivered on 26 December 1901 before the Missouri State Teachers' Association (white) on behalf of the Missouri State Teachers' Association (African American). The statue of John Brown still stands in Kansas City, Kansas. Although founded for African Americans, the school claimed that its doors were open to all races, creeds, and colors. The evidence available suggests that only African American students attended the school. See *Twenty-sixth Biennial Report of Western University and State Industrial Department*, 12, KC.

Chapter Six

1 *Topeka Daily Capital*, 26 September and 17 October 1926; *Kansas City Journal-Post*, September 26, 1926.

2 "Haskell Celebration" (Special Issue), *IL*, 29 October 1926; see also *IL*, 5, 12, and 19 November 1926.

3 "Haskell Celebration."

4 U.S. Congress, House, *The Indian Problem*, 33.

5 Meriam, *The Problem of Indian Administration*. Also see Peairs, "Indians Trained to Compete on Even Terms with Other Races," *School Life* 11 (April 1926), KSHS, 145; Ahern, "An Experiment Aborted," 268.

6 *Kansas City Times*, 30 October 1926; *Topeka Daily Capital*, 17 October 1926.

7 "Haskell Celebration," 12.

8 Frank O. Jones to Fellow Members of the Haskell Alumni Association, 25 May 1926, box 181, file I–J, HI, RG 75, NARA; Bloom, *To Show What an Indian Can Do*, 46.

9 *Topeka Daily Capital*, 26 September 1926. Rader argues that the homecoming offered examples of diversity among Native American tribes, but I argue that the similarities were more important to the press, Haskell officials, and visitors themselves. See Rader, "The Greatest Drama in Indian Life," 438.

10 *Kansas City Times*, 27 October 1926; "Haskell Celebration," 7.

11 "Haskell Celebration," 7.

12 *Kansas City Kansan*, 28 October 1926.

13 *Topeka Daily Capital*, 29 October 1926; *Topeka State Journal*, 19 November 1926; "Haskell Celebration," 6.

14 Lynn-Sherow and Bruce, "'How Cola' from Camp Funston," 96.

15 *Kansas City Times*, 27 October 1926. The *Times* reported that the four buffalo were shipped from Cache, Oklahoma, at a cost of $1,500. The account in the *Topeka Daily Capital* that same day reported four buffalo were "sacrificed" for the barbecue. The *Indian Leader* reported that only four beeves were used in the

barbecue and the Haskell yearbook listed the number as twenty. See "Haskell Celebration," 6; *Haskell Annual* (1927), HCCM; McDonald, *John Levi of Haskell*, 46.

16 "The New Stadium," 27–30 October 1926, photocopy, Stadium Dedication file, 11, 17, HCCM.

17 *IL*, 21 May 1926; "Haskell Celebration," 5.

18 Mossman quoted in Bloom, *To Show What an Indian Can Do*, 40.

19 McDonald, *John Levi of Haskell*, 46; *Kansas City Times*, 27 October 1926.

20 "Haskell Celebration," 8–9; *Topeka Daily Capital*, 17 October 1926.

21 "Haskell Celebration," 8; *Haskell Annual*, 1927, HCCM.

22 *Lawrence Journal-World* quoted in "Haskell Celebration," 8; Photographs, Stadium Dedication file, HCCM.

23 In 1909, the Commercial Club of Chapman, Kansas, asked the superintendent of Haskell to arrange a performance of *Hiawatha*. Originally the school would have charged $1,000 for the performance, but through a series of negotiations, Superintendent Hervey B. Peairs agreed to a $500 charge with a smaller cast of twenty to twenty-eight students rather than the forty-three who performed previously, as long as the club paid for the proper stage, scenery, lighting, and local expenses. E. F. Halbert to Dear Sir [Hervey B. Peairs], 20 July 1909; Superintendent [Peairs] to Mr. E. F. Halbert, 21 July 1909; E. F. Halbert to Dear Sir [Peairs], 22 July 1909; Superintendent [Peairs] to Mr. E. F. Halbert, 23 July 1909; Superintendent [Peairs] to My dear Sir [YMCA secretary], 2 June 1909, "Hiawatha," 1909 and 1920 file, Subject Correspondence, HI, RG 75, NARA. For the regular June 1909 performance, Peairs suggested a cast of forty students for the rate of $1,500. Also see *Topeka Daily Capital*, 1 July 1906, for earlier performance.

24 Trachtenberg, *Shades of Hiawatha*, 52, 89.

25 Superintendent [Hervey B. Peairs] to Miss Genevive Hurley, 4 April [1910]; Superintendent [Peairs] to Mr. E. F. Halbert, 23 July 1909, "Hiawatha," 1909 and 1920, Subject Correspondence, HI, RG 75, NARA.

26 Rader, "The Greatest Drama in Indian Life," 429–50; Philip J. Deloria, *Playing Indian*, 7, 122.

27 For example, as a college student, Roe Cloud participated in end-of-semester class competitions and celebrations dressed in Native American costume like his classmates. See Henry [Roe Cloud] to Mother [Mary Roe], 16 May 1910, RFP. For more on Roe Cloud's negotiations with Indian stereotypes while at Yale between 1906 and 1910, see Pfister, *The Yale Indian*, 46–56. In 1911, a teacher in the Sewing Department of Lincoln High School, an African American high school located in Kansas City, Missouri, requested information from Haskell Institute about how to acquire costumes for its own performance of *Hiawatha*. See Frederika Daparage[?] to President, Haskell Institute, 10 April 1911, "Hiawatha," 1909 and 1920 file, Subject Correspondence, HI, RG 75, NARA.

28 *Kansas City Times*, 30 October 1926; Bloom, *To Show What an Indian Can Do*, 47–48; Philip J. Deloria, *Playing Indian*, 7.

29 The *Topeka Daily Capital*, 17 October 1926, reported that the stadium, "a monument of masonry costing about $250,000," was started in April 1924 by Sena-

tor Charles Curtis, a member of the Kaw tribe. "Many contributions by white men were refused," the newspaper added. Child recorded that the money raised totaled $185,000; see *Boarding School Seasons*, 4. Another total was reported as $166,000. Also see McDonald, *John Levi of Haskell*, 53; "A Walking Tour of Haskell," HCCM; *Lawrence Journal-World*, 19 February 1925.

30 "The New Stadium," 42; *Kansas City Journal-Post*, 26 September 1926. On 29 October 1926, the *Kansas City Times* reported that the Haskell stadium was bought and paid for with "wampum": "Not a cent of white money went into the beautiful structure." Bloom notes that the stadium had only 10,500 seats when built; see *To Show What an Indian Can Do*, 37.

31 McDonald, *John Levi of Haskell*, 43.

32 Pfister, *The Yale Indian*, 147; *Lawrence Journal-World*, 19 February 1925; "Haskell Celebration," 5; "The New Stadium," 12, 14; Horne and McBeth, *Essie's Story*, 37; *Kansas City Kansan*, 28 October 1926.

33 "John Levi," unnamed periodical, Stadium Dedication, 1926, Contributors file, HCCM.

34 *Kansas City Star*, 10 October 1926; McDonald, *John Levi of Haskell*, 49.

35 "Haskell Celebration," 12; Paul, "'In Honor of Those Who Served,'" 144; Trout, "Forgotten Reminders," 202, 210. Trout overlooked Haskell's Memorial Arch in his list of World War I memorials. The Liberty Memorial in Kansas City went through a rededication in 2004 and is now called the National World War I Museum.

36 "Haskell Celebration," 4, 14.

37 Vance quoted in Lynn-Sherow and Bruce, "'How Cola' from Camp Funston," 86.

38 Lynn-Sherow and Bruce, "'How Cola' from Camp Funston," 94.

39 *IO*, March 1928; unidentified soldier quoted in Mrs. Walter C. [Mary] Roe, "The American Indian—in Two Continents," *Record of Christian Work* (November 1929), 660, RFP.

40 Plenty Coups quoted in Tate, "From Scout to Doughboy," 417.

41 Tate, "From Scout to Doughboy," 418; Lynn-Sherow and Bruce, "'How Cola' from Camp Funston," 96–97.

42 For an overview of the growth of football at Carlisle Institute, see Jenkins, *The Real All Americans*.

43 *IO*, October–November 1925; James, *The Moral Equivalent of War*.

44 *IO*, April 1924; emphasis in original.

45 Philip J. Deloria, *Indians in Unexpected Places*, 109–35; Bloom, *To Show What an Indian Can Do*, 44. For an argument about football and its ancillary behaviors as a challenge to white power during the early twentieth century, see Rader, "The Greatest Drama in Indian Life," 429–50.

46 Trachtenberg, *Shades of Hiawatha*, xvii. Also see Pfister, *The Yale Indian*; Maddox, *Citizen Indians*.

47 Memorandum to the President of the United States from Society of American Indians, 10 December 1914; Henry Roe Cloud, "Education of the American Indian" (1914), RFP.

48 *IO*, March 1928; Gere, "Indian Heart/White Man's Head," 65.

49 Some historians write that Ella Cara Deloria was born in 1889. Janet Finn lists her birth year as 1888; so does Beatrice Medicine. Agnes Picotte lists her birthday as January 31, 1899. See Medicine, "Ella C. Deloria"; Finn, "Ella Cara Deloria and Mourning Dove"; Picotte, "Biographical Sketch of the Author." Roe Cloud wrote in his autobiographical essay that he was born in the winter of 1884, but other sources say that he was born in 1882 or 1886. See Roe Cloud, "From Wigwam to Pulpit"; Ramirez, "Henry Roe Cloud: A Granddaughter's Native Feminist Biographical Account."

50 "Significance of the American Indian Institute in Indian Affairs," n.d., Records of the American Indian Institute, 1908–1954; Henry [Roe Cloud] to My dear Mother [Mary Roe], 6 July 1914; Alumnus Questionnaire, 16 February 1926, RFP.

51 *Southern Workman*, February 1924; Murray, "Ella Deloria," 50–52, 57.

52 Philip J. Deloria, *Playing Indian*, 122. Deloria also analyzes the roles of Arthur C. Parker and Charles Eastman, two "Indian mediators" whom he argues are "difficult to situate culturally." See *Playing Indian*, 95–127, for a more comprehensive discussion of twentieth-century Native American leaders who tried to bridge Native American and white American cultures.

53 Nakota was the third dialect of the Sioux language. In her ethnographic work, Ella Cara Deloria would record language and stories in all three Sioux dialects. See Gardner, "Speaking of Ella Deloria."

54 Margaret Mead to Dear Sir [Chair, Publications Committee, American Philosophical Society], n.d., Dakota Ethnography: Box 1, The Dakota Way of Life file, EDA.

55 Medicine, "Ella Deloria," 29.

56 Margaret Mead to Dear Sir, n.d., and Franz Boas to Whom It May Concern, 7 July 1937, in Ella Deloria: Personal and Professional Papers, Material Received from Vine Deloria, Sr., 19 October 1979, EDA.

57 Gardner, "Pageant Pence," unpublished manuscript cited with permission from author.

58 Ella Deloria quoted in DeMallie, "Afterword," 237.

59 Philip J. Deloria, *Playing Indian*, 122.

60 "Tonight! Big Indian Meeting at the Y.M.C.A.," n.d., RFP. The flyer incorrectly listed the speaker as "Rain Roe Cloud of Yale University."

61 Philip J. Deloria, *Playing Indian*, 122; Medicine, "Ella Deloria," 23–30; Finn, "Ella Cara Deloria and Mourning Dove," 133; Hertzberg, "Nationality, Anthropology, and Pan-Indianism," 47–48; Pfister, *The Yale Indian*, 76.

62 Haskell did not establish a village for guests in 1927, but some chose to sleep on the school grounds. See *IL*, 11–12 November 1927. Haskell did establish a village in 1934 during the celebration of the school's fiftieth anniversary. See *IL*, 23 November 1934. For the pageant, see Ella Deloria, "Indian Progress: A Pageant Commemorating a Half Century of Endeavor among the Indians of North America," unpublished play, Haskell Institute, 1927, "Deloria, Ella," Vertical file, HCCM. Also see a summary of the pageant in the *Topeka Daily Capital*, 10 November 1927.

63 Pfister, *The Yale Indian*, 67–68.

64 Ella Deloria, "Indian Progress."

65 ECD [Ella Cara Deloria] to HLB, 16 December 1927, quoted in Gardner, "Pageant Pence."

66 *Topeka Journal*, 7 and 14 November 1927; *Topeka Daily Capital*, 10 November 1927.

67 Ella Deloria, "Oicimani Hanska Kin (The Fifty Years' Trail)," printed program, 1920; Ella Deloria, "The Life-Story of a People," printed program, 1941, Ella Deloria: Personal and Professional Papers, Materials Received from Vine Deloria, Sr., EDA.

68 Ella Deloria to Dr. [Franz] Boas, 17 November 1926 [or 1927?], Vertical file, HCCM. Deloria sent the pageant to Boas, although she did not "expect for a moment to arrest a scientist's attention with the program . . . but I am sending it for you to look over."

69 *IL*, 17 March 1933 and 12 January 1934.

70 "Haskell Institute Home Coming Anniversary," 5 November 1934, *Kansas City Star/Times* Clippings, Kansas City Public Library, Kansas City, Missouri; *Kansas City Star*, 30 September 1934; *Kansas City Times*, 8 November 1934.

71 Henry Roe Cloud, "Haskell and Her New Frontiers," *IL*, 8 June 1934 (Commencement Issue), 14–17; *Wichita Eagle*, 13 December 1900; Tetzloff, "'To do some good among the Indians,'" 146; Anson Phelps Stokes Jr. to My dear Chancellor [Frank] Strong, 30 July 1913, Series: Health, Education and Welfare, Subseries 3: American Indian Institute, 1873–1942, Board of National Missions Collection, Presbyterian Historical Society, Philadelphia, Pennsylvania; *Wichita Eagle*, 16 October 1927 and 5 May 1933; Crum, "Henry Roe Cloud," 173–74; Pfister, *The Yale Indian*, 147–49; Trachtenberg, *Shades of Hiawatha*, 302.

72 *IO*, May 1927. This biographical reference specifically states that the young Henry was "taken away" from the Winnebago Reservation to attend school. Also see Tetzloff, "'To do some good among the Indians,'" 10–12.

73 Henry Roe Cloud, "An Anthropologist's View of Reservation Life" (1941), RFP.

74 Roe Cloud, "Haskell and Her New Frontiers." Mount Hermon School was founded in Massachusetts by Dwight L. Moody, a prominent evangelist, in 1881.

75 Roe Cloud quoted in *Southern Workman*, January 1915, RFP, 15–16.

76 Roe Cloud, "Haskell and Her New Frontiers," 14–17.

77 *IL*, 2 March 1934. Also see *IO*, 10 December 1923.

78 Henry [Roe Cloud] to My dear Mother [Mary Roe], 27 October 1915; Henry to Dear Mother, 27 July 1914, RFP. Roe Cloud is quoted using the term "Red Man" in *Wichita Eagle*, 30 October 1918.

79 Henry Roe Cloud, "The North American Indian of To-Day," *Good Reading for the Home*, November 1913, 491–92, RFP.

80 *IO*, March 1924; Henry Roe Cloud, "A Study in Contrasts," RFP. Roe Cloud thought that Wichita provided the right climate, fertile ground, and available land to encourage agriculture and stock raising. Within two years, the school had acquired sixty acres of land, three buildings, and equipment for dairy farming for the purpose of raising money to sustain the institution. In 1924, students farming yielded nearly 6,000 bushels of wheat.

81 The quotation is taken from a photocopy of a document, likely page 41 from the college yearbook, *Wichita State University Parnassus* (1919), Department of Special Collections, Wichita State University, Wichita, Kansas. Also see "The American Indian Institute at Wichita, Kansas," Records of the American Indian Institute, Presbyterian Historical Society; *IO*, 10 December 1923, 2, 6; *IO*, 10 February 1924, 3; "Facts about the American Indian Institute" (1920), RFP.

82 *IL*, 15 and 22 September 1933.

83 *IO*, May 1924.

84 *IO*, February–March 1926 and May 1927; Crum, "Henry Roe Cloud," 174–75; Pfister, *The Yale Indian*, 137–39.

85 Crum, "Henry Roe Cloud," 178; Granzer, "Education at Haskell Institute," 219, 229–31.

86 Lohman, *A History of the Class of 1910, Yale College*, 109.

87 Crum, "Henry Roe Cloud," 182–83.

88 U.S. Congress, House, *The Indian Problem*, 2, 29.

89 *IL*, 17 March 1933. The Committee of One Hundred listed 92,000 students under the federal government's charge. See U.S. Congress, House, *The Indian Problem*, 30.

90 *IO*, May 1924.

91 Ibid.

92 All of Roe Cloud's daughters attended college: Elizabeth Marion graduated from Wellesley College; Lillian Alberta attended the University of Kansas for two years; Anne Woesha graduated from Vassar and received two master's degrees, including one from Stanford University, and a Ph.D. from the University of Nebraska; and Ramona Clark graduated from Vassar. Ramona later taught Native American studies at a community college in Fresno, California. See Pfister, *The Yale Indian*, 75n, 194; North, quoted in Crum, "Henry Roe Cloud," 177; Meriam, *The Problem of Indian Administration*, 352–53, 419.

93 Ella Deloria and her sister Susan were hired to operate their former school together in Wakpala, South Dakota. Ella Deloria lived out her last years in Vermillion and died on 12 February 1971. This school is sometimes referred to as All Saints.

94 Medicine, "Ella Deloria," 24. See Albert C. Spaulding [Program Director for Anthropology, National Science Foundation] to Ella Deloria, 8 February 1962; Material Received from Vine Deloria Sr.; untitled newspaper clipping, 22 October 1943, Ella Deloria's Scrapbook, 21; "Miss Ella C. Deloria Honored," newspaper clipping, n.d., Ella Deloria's Scrapbook, 26; Lloyd R. Moses to Vine Deloria Sr. [Position Announcement], 1974, Ella Deloria: Personal and Professional Papers, EDA.

Conclusion

1 Thurgood Marshall to Charles S. Scott [stamped received 6 April 1955], file 29, box 2, Charles S. Scott Collection, KC; *Topeka Capital-Journal*, 5 and 7 March 1989.

2 *Topeka Capital-Journal*, 11 August 1988; *Bulletin of the Shawnee County Historical Society*, Number 42 (December 1965), Shawnee County Clippings, KSHS, 21–22.

3 Kluger, *Simple Justice*, 386.

4 Ibid., 386–87.

5 Douglas, *Jim Crow Moves North*, 10–11; Fairclough, *A Class of Their Own*, 6.

6 Crum, "Henry Roe Cloud, A Winnebago Indian Reformer," 177.

7 Josephy, Nagel, and Johnson, *Red Power*, 1.

8 Mankiller quoted in ibid., 40.

9 Mankiller and Wallis, *Mankiller*, 193; also see ibid., 185–206.

10 O. L. Plucker [Superintendent of Schools] to Mr. W. R. Channell and Bill D. Todd, 13 January 1967, SHSR.

11 These numbers are based on 2000–2001 enrollment statistics at Sumner Academy, Kansas City, Kansas.

12 Matthews, "Best High Schools in America," 49–54. The author of this article devised a ratio to rank public schools across the nation based on the number of advanced placement or international baccalaureate tests taken by all students at a school in 2002. That number was then divided by the number of graduating seniors. Sumner Academy ranked ninety-ninth.

13 Okihiro, *Margins and Mainstreams*, ix.

Bibliography

Primary Sources

MANUSCRIPT AND ARCHIVE COLLECTIONS

Bonner Springs, Kansas
  Wyandotte County Historical Society and Museum
    Western University Collection
Chamberlain, South Dakota
  Dakota Indian Foundation
    Ella Deloria Archive
Fort Scott, Kansas
  Arnold Schofield Private Collection
  Minutes of School Board Meetings, Unified School District 234, Fort Scott,
    Kansas
  Kirk Sharp Private Collection
Kansas City, Kansas
  Kansas City, Kansas Public School District Office Archives
    Sumner High School Records
Kansas City, Missouri
  Kansas City Public Library
    Kansas City Star/Times Clippings
  National Archives and Records Administration–Central Plains Region
    Record Group 21, Records of the District Courts of the United States
      Law Case Files
    Record Group 75, Records of the Bureau of Indian Affairs
      Records of the Education Division, 1874–1948
      Records of Haskell Indian Junior College
      Hervey B. Peairs Papers, 1917–59
      Records of the Potawatomi Agency
      Student Case Files, 1884–1920
Lawrence, Kansas
  Haskell Indian Nations University Cultural Center and Museum
  Kansas Collection, Kenneth Spencer Research Library, University of Kansas
    Libraries
    Greene B. Buster Collection

Kansas Industrial and Educational Institute Announcements and Reports, 1911–26
  Kansas Vocational School Reports, 1924–48
  Charles S. Scott Collection
  Sumner High School Collection
  Bishop William Tecumseh Vernon Collection
New Haven, Connecticut
  Yale University, Sterling Memorial Library, Manuscript and Archives Collection
    Roe Family Papers
Palo Alto, California
  Elizabeth "Jing" Lyman Private Collection
Philadelphia, Pennsylvania
  Presbyterian Historical Society
    Records of the American Indian Institute
    Board of National Missions Collection
Topeka, Kansas
  Central Congregational Church
    Central Congregational Church Collection
    Charles M. Sheldon Memorial Room
  Kansas State Historical Society
    Central Congregational Church Collection
    Governor's Records
    Haskell Institute Clippings, Volume 1, 1885–1938
    Kansas State Legislative Documents, Volume 4, 1862–99
    Negroes Clippings
    Pamphlets Collection
    Shawnee County Clippings
    Charles Sheldon Papers
    Quindaro Pamphlets (Miscellaneous), Volume 1
  Topeka and Shawnee County Public Library
    Topeka Room Collection
Wichita, Kansas
  Department of Special Collections, Wichita State University

NEWSPAPERS

(All periodicals were published in Kansas unless otherwise noted)

Afro-American Advocate
  (Coffeyville)
Halstead Independent
Kansas City (Mo.) Call
Kansas City (Mo.) Journal/
  Journal-Post
Kansas City Kansan
Kansas City (Mo.) Star

Kansas City (Mo.) Times
Kansas State Journal
Lawrence Journal-World
Leavenworth Advocate
Leavenworth Times
Mennonite (Newton)
Topeka Capital-Journal/
  Journal

Topeka Colored Citizen
Topeka Commonwealth
Topeka Daily Capital
Topeka Daily Herald
Topeka Plaindealer
Topeka State Journal
Topeka Weekly Times
Wichita Eagle

Annual Report of the Commissioner of Indian Affairs to the Secretary of Interior. Washington: Government Printing Office, 1890.

Annual Report of the Commissioner of Indian Affairs. Washington: Government Printing Office, 1895.

"Articles of Corporation and By-Laws of the Kansas Freedmen's Relief Association." Topeka, Kans.: F. P. Baker and Sons, 1879.

Boas, Franz, and Ella Cara Deloria. *Dakota Grammar.* Washington: Government Printing Office, 1941.

Cloud, Henry Roe. "From Wigwam to Pulpit: A Red Man's Own Story of His Progress from Darkness to Light." *Missionary Review of the World* 28 (May 1915): 329–39.

Deloria, Ella Cara. *Dakota Texts.* New York: G. E. Stechert and Co., 1932.

———. *Speaking of Indians.* New York: Friendship Press, 1944.

———. *Waterlily.* Lincoln: University of Nebraska Press, 1988.

"Exodusters." In *First Annual Report of the Bureau of Labor and Industrial Statistics,* 248–57. Topeka, Kans.: T. D. Thacher, 1886.

Hare, Caroline, ed. *The Life and Letters of Elizabeth L. Comstock.* Philadelphia, Pa.: J. C. Winston and Co., 1895.

Haviland, Laura Smith. *A Woman's Life-Work: Labors and Experience of Laura S. Haviland.* Chicago, Ill.: C. U. Waite and Co., 1887.

Krehbiel, Christian. *Prairie Pioneer: The Christian Krehbiel Story.* Newton, Kans.: Faith and Life Press, 1961.

Meriam, Lewis, et al. *The Problem of Indian Administration: Report of a Survey Made at the Request of Hubert Work, Secretary of the Interior, and Submitted to Him, February 21, 1928.* Baltimore, Md.: Johns Hopkins Press, 1928.

Meserve, Charles F. *A Tour of Observation among Indians and Indian Schools in Arizona, New Mexico, Oklahoma, and Kansas.* Philadelphia, Pa.: Office of the Indian Rights Association, 1894.

Office of Superintendent of Indian Schools. *Course of Study for the Indian Schools of the United States, Industrial and Literary.* Washington: Government Printing Office, 1901.

Parks, Gordon. *A Choice of Weapons.* New York: Harper & Row, 1966.

———. *Half-Past Autumn: A Retrospective.* Boston, Mass.: Little, Brown/Corcoran Gallery of Art, 1997.

———. *The Learning Tree.* New York: Ballantine Books, 1963.

———. *Voices in the Mirror: An Autobiography.* New York: Doubleday, 1990.

Peairs, Hervey B. "The Difference in the Starting Point of the Indian Child as Compared with That of the Average Civilized Child." *State Normal Monthly* 4 (February 1897): 67–70.

Proceedings of the Annual Meeting of the Lake Mohonk Conference of Friends of the Indian [1883–1916, 1929]. New York: Clearwater Publishing Co., 1975. Microfilm.

Proceedings of the First [and Second] Lake Mohonk Conference on the Negro Question [1890–91]. New York: Clearwater Publishing Co., 1975. Microfilm.

Sheldon, Charles M. *In His Steps: "What Would Jesus Do?"* Chicago, Ill.: Advance Publishing Company, 1898.

State Superintendent of Public Instruction of Kansas. *Fifteenth Biennial Report, for the Years Ending June 30, 1905 and June 30, 1906.* Topeka, Kans.: State Printing Office, 1906. ⟨http://brownvboard.org/research/handbook/sources/misc/1905edrept.htm⟩. 16 July 2009.

U.S. Bureau of the Census. *Fourteenth Census, 1920.* Volume 3, Population—Kansas, 1920, 1910, 1900. Washington: Government Printing Office, 1921.

———. *Ninth Census, 1870.* Volume 1, Table 1, Population, 1870–1790 by States and Territories, in Aggregate, and as White, Colored, Free-Colored, Slave, Chinese, and Indian. Washington: Government Printing Office, 1872.

———. *Tenth Census, 1880.* Volume 1, Table 4, Population, by Race and by States and Territories, 1880, 1870, 1860. Washington: Government Printing Office, 1882.

———. *Thirteenth Census, 1910.* Volume 2, Reports by States Alabama–Montana. Washington: Government Printing Office, 1913.

U.S. Congress. House. *The Indian Problem: Resolution of the Committee of One Hundred Appointed by the Secretary of the Interior and a Review of the Indian Problem.* 68th Cong., 1st sess., 1924, H. Doc. 149.

Vernon, William Tecumseh. *The Upbuilding of a Race; or, The Rise of a Great People: A Compilation of Sermons, Addresses and Writings on Education, the Race Question and Public Affairs.* Quindaro, Kans.: Industrial Students Printers, 1904.

Washington, Booker T. *Up from Slavery: An Autobiography.* 1901. New York: Dover Publications, 1995.

Secondary Sources

UNPUBLISHED WORKS

Bell, Genevieve. "Telling Stories Out of School: Remembering the Carlisle Indian Industrial School, 1879–1918." Ph.D. diss., Stanford University, 1998.

Burgess, Larry E. "The Lake Mohonk Conferences on the Indian, 1883–1916." Ph.D. diss., Claremont Graduate School, 1972.

Gardner, Susan. "Pageant Pence." Working paper, University of North Carolina at Charlotte, 2006.

Goddard, Geneva. "A Study of the Historical Development and Educational Work of Haskell Institute." Master's thesis, Kansas State Teachers College–Emporia, 1930.

Granzer, Loretta Mary. "Indian Education at Haskell Institute, 1884–1937." Master's thesis, University of Nebraska, 1937.

Israelson, Chad. "The Haskell Indians: Sports at a Native American Boarding School, 1920–1940." Master's thesis, University of Nebraska, 1995.

Jacobs, Margaret D. "Gender and Colonialism in the American West." Paper presented to the Conference of the International Federation for Research in Women's History, Sydney, Australia, July 2005. ⟨http://www.historians.ie/women/jacob.pdf⟩. 20 September 2006.

Krauthamer, Barbara. "Blacks on the Borders: African-Americans' Transition from Slavery to Freedom in Texas and the Indian Territory, 1836–1907." Ph.D. diss., Princeton University, 2000.

Lawrence, Dennis. "The Impact of Local, State and Federal Government Decisions on the Segregation and Subsequent Integration of Sumner High School in Kansas City, Kansas." Ph.D. diss., University of Kansas, 1977.

McGuinn, Nellie. "The Kansas City, Kansas, Public School System, 1819–1961." Unpublished manuscript, 1987. Kansas City, Kansas Public School District Office.

Murray, Janette K. "Ella Deloria: A Biographical Sketch and Literary Analysis." Ph.D. diss., University of North Dakota, 1974.

Smith, Thaddeus T. "Western University: A Ghost College in Kansas." Master's thesis, Kansas State College of Pittsburg, 1966.

Tetzloff, Jason M. "'To do some good among the Indians': Henry Roe Cloud and Twentieth Century Native American Advocacy." Ph.D. diss., Purdue University, 1996.

PUBLISHED WORKS

Adams, David Wallace. *Education for Extinction: American Indians and the Boarding School Experience, 1875–1928.* Lawrence: University Press of Kansas, 1995.

———. "Education in Hues: Red and Black at Hampton Institute, 1878–1893." *South Atlantic Quarterly* 76 (1977): 159–76.

———. "From Bullets to Boarding Schools." In *The American Indian Experience*, edited by Philip Weeks, 218–39. Arlington Heights, Ill.: Forum Press, 1988.

———. "Fundamental Considerations." *Harvard Educational Review* 58 (spring 1988): 1–28.

Ahern, Wilbert H. "Assimilationist Racism: The Case of the 'Friends of the Indian.'" *Journal of Ethnic Studies* 4 (summer 1976): 23–32.

———. "An Experiment Aborted: Returned Indian Students in the Indian School Service, 1881–1908." *Ethnohistory* 44 (spring 1997): 263–304.

Anderson, James D. *The Education of Blacks in the South, 1860–1935.* Chapel Hill: University of North Carolina Press, 1988.

Archuleta, Margaret, Brenda J. Child, and K. Tsianina Lomawaima, eds. *Away from Home: American Indian Boarding School Experiences, 1879–2000.* Phoenix, Ariz.: Heard Museum, 2000.

Athearn, Robert G. *In Search of Canaan: Black Migration to Kansas, 1879–80.* Lawrence: Regents Press of Kansas, 1978.

Bardolph, Richard. "The Distinguished Negro in America, 1770–1936." *American Historical Review* 60 (April 1955): 527–47.

Bederman, Gail. *Manliness and Civilization: A Cultural History of Gender and Race in the United States, 1880–1917.* Chicago: University of Chicago Press, 1995.

Blair, Ed. *History of Johnson County, Kansas.* Lawrence, Kans.: Standard Publishing, 1915.

Bloom, John. *To Show What an Indian Can Do: Sports at Native American Boarding Schools.* 1997. Minneapolis: University of Minnesota Press, 2005.

Bond, Horace Mann. *The Education of the Negro in the American Social Order*. 1934. New York: Octagon Books, 1966.

Brady, Marilyn Dell. "Kansas Federation of Colored Women's Clubs, 1900–1930." *Kansas History: A Journal of the Central Plains* 9 (spring 1986): 19–30.

"A Brief History of Fort Scott African American Schools" [National Park Service bulletin]. Washington: Government Printing Office, n.d.

Brooks, James F. *Captives and Cousins: Slavery, Kinship, and Community in the Southwest Borderlands*. Chapel Hill: University of North Carolina Press, 2002.

———, ed. *Confounding the Color Line: The Indian-Black Experience in North America*. Lincoln: University of Nebraska Press, 2002.

Burgess, Larry E. *The Lake Mohonk Conference of Friends of the Indian: Guide to the Annual Reports*. New York: Clearwater Publishing, 1975.

Burton, Antoinette M. "The White Woman's Burden: British Feminists and 'The Indian Woman,' 1865–1915." In *Western Women and Imperialism: Complicity and Resistance*, edited by Nupur Chaudhuri and Margaret Strobel, 137–57. Bloomington: Indiana University Press, 1992.

Burton, Katherine. *The Golden Door: The Life of Katharine Drexel*. New York: P. J. Kennedy and Sons, 1957.

Buster, Greene B. *Brighter Sun*. New York: Pageant Press, 1954.

Carper, James C. "The Popular Ideology of Segregated Schooling: Attitudes toward the Education of Blacks in Kansas, 1854–1900." *Kansas History: A Journal of the Central Plains* 1 (winter 1978): 254–65.

Child, Brenda. *Boarding School Seasons: American Indian Families, 1900–1940*. Lincoln: University of Nebraska Press, 1998.

Coulter, Charles E. *"Take Up the Black Man's Burden": Kansas City's African American Communities, 1865–1939*. Columbia: University of Missouri Press, 2006.

Cox, Thomas C. *Blacks in Topeka, Kansas, 1865–1915: A Social History*. Baton Rouge: Louisiana State University Press, 1982.

Crum, Steven J. "Henry Roe Cloud, a Winnebago Indian Reformer: His Quest for American Indian Higher Education." *Kansas History: A Journal of the Central Plains* 11 (autumn 1988): 171–84.

Danforth, Mildred. *A Quaker Pioneer: Laura Haviland, Superintendent of the Underground*. New York: Exposition Press, 1961.

Deloria, Philip J. *Indians in Unexpected Places*. Lawrence: University Press of Kansas, 2004.

———. *Playing Indian*. New Haven: Yale University Press, 1998.

DeMallie, Raymond J. Afterword. In *Waterlily*, by Ella Cara Deloria, 233–38. Lincoln: University of Nebraska Press, 1988.

Donato, Ruben, and Marvin Lazerson. "New Directions in American Educational History: Problems and Prospects." *Educational Researcher* 29 (November 2000): 1–5.

Douglas, Davison M. *Jim Crow Moves North: The Battle over Northern School Segregation, 1865–1954*. New York: Cambridge University Press, 2005.

Dudziak, Mary L. "The Limits of Good Faith: Desegregation in Topeka, Kansas, 1950–1956." *Law and History Review* 5 (autumn 1987): 351–91.

Edwards, Laura F. "Status without Rights: African Americans and the Tangled History of Law and Governance in the Nineteenth-Century U.S. South." *American Historical Review* 112 (April 2007): 365–93.

Ellis, Clyde. *To Change Them Forever: Indian Education at the Rainy Mountain Boarding School, 1893–1920*. Norman: University of Oklahoma Press, 1996.

Elson, Ruth Miller. *Guardians of Tradition: American Schoolbooks of the Nineteenth Century*. Lincoln: University of Nebraska Press, 1964.

Fairclough, Adam. *A Better Day Coming: Blacks and Equality, 1890–2000*. New York: Viking Press, 2001.

———. *A Class of Their Own: Teachers in the Segregated South*. Cambridge, Mass.: Belknap Press of Harvard University Press, 2007.

———. *Teaching Equality: Black Schools in the Age of Jim Crow*. Athens: University of Georgia Press, 2001.

Fear-Segal, Jacqueline. *White Man's Club: Schools, Race, and the Struggle of Indian Acculturation*. Lincoln: University of Nebraska Press, 2007.

Finn, Janet L. "Ella Cara Deloria and Mourning Dove: Writing for Cultures, Writing against the Grain." In *Women Writing Culture*, edited by Ruth Behar and Deborah A. Gordon, 131–47. Berkeley: University of California Press, 1995.

Foner, Eric. *Free Soil, Free Labor, Free Men: The Ideology of the Republican Party before the Civil War*. New York: Oxford University Press, 1995.

"Fort Scott." National Park Service bulletin. Washington: Government Printing Office, n.d.

Frank, Thomas. *What's the Matter with Kansas?: How Conservatives Won the Heart of America*. New York: Metropolitan Books, 2004.

"Free to Learn." Fort Scott National Historic Site pamphlet. Washington: Government Printing Office, n.d.

Fultz, Michael. "African American Teachers in the South, 1890–1940: Powerlessness and the Ironies of Expectations and Protest." *History of Education Quarterly* 35 (winter 1995): 401–22.

Gardner, Susan. "Speaking of Ella Deloria." *American Indian Quarterly* 24 (summer 2000): 456–82.

Gere, Anne Ruggles. "Indian Heart/White Man's Head: Native-American Teachers in Indian Schools, 1880–1930." *History of Education Quarterly* 45 (spring 2005): 38–65.

Gibson, Campbell, and Kay Jung. "Historical Census Statistics on Population Totals by Race, 1790 to 1990, and by Hispanic Origin, 1970 to 1990, for the United States, Regions, Divisions, and States." Population Division, U.S. Census Bureau, 2005. ⟨http://www.census.gov/population/www/documentation/twps0076/twps0076.html⟩. 6 June 2009.

Giddings, Paula. *Where and When I Enter: The Impact of Black Women on Race and Sex in America*. New York: W. Morrow, 1984.

Gilmore, Glenda Elizabeth. *Gender and Jim Crow: Women and the Politics of White Supremacy in North Carolina, 1896–1920*. Chapel Hill: University of North Carolina Press, 1996.

Goffman, Ervin. *Asylums: Essays on the Social Situation of Mental Patients and Other Inmates.* Chicago, Ill.: Aldine Publishing, 1961.

Greenbaum, Susan D. *The Afro-American Community in Kansas City, Kansas.* Kansas City, Kans.: Department of Community Development, 1982.

Greene, Peggy. "Dr. Sheldon and Tennesseetown." *The Melting Pot: Shawnee County's Ethnic Communities.* Bulletin No. 58. Topeka, Kans.: Shawnee County Historical Society, November 1981.

Hagan, William T. "How the West Was Lost." In *Indians in American History: An Introduction,* edited by Frederick E. Hoxie, 179–202. Arlington Heights, Ill.: Harlan Davidson, 1988.

Handy, Robert T. *A Christian America: Protestant Hopes and Historical Realities.* New York: Oxford University Press, 1971.

———. "The Protestant Quest for a Christian America, 1830–1930." *Church History* 22 (March 1953): 8–20.

Hanson, Joyce A. *Mary McLeod Bethune and Black Women's Political Activism.* Columbia: University of Missouri Press, 2003.

Harmon, Alexandra. "When Is an Indian Not an Indian?: The 'Friends of the Indian' and the Problems of Indian Identity." *Journal of Ethnic Studies* 18 (summer 1990): 95–123.

Haywood, C. Robert. *Victorian West: Class and Culture in Kansas Cattle Towns.* Lawrence: University Press of Kansas, 1991.

Hertzberg, Hazel Whitman. "Nationality, Anthropology, and Pan-Indianism in the Life of Arthur C. Parker (Seneca)." *Proceedings of the American Philosophical Society* 123 (February 1979): 47–72.

———. *The Search for an American Indian Identity: Modern Pan-Indian Movements.* Syracuse, N.Y.: Syracuse University Press, 1971.

Higginbotham, Evelyn Brooks. *Righteous Discontent: The Women's Movement in the Black Baptist Church, 1880–1920.* Cambridge, Mass.: Harvard University Press, 1993.

Hine, Robert V., and John Mack Faragher. *The American West: A New Interpretive History.* New Haven, Conn.: Yale University Press, 2000.

Hodes, Martha. "The Mercurial Nature and Abiding Power of Race: A Transnational Family Story." *American Historical Review* 108 (February 2003): 84–118.

Hodge, L. C. "Problem of Self-Help: A Practical Solution Has Been Made in This Western City—Some Interesting Details." *Civic Pride* 1 (May 1904): 73–76.

Horne, Esther Burnett, and Sally McBeth. *Essie's Story: The Life and Legacy of a Shoshone Teacher.* Lincoln: University of Nebraska Press, 1998.

Hoxie, Frederick E. "The Curious Story of Reformers and the American Indians." In *Indians in American History: An Introduction,* edited by Frederick E. Hoxie, 205–30. Arlington Heights, Ill.: Harlan Davidson, Inc., 1988.

———. *A Final Promise: The Campaign to Assimilate the Indians, 1880–1920.* Lincoln: University of Nebraska Press, 1984.

Hurtado, Albert L. *Intimate Frontiers: Sex, Gender, and Culture in Old California.* Albuquerque: University of New Mexico Press, 1999.

Jacobson, Matthew Frye. *Whiteness of a Different Color: European Immigrants and the Alchemy of Race*. Cambridge, Mass.: Harvard University Press, 1998.

James, William. *The Moral Equivalent of War*. New York: American Association for International Conciliation, 1910.

Jenkins, Sally. *The Real All Americans: The Team That Changed a Game, a People, a Nation*. New York: Doubleday, 2007.

Jensen, Katherine. "Civilization and Assimilation in the Colonized Schooling of Native Americans." In *Education and the Colonial Experience*, edited by Philip G. Altbach and Gail P. Kelly, 2nd ed., 155–79. New Brunswick, N.J.: Transaction, 1984.

Jones, Jacqueline. "Women Who Were More than Men: Sex and Status in Freedmen's Teaching." *History of Education Quarterly* 19 (spring 1979): 47–59.

Josephy, Alvin M., Jr., Joane Nagel, and Troy Johnson, eds. *Red Power*. 2nd ed. New York: Oxford University Press, 1997.

Katz, William Loren. *Black Indians: A Hidden Heritage*. New York: Atheneum, 1986.

Keller, Robert H., Jr. *American Protestantism and United States Indian Policy*. Lincoln: University of Nebraska Press, 1983.

Kerber, Linda K. "The Abolitionist Perception of the Indian." *Journal of American History* 62 (September 1975): 271–95.

Kluger, Richard. *Simple Justice: The History of* Brown v. Board of Education *and Black America's Struggle for Equality*. 1975. New York: Vintage Books, 1977.

Kousser, J. Morgan. "Before *Plessy*, before *Brown*: The Development of the Law of Racial Integration in Louisiana and Kansas." In *Toward a Usable Past: Liberty under State Governments*, edited by Paul Finkelman and Stephen C. Gottlieb, 213–70. Athens: University of Georgia Press, 1991.

Lindsey, Donal F. *Indians at Hampton Institute, 1877–1923*. Chicago: University of Illinois Press, 1995.

Litwack, Leon F. *Been in the Storm So Long: The Aftermath of Slavery*. New York: Alfred A. Knopf, 1979.

———. *Trouble in Mind: Black Southerners in the Age of Jim Crow*. New York: Vintage Books, 1998.

Lohman, Carl A. *A History of the Class of 1910, Yale College*. New Haven, Conn.: Class Secretaries Bureau, 1926.

Lomawaima, K. Tsianina. *They Called It Prairie Light: The Story of Chilocco Indian School*. Lincoln: University of Nebraska Press, 1994.

Lynn-Sherow, Bonnie, and Susannah Ural Bruce. "'How Cola' from Camp Funston: American Indians and the Great War." *Kansas History: A Journal of the Central Plains* 24 (summer 2001): 84–97.

Maddox, Lucy. *Citizen Indians: Native American Intellectuals, Race, and Reform*. Ithaca, N.Y.: Cornell University Press, 2005.

Mankiller, Wilma, and Michael Wallis. *Mankiller: A Chief and Her People*. New York: St. Martin's Press, 1993.

Manuel, Verna, and Larry Oskiniko. *Two Plays about Residential School*. Vancouver, B.C.: Living Traditions, 1998.

Matthews, Jay. "Best High Schools in America." *Newsweek*, 2 June 2003, 49–54.

McDonald, Frank W. *John Levi of Haskell*. Lawrence, Kans.: World Company, 1972.

McPherson, James M. *The Abolitionist Legacy: From Reconstruction to the NAACP*. Princeton, N.J.: Princeton University Press, 1975.

———. "White Liberals and Black Power in Negro Education, 1865–1915." *American Historical Review* 75 (June 1970): 1357–86.

Medicine, Bea. "Ella C. Deloria: The Emic Voice." *MELUS* 7 (winter 1980): 23–30.

Mihesuah, Devon. *Cultivating the Rosebuds: The Education of Women at the Cherokee Female Seminary, 1851–1909*. Chicago: University of Illinois Press, 1993.

Miles, Tiya. *Ties That Bind: The Story of an Afro-Cherokee Family in Slavery and Freedom*. Berkeley: University of California Press, 2002.

Miles, Tiya, and Sharon P. Holland, eds. *Crossing Waters, Crossing Worlds: The African Diaspora in Indian Country*. Durham, N.C.: Duke University Press, 2006.

Milk, Theresa. *Haskell Institute: 19th Century Stories of Sacrifice and Survival*. Lawrence, Kans.: Mammoth Publications, 2007.

Miller, Lillian M. "'Aunt Laura': The Story of Laura Haviland." *Northwest Ohio Quarterly: A Journal of History and Civilization* 14 (autumn 1952): 199–210.

Miller, Timothy. "Charles M. Sheldon and the Uplift of Tennesseetown." *Kansas History: A Journal of the Central Plains* 9 (autumn 1986): 125–37.

———. *Following in His Steps: A Biography of Charles M. Sheldon*. Knoxville: University of Tennessee Press, 1988.

Milner, Clyde A., II, and Floyd A. O'Neil, eds. *Churchmen and the Western Indians, 1820–1920*. Norman: University of Oklahoma Press, 1985.

Naylor, Celia E. *African Cherokees in Indian Territory: From Chattel to Citizens*. Chapel Hill: University of North Carolina Press, 2008.

Novak, Steven J. "The Real Takeover of the BIA: The Preferential Hiring of Indians." *Journal of Economic History* 50 (September 1990): 639–54.

O'Brien, Sharon. *American Indian Tribal Governments*. 1989. Norman: University of Oklahoma Press, 1993.

Okihiro, Gary Y. *Margins and Mainstreams: Asians in American History and Culture*. Seattle: University of Washington Press, 1994.

Painter, Nell Irvin. *Exodusters: Black Migration to Kansas after Reconstruction*. New York: Alfred A. Knopf, 1976.

Parker, Arthur. "Race Assimilation in America, with Special Reference to the American Indian." *American Indian Magazine* 4 (October–December 1916): 285–304.

Pascoe, Peggy. *Relations of Rescue: The Search for Female Moral Authority in the American West, 1874–1939*. New York: Oxford University Press, 1990.

Paul, Eli. "'In Honor of Those Who Served': Introduction." *Kansas History: A Journal of the Central Plains* 29 (autumn 2006): 142–45.

Peavler, David J. "Drawing the Color Line in Kansas City." *Kansas History: A Journal of the Central Plains* 27 (autumn 2005): 188–201.

Perales, Marian. "Empowering 'the Welder': A Historical Survey of Women of Color in the West." In *Writing the Range: Race, Class, and Culture in the Women's West*, edited by Elizabeth Jameson and Susan Armitage, 21–41. Norman: University of Oklahoma Press, 1997.

Pfister, Joel. *The Yale Indian: The Education of Henry Roe Cloud.* Durham, N.C.: Duke University Press, 2009.

Picotte, Agnes. "Biographical Sketch of the Author." In *Waterlily*, by Ella Cara Deloria, 229–31. Lincoln: University of Nebraska Press, 1988.

Pratt, Richard Henry. *Battlefield and the Classroom: Four Decades with American Indians, 1867–1904.* Edited by Robert M. Utley. New Haven, Conn.: Yale University Press, 1964.

Prucha, Francis Paul. *American Indian Policy in Crisis: Christian Reformers and the Indian, 1865–1900.* Norman: University of Oklahoma Press, 1976.

———. *The Great Father: The United States Government and the American Indians.* Abridged ed. Lincoln: University of Nebraska Press, 1986.

———. *Indian Policy in the United States: Historical Essays.* Lincoln: University of Nebraska Press, 1981.

———. *The Indians in American Society: From the Revolutionary War to the Present.* Berkeley: University of California Press, 1985.

———, ed. *Americanizing the American Indians: Writings by the "Friends of the Indian," 1880–1900.* Cambridge, Mass.: Harvard University Press, 1973.

Rader, Benjamin G. "'The Greatest Drama in Indian Life': Experiments in Native American Identity and Resistance at the Haskell Institute Homecoming of 1926." *Western Historical Quarterly* 35 (winter 2004): 429–52.

Ramirez, Renya K. "Henry Roe Cloud: A Granddaughter's Native Feminist Biographical Account." *Wicaso Sa Review Journal* 24 (fall 2009): 77–103.

Rury, John L. "Vocationalism for Home and Work: Women's Education in the United States, 1880–1930." *History of Education Quarterly* 24 (spring 1984): 21–44.

Saunt, Claudio. *Black, White, and Indian: Race and the Unmaking of an American Family.* New York: Oxford University Press, 2005.

Schwendemann, Glen. *Nicodemus: Negro Haven on the Solomon.* Topeka, Kans.: State of Kansas Commission on Civil Rights, 1971.

Scott, Joan W. "Gender: A Useful Category of Historical Analysis." *American Historical Review* 91 (December 1986): 1053–75.

Sculle, Keith A. "'The New Carlisle of the West': Haskell Institute and Big-Time Sports, 1920–1932." *Kansas History: A Journal of the Central Plains* 17 (autumn 1994): 192–208.

Sheridan, Richard B. "From Slavery in Missouri to Freedom in Kansas: The Influx of Black Fugitives and Contrabands into Kansas, 1854–1865." *Kansas History: A Journal of the Central Plains* 12 (spring 1989): 28–47.

Stampp, Kenneth. *The Peculiar Institution: Slavery in the Ante-bellum South.* 1956. New York: Vintage Books, 1964.

Stoler, Ann Laura. *Carnal Knowledge and Imperial Power: Race and the Intimate in Colonial Rule.* Berkeley: University of California Press, 2003.

———. "Tense and Tender Ties: The Politics of Comparison in North American History and (Post) Colonial Studies." *Journal of American History* 88 (December 2001): 829–65.

Takaki, Ronald. *A Different Mirror: A History of Multicultural America.* Boston, Mass.: Little, Brown and Co., 1993.

Tate, Michael L. "From Scout to Doughboy: The National Debate over Integrating American Indians into the Military, 1891–1918." *Western Historical Quarterly* 17 (October 1986): 417–37.

Taylor, Quintard. *In Search of the Racial Frontier: African Americans in the American West, 1528–1990*. New York: W. W. Norton and Co., 1998.

Trachtenberg, Alan. *Shades of Hiawatha: Staging Indians, Making Americans, 1880–1930*. New York: Hill and Wang, 2004.

Trafzer, Clifford E., Jean A. Keller, and Lorene Sisquoc, eds. *Boarding School Blues: Revisiting American Indian Educational Experiences*. Lincoln: University of Nebraska Press, 2006.

Trennert, Robert A. *Alternative to Extinction: Federal Indian Policy and the Beginnings of the Reservation System, 1846–1851*. Philadelphia, Pa.: Temple University Press, 1975.

———. "Educating Indian Girls and Women at Nonreservation Boarding Schools, 1878–1920." *Western Historical Quarterly* 13 (July 1982): 271–90.

———. "From Carlisle to Phoenix: The Rise and Fall of the Indian Outing System, 1878–1930." *Pacific Historical Review* 52 (August 1983): 267–91.

———. *The Phoenix Indian School: Forced Assimilation in Arizona, 1891–1935*. Norman: University of Oklahoma Press, 1988.

Trout, Steven. "Forgotten Reminders: Kansas World War I Memorials." *Kansas History: A Journal of the Central Plains* 29 (autumn 2006): 200–215.

Tyack, David B. *The One Best System: A History of American Urban Education*. Cambridge, Mass.: Harvard University Press, 1974.

Tyack, David B., and Larry Cuban. *Tinkering toward Utopia: A Century of Public School Reform*. Cambridge, Mass.: Harvard University Press, 1995.

Tyack, David B., and Elisabeth Hansot. *Learning Together: A History of Coeducation in American Public Schools*. New Haven, Conn.: Yale University Press, 1990.

Tyler, S. Lyman. *A History of Indian Policy*. Washington: U.S. Department of the Interior, 1973.

Underwood, June O. "Civilizing Kansas: Women's Organizations, 1880–1920." *Kansas History: A Journal of the Central Plains* 7 (winter 1984–85): 291–306.

Van Meeter, Sondra. "Black Resistance to Segregation in the Wichita Public Schools, 1870–1912." *Midwest Quarterly* 20 (October 1978): 64–77.

Vučković, Myriam. *Voices from Haskell: Indian Students between Two Worlds, 1884–1928*. Lawrence: University Press of Kansas, 2008.

Wall, Wendy. "Gender and the 'Citizen Indian.'" In *Writing the Range: Race, Class, and Culture in the Women's West*, edited by Elizabeth Jameson and Susan Armitage, 202–29. Norman: University of Oklahoma Press, 1997.

White, Deborah Gray. *Ar'n't I a Woman?: Female Slaves in the Plantation South*. New York: W. W. Norton, 1985.

———. *Too Heavy a Load: Black Women in Defense of Themselves, 1894–1994*. New York: W. W. Norton, 1999.

Williams, Heather Andrea. *Self-Taught: African American Education in Slavery and Freedom*. Chapel Hill: University of North Carolina Press, 2005.

Wolters, Raymond. *The New Negro on Campus: Black College Rebellions in the 1920s.* Princeton, N.J.: Princeton University Press, 1975.

Woods, Randall B. "After the Exodus: John Waller and the Black Elite, 1878–1900." *Kansas Historical Quarterly* 43 (summer 1977): 172–92.

———. "Integration, Exclusion, or Segregation?: The 'Color Line' in Kansas, 1878–1900." *Western Historical Quarterly* 14 (April 1983): 181–98.

Woodson, Carter Godwin. *The Mis-Education of the Negro.* Washington: Associated Publisher, 1933.

Woodward, C. Vann. *The Strange Career of Jim Crow.* New York: Oxford University Press, 1955.

Index